Sovereignty
The Empirical Path of Odhinn

Heathen Blodharn

Cadmus Publishing
www.cadmuspublishing.com

Questions, comments, or criticisms should be directed to the author:

Heathen Blodharn

heathenblodharn@gmail.com

Copyright © 2022 Heathen Blodharn

Published by Cadmus Publishing
www.cadmuspublishing.com
Port Angeles, WA

ISBN: 978-1-63751-255-5

All rights reserved. Copyright under Berne Copyright Convention, Universal Copyright Convention, and Pan-American Copyright Convention. No part of this book may be reproduced, stored in a retrieval system, or transmitted in any form, or by any means, electronic, mechanical, photocopying, recording or otherwise, without prior permission of the author.

Introduction

This book is the culmination of a lifetime dedicated to seeking Truth, wherever it may be found, and the experiences that come from living with Intent; I can only hope to inspire others the way the Gods and Goddesses inspire me every day. This book can only serve that purpose however: as an inspiration, as no person can tell another how to nourish their spirit; one can only offer the other advice or the wisdom gained by their individual experience and each of us must decide for ourselves what to do with it. To that end then, I recommend that every person conduct their own studies and experiments to learn what works for them, as this book is what works for me and may serve you as well, though there are no guarantees. Effective Evolution can only be brought about by consciously striving at all times to be Godlike and this begins, of necessity, by banishing the chaos giants from your garden, then seeking Truth in all things.

Ultimately, I propose to address three primary issues of importance herein: that which is, that which is becoming, and that which should be. Obviously, this is a very basic introduction to the Empirical Path of Odhinn, as a single volume is unlikely to capture its complexities, though I do hope to inspire others to pick up the torch of illumination and light the way along the Path for subsequent generations, to reclaim Tradition from montheistic ignorance, and enlighten Fólk to the wisdom of our ancestors. It is with this in mind that I prepared the following, to serve as a foundation from which a strong structure may be built; far from being comprehensive this book is only intended to be the seed of a new orientation and, as with any pod, it must first be planted, nourished, and nurtured if it is to grow and blossom.

I have been frustrated for quite a while now by the sheer lack of sincerity in the so-called "revival" of the Northern European traditions: from the absence of a true philosophical foundation upon which a strong spirituality can be built, to the disregard and outright contempt for those Fólk who came before us, our heritage and culture. Most "scholars" simply use their so called "expertise" to substantiate the monotheistic myth, often to the detriment of all else, while simultaneously disparaging and demonizing anything that does not correspond with the one omnipotent god narrative that has been espoused exponentially for well over a thousand years. Far from being uncouth or uncultured cave-dwellers, our distant ancestors laid the foundation for Western civilization long before anyone had thought to elevate one god above the others and no amount of revisionist history can change this fact. Today, too many rely on these selfsame scholars to interpret writings, carvings, items, etc. from the pre-monotheistic period, people who cannot even conceive of how our ancestors thought or felt, what they believed or practiced, and as a result we get phalluses and fertility, savages and solar cults simply because they do not understand the Fólk-Soul, let alone believe there is anything sacred or spiritual to be found beyond their myopic monotheism. It is long past time that we reclaim the narrative and development of our spirituality by producing material for the Fólk, by the Fólk.

I make no assertions to expertise, though neither do I need a piece of paper from another individual to be able to relay what I know with confidence to be true and relevant. I am a Natural Philosopher, in the vein of many great Fólk before me who believed that philosophy is the middle ground (the Midgardh if you will), between theology and science, and it is with this in mind that I present the following.

Heathen Blodharn
Vinland 4215 A.A.S.

"Philosophy is the train of thought that finally sees into its own inadequacy and realizes the need for an absolute action that originates from within."

– Julius Evola

Table of Contents

I. Archegnosis: A Brief History 1
II. Odhinism: Religion vs. Spirituality. 17
III. Ørlag: Primal Law. 47
IV. Önd ok Óð: Instinct, Intellect, Impulse 68
V. Lá ok Litu Goða: Genetic Memory 97
VI. Ár ok Aldr: Time and Eternity 117
VII. Ragnarokr: Death and Eternal Existence 135
VIII. Sovereignty. 147
IX. Rúna: The Mysteries. 164
A Note to Female Fólk. 189
Meginsmal 191
Glossary of Old Norse. 210
Other Words & Terms 215

ARCHEGNOSIS: A BRIEF HISTORY

"At the edge of history, history itself can no longer help us, and only myth remains equal to reality."

– William Irwin Thompson

Out of the mists of history, however, emanates an ephemeral phenomena that can only be referred to as a "plebeian perspective": a framework for modern society of views, values, morality, beliefs, perceptions, and judgments in which multiple religions, philosophies, cultures, and ideals all contribute to a single vulgar worldview, an inorganic outlook manifesting from the masses wherein there is no Absolute or sacred principle.

Mainstream society regards the individuality of Tradition with trepidation, anxiety, and apprehension, seeing in its unique stance a threat to the status quo, not in terms of what is right or wrong, but solely in reference to the plebeian perspective. Those who participate in the social construct of this commonly accepted worldview have no choice but to live with the conscious "realities" that permeate their belief system; they absorb this collective dogma unconsciously because they either know no better or do not care enough to manifest their own will. Either way the result remains the same: the plebeian perspective intrinsically influences how they interpret everything they see, perceive, and understand.

Individually each of us is Sovereign over our inner sanctum and like a magnet we attract the facts that we allow entry into our conscious reality, that which we accept as truth. Yet today, more than any other period of time, this reality is subject to the capricious view that one man's truth is another's delusion, with a blatant disregard for the Absolute. As a result of the vast amount of information readily available to all and sundry, truth has been submerged in a sea of redundancy, borne out by the fact that all who wish to substantiate personal predilections, no matter how perverse or overtly contrary to nature, may do so freely, with little effort and often with the full support of the plebeian perspective to lean on.

On the other hand, those who would dare to deviate from or disregard this plebeian perspective are considered outcasts or "social misfits," deemed mentally unstable and locked away or exiled to the edge of history, when in fact it is often a genuine concern for Fólk that compels them to free themselves from the fetters of the societal norm in the first place. Any who dare to dispute "history" are likewise determined to be in denial, denounced, and stigmatized as subversives.

Where once it was considered the ultimate shame to be banished from the tribe, it now becomes necessary to remove oneself from society at large and proceed to the outer limits of known experience, the boundaries of contemporary culture, just to get a glimpse beyond the plebeian perspective, begin to understand the timeless truths absent from modern education, and act in accordance with the Absolute. The rare individual who does so stands at the edge of history, where past and future collide in an absolute present, obliterating the plebeian perspective of communal collectivism and reject all forms of historicism; not as a revolution, but as a reaction, a return to Tradition.

Societies, so long as they can be called such, continue to take the same steps along the path to perdition. Initially, we see a struggle to exist as a community of likeminded individuals wherein virtue is determined by common weal against the woe of the outsider, and love of one's own is the primal driving force for all. As the community settles, they become soft, since the threat from beyond its borders has been neutralized and it is in this peaceful environment that self-mutilation begins and love of one's own becomes a struggle for power. Compassion, fairness, and assistance transform into craftiness, vengefulness, and competition, all of which lead to a weakening of the will which ultimately had seen the creation of the community as something superior, but now borders on mediocrity. Finally, the virtues this society was founded upon are upended, everything high-minded and noble, even the spirit of struggle for something superior, is deemed immoral, as the plebeian perspective takes firm hold on the community, to the point that criminals, perverts, and every type of immoralist is placed into positions of prominence, while the free-thinkers and culture-creating strata are consistently forced to the fringes and eventually the process begins anew.

Sovereignty is a spiritual and social movement towards the Absolute; it recognizes the individuality necessary for spiritual nourishment, as well as the independence of truly noble Fólk. Absolute in this sense means above or beyond time, the realization of the supraconscious state of godhead. A strong society is one that mirrors Eternity and a spiritual system that does not perpetuate this as well is counterproductive to the Ideal of the Fólk-Soul. A Sovereign recognizes the importance of Tradition, embraces the timeless truths found in ancestral teachings, and understands the significance of mythology to our Fólk. Where history fails to substantiate mythology, it is the former that must be brought into question by utilizing the Traditional method for determining truth; mythology is indeed a far more accurate account of actual events, as it is typically the accepted chronicle of an entire tribe, containing the timeless truths of these Fólk, as perceived and understood according to their nature, culture, and tradition.

A prime example of this is the Iliad, which describes the events of the Trojan War, something so-called scholars and historians alike considered a mere legend or fairy tale until amateur archeologist Heinrich Schliemann located the famed city of Troy and subsequent evidence of the Trojan War came to light. Mythology, far from being merely exaggerations of the imagination or the barbarous fancies of an uncivilized people, can be seen as the collective memory of the most distant events, while history often remains the work of one individual at the insistence of the ruling power of the time, fraught with all the frailties that entails: from personal perspective, prejudices, and predilections being woven through the tapestry of the narrative as "fact," to the heavy influence of the plebeian perspective, concerned with the thing that seems rather than what is.

Sovereignty: The Empirical Path of Odhinn

True history is, or should be, that which is able to trace the evolution of the spirit that animates our Fólk-Soul, from creation as such, to realization, with impeccable accuracy; something scholars and historians alike fail miserably to do, despite their so-called scientific mechanistic means, methods, and theories. The mythographer on the other hand is able to trace the timeless truths of a tribe, as Traditional man considered it the greatest infamy to inaccurately record or remember the deeds of our ancestors, and this belief lasted through the Heathen Era.

Seen in this light, it can be no coincidence that, though we stand upon the precipice of a new era, the Wolf Age waning, the ranks of those who would question the status quo continue to swell; despite all attempts to suppress Tradition in the name of progress, eradicate European culture and heritage with the doctrine of inclusion, and in the face of those innumerable forces that would stifle or inhibit the natural evolution of the philogenesis, all are still alive and thriving. This attests to the strength and fortitude of the Heathen spirit and its unconquerable nature.

For the better part of two centuries there has been a general restlessness across Europe reflected in her descendants around the globe, a discontentment that can only be characterized as dissatisfaction with the current state of spirituality and its fragmentary existence. Many Fólk have termed this the Great Reawakening, an apt and appropriate appellation considering unfolding events all around the world. How or why this awakening began we will likely never know, nor does it matter, as Carl Jung's *Ergriffenheit* had taken firm hold of Fólk by the time Friedrich Nietzsche declared god to be dead and suggested all good Europeans move beyond good and evil; all of which resulted in the Radical Traditionalism of Julius Evola, perhaps the greatest modern philosopher. Either way, there can be no doubt that the long slumbering consanguineous unconscious of Arya has begun to stir, awakening to its anaryan surroundings and started to shed the shackles of stagnation that have kept it bound for a millennium or more. The volksgeist is alive and thriving once more.

The strongest evidence of this is the resurgence of all things spiritual, natural, and Folkish, though only recently have most begun to realize the relationship each of these has to the others and the importance of each. Perhaps ironically, after at least three failed attempts at unifying Europe (each influenced by the church), we now find a nearly united Europe, seeking a cultural identity of its own and it is imperative that the Sovereign step forward to offer one based upon Tradition, one that emanates directly from the Fólk-Soul, and most importantly, with an eye to the future of our Fólk as a whole. This can be found along the Path of Odhinn.

As a Fólk we have long forged our own paths, daring to venture forth when nobody else would; we have founded and built nearly every great civilization that has ever existed, influenced the rest, conquered and inhabited almost every square mile of this planet and explored those regions that were inhospitable; we have developed systems of philosophical thought that most cannot even fathom, been at the forefront of scientific discoveries, technological advancements and the innovations that characterize progress in today's societies; we have offered some of the greatest minds to ever live, from poets, playwrights, and singers, to scientists, philosophers, and explorers. Thus is the heritage we hope to preserve, the Tradition we must once again embrace as sacred, that desire to be the best, to seek out and gain wisdom, to grow, thrive, evolve, and advance, not just as individuals, but as a Fólk. Our greatest gift to the world was spirituality, something we squandered along the way, but can regain with Sovereignty.

It is significant that no skeletal remains of any person or civilization not indigenous to Europe have ever been found on or in her soil, the *Óðal* land of our Fólk, while remnants of our ancestors have been located all over the world; from the Solutreans of modern day Northern Spain and Southern France, of whom it has been determined introduced the famous Clovis point to North America some 20,000 years ago, to the hundreds of mummified bodies found in the Taklimakan desert region of the Tarim Basin in Northwest China, all of whom were so pristinely preserved as to allow for them to be indisputably identified as early Fólk with reddish-blond hair, blue eyes, and wearing Celtic styled clothing, thriving in this area at least 4,000 years ago. The remains of prehistoric Fólk have been found everywhere from North Africa to modern Iran, Iraq, Turkey, the entire Fertile Crescent, Afghanistan, Russia, India, and South America, as well as Japan, where the Caucasoid Ainu still exist; all attesting to the inquisitive instinct of our Fólk and our desire to explore, seek out knowledge and wisdom wherever it is to be found, and all in an effort to expand our collective conscious, to achieve ever greater feats.

The history of our Fólk and accomplishments are beyond the scope of the current undertaking, however, some of the more significant events and developments are worth noting and are necessary to a proper understanding of our spiritual evolution.

c200,000bp: First known altars found in Swiss-German Alps.

c35,000bp: Earliest known spiritual practices anywhere in the world are found in Western Europe. First known script in the world found in Europe. Earliest statuettes/figurines/pendants found in Europe.

c20,000bp: Solutreans introduce Clovis point to North America.

c16,000bp: Antarctica located 2,000 miles to the North of current location.

c12,000bp: Last Ice Age ends; primary habitation for Europeans (currently the English Channel) is flooded.

c10,000bp: First civilization thrives in what is today Germany, Slovakia, and the Czech Republic; Cheddar Man thrives in the British Isles.

c8,000bp: Settlement thriving just off the Isle of Wight.

c5,200bce: Fólk inhabit Malta.

c5,000bce: Longest continually existing city is built in what is today Sweden; Gosek henge, the oldest known solar observatory, is built and sanctified in modern day Germany.

c3,800bce: Megaliths built on Malta.

c3,200bce: Construction of Stonehenge completed (begun as early as c6,000bce); Newgrange is built.

3,114bce: Meteor hits Austria.

c3,000bce: Montevecchia built in Northern Italy; Ring of Brodgar built in Orkney.

c2,720bce: Hellenikon pyramid built in Greece.

c2,660bce: Silbury Hill built in England.
c2,500bce: Durrington Walls is thriving short distance from Stonehenge.

2,213bce: Hale-Bopp comet passes earth.

c2,200bce: Summer solstice leaves Leo for Cancer; Bactria-Margiana Archaeological Complex (Oxus civilization) is thriving; Major flooding at Lough Neagh in Northern Ireland; Taklimakan Fólk thriving in Northwestern China; Maltan Fólk disappear.

2,193bce: Aldland sinks.

c1,550bce: Volcano erupts on Santorini.

c1,500bce: Aryans enter the Indus Valley with the Rig Veda.

c1,350bce: Akhenaten declares there is only one god.

c1,300bce: Moses found on the Nile.

c1,200bce: Goloring henge is built in the Koberner Forest, said to be a sacred Druid site.

1,188bce: Trojan War.

c700-600bce: Paradigm shift in consciousness from right brain creativity to left brain logic occurs, leading to the creation of a number of schools of thought and spiritual systems.

c70bce: The Odhinn of the Ynglinga renews Odhinism.

It is likely that our Ur-Fólk were the Hyperboreans and that it was these ancestors that handed down all forms of philosophy and spirituality initially; there can be no doubt that this knowledge and wisdom evolved naturally in Europe until the monotheistic crusades attempted to eradicate Odhinism. Even the Greeks attest to the fact that Apollo had migrated

Sovereignty: The Empirical Path of Odhinn

from the land of the Hyperboreans and his worship extended all the way to Troy at the very least. We need not go that far back to explore the sacred spirituality and motifs of our Fólk, however, but instead simply examine the oral and written sources we have according to the Traditional method of Evola and allow Instinct to guide us to the truth.

> *"During the past fifty years learned men of many nations have investigated philology and comparative mythology so thoroughly that they have ascertained beyond the possibility of doubt that English, together with all the Teutonic dialects of the continent, belongs to that large family of speech which comprises, besides Teutonic, Latin, Greek, Slavonic, and Celtic, the languages of India and Persia. It has also been proved that the various Tribes who started from the central home to discover Europe in the North and India in the South, carried away with them, not only a common language, but a common faith and a common mythology. These are facts which may be ignored, but cannot be disputed."*

This comes from the seminal work "Myths of the Norsemen," published in 1909 by Helene Adeline Guerber, long before the corruption that came about post-WWII, with most so-called scholarly works proposing to be examinations of our mythology or way of life. Most people today understand on some superficial level that all of the "Indo-European" mythology is linked, however, many do not realize that all of it comes from our Fólk-Soul, nor that, despite the fact that so much has evolved separately over time, it still relies on common motifs and symbology to achieve Sovereignty. The proof of this is found in our languages.

The spoken word is the primary vehicle for cultural and spiritual practices and beliefs, for without it no two people can share the beliefs and behaviors that become custom, convention, and culture. Today we are well aware that there existed a proto-language from which our family of languages descends and in the early days of etymology this was referred to as Aryan, likely derived from both the people who spoke it, as well as the area from which this proto-language derived. Since WWII this family of languages has been known as Indo-European, though this is a misnomer considering no language in our tree originated outside of Europe, nor from any but our Fólk.

The importance of this distinction is found most prominently in the wisdom of the Rig Veda: as an oral source it was wholly Aryan, though as a written text it was corrupted by the Dravidians, those the Aryans had conquered in the Indus Valley.

> *"The Aryans came from outside India. We actually have genetic evidence for that. Very clear genetic evidence from a marker that arose on the Southern steppes of Russia and the Ukraine around 5,000 to 10,000 years ago, and it is subsequently spread to the East and South through central Asia, reaching India."*
>
> — Spencer Wells

These Aryans were likely the Tocharians, those Fólk found in the Taklimakan Desert, perhaps even the Ainu; these Aryans migrated to the East and West long before reaching India or even Iran. Often overlooked is that these Aryans also went West and it is likely that the Rig Veda is the root of the Edda, existing as an oral tradition in Europe for more than 2,000 years because our Fólk considered speech sacred, believing the spoken word and song to be a gift from the Gods through the end of the Heathen Era. Inscribing symbols and characters was thought to be the province of magic and divination, thus to record the wisdom of the Gods via inscription was to make it profane, the ultimate sacrilege. This is why oral traditions persisted through the Middle Ages in Europe and some remnants can still be found to this day. Contrary to popular opinion, prehistoric European man was not incapable of writing; he merely had no desire to do so, as the spoken verse and *galdr* were considered far superior to the written word.

The linguistic center of gravity premise postulates that the roots of a language family tree are found firmly grounded in the region of greatest variation and in the case of Aryan this would be Eastern Europe in the area known today as Ukraine into Western Kazakhstan; this then marks the likely point of origin for not only our linguistic roots, but cultural, philosophic, and spiritual source as well. Interestingly, there is only one river specifically mentioned in our proto-language and that is the river Don or *danu*. In the Ynglinga Saga this river is called the Tanais and was said to separate Sweden and Sweden the Great; where the rivers Don and

Volga are closest was known as the Tanakvisl or the Vanaforks, due to the fact that *Vanaland* or Vanaheim, the home of the *Vanir*, is located here.

The *Tuatha de Danaan* are considered the greatest of the Celtic Gods and most Fólk regard them as the Goddess Danu's Fólk, though this is only partially true; a more accurate interpretation of *Tuatha de Danaan* would be Tribe of the river Don, and as such, is likewise the *Vanir*. It is well known that the earliest inhabitants of the British Isles were Celts and among these the Welsh remain the purest of indigenous peoples, as they were never conquered nor subjugated in any substantial way. The Welsh are known as Cambrians, derived from Cymri, which is identical to Cimbri and Cimmerians, the Fólk that both Greek and Roman historians note as having originated from North of the Black Sea, to spread across the Northwest of Europe. Interestingly, it is in modern Wales that the earliest Fólk, the henge builders, are said to have first arrived from the mainland before dispersing into Ireland and England.

The Aryans likewise are known to have come from the lower Volga North of the Caucasus Mountains and recent research has revealed these Fólk as the Yamnaya, a people who are said to have domesticated the horse some 6,000 years ago in the region around modern day Botai, Kazakhstan. These Yamnaya spoke proto-Aryan, the original language of our Fólk and this language, along with the cultural and spiritual beliefs it embodied, dominated Europe within a short period of time. Snorri says, "The land in Asia to the East of the Tanakvisl was called Asaland or Asaheim and the chief town in the land was called Asagardh." It is likely that Asia gets its very name from the *Aesir*, however, there can be no doubt that this Asaland is the original home of the Aryans/Yamnaya. Marijia Gimbutas has demonstrated that the Aryans must have still been flourishing in this area in the third millennium before common era, while linguists and archaeologists alike agree that these Fólk must still have been together when the horse (**èkwos*) was first domesticated, but had likely begun their migration in every direction by 2,300bce. Interestingly, Snorri also referred to an Old Asgardh as a place, as well as a language:

"Who is the highest and most ancient of gods?"
"High said: 'He is called All-Father in our language,
but in Old Asgardh he had twelve names.'"

Here Snorri is clearly referring to a language, seemingly to distinguish what the *Aesir* spoke from that spoken in Scandinavia during Gylfi/Gangleri's time. The spread of this original "Old Asgardh" language is associated with Y-chromosome haplogroup R1a1, which is identified with genetic marker M17. Philologists have identified the region North of the Caspian and Aral Seas as the original homeland of the Aryan family of languages, thus the proto-language of our Fólk. The genetic legacy of India substantiates this as well:

> *"Analysis of these data demonstrates that the upper castes [Aryans] have a higher affinity to Europeans than to Asians and the upper castes are significantly more similar to Europeans than are the lower castes. Collectively, all five datasets show a trend toward upper castes being more similar to Europeans, whereas lower castes are more similar to Asians."*
>
> – Michael Bamshad, et. al.

While the indigenous name of these Fólk cannot be ascertained with certainty, nor reconstructed, and despite modern scholars referring to them as Yamnaya, *aryo* was sometimes held as a self-identification and has been attested to as an ethnic designation, from which we get Aryan. To the West its cognates *aeth/óð* and *aire* have been used by Fólk to indicate noble descent.

From this then we can identify the *Vanir*/Danaan (Celts) and *Aesir*/Aryans as the two tribes of Fólk referred to in our wisdom teachings, as well as the Gods and Goddesses; this is an important distinction for several reasons, the most significant of which can be seen in the mention of the first war in the world:

that man hon fólkvíg the Fólk-war she recalls
fyrst i heimi first in homes
(Voluspa 21)
fleygdhi Odhinn flew Odhinn
ok i fólk umskaut in and around Fólk
that var enn fólkvíg was that one Fólk-war
fyrst i heimi first in homes
(Voluspa 24)

Sovereignty: The Empirical Path of Odhinn

Left out of every translation of the Voluspa for some strange reason is any mention of this *fólkvíg*, literally "Fólk conflict" or civil war, referring to a battle between a people connected biologically, linguistically, culturally, and spiritually. This first war in the homes of Fólk, Vanaheim and Asaheim presumably, was between the *Vanir* and *Aesir*, Celt and Aryan, the result of which was a treaty with an agreement to share worship; this syncretism of *Vanir* earth veneration and knowledge, with *Aesir* sky worship and wisdom is what we know Odhinism to be today. As part of this treaty Kvasir as "perfected wisdom" was the result of the pact among *Aesir* and *Vanir*, a being that "travelled widely through the worlds teaching people knowledge." It is not difficult to imagine the Tanais as the Van-Aes and not just according to fólk etymology, but in recognition of the coming together of two tribes. Nor would it be much of a stretch to believe that many Fólk would be unhappy with such a blending, electing to keep their identity intact and so we have Aryans migrating East and South, while the *Tuatha de Danaan* were pushed westward, each maintaining their respective linguistic, cultural, and spiritual beliefs for a time—long enough for us to have remnants of both aside from the other.

Too often when studying the spiritual and historical beliefs and practices of a people, particularly from prehistoric recorded traditions, we find that, though two tribes originating from the same source should have similar customs or wisdom teachings, they often differ, even to the point of opposing one another. This is seen in the Edda and Rig Veda: though there are similarities between them, there also remain a number of differences as well and this can be attributed to who recorded each, in addition to the way in which each evolved apart from the other. The Aryans, after assimilating with the Dravidians of the Indus Valley, recorded the Rig Veda in fixed form and due to the latter's elevation of the priests to positions of prominence, it remained this way for generations; this is and has been the practice of priests around the world, even the Druids, and is the reason most spiritual paths stagnate, suffocating from their religious dogmatism. The Edda, however, was allowed to evolve naturally with the Fólk, until a monotheistic priest elected to record what lays he could learn, likely in corrupt form. This can also be seen in cultures as close as the Avestan and Vedic as well, both deriving from the Aryans, but different in many ways.

Archegnosis: A Brief History

With this in mind it can be daunting for the seeker to separate truth from falsehood, though it need not be overwhelming. Ultimately, how each of us nourishes our spirit is solely determined by the self; no text or so-called expert, no guru, *goði* or god can explain exactly what is needed or necessary to nourish our individual spirit.

> *"One's self alone is aware*
> *What within lay lingering*
> *A man his mind alone has ascertained"*
>
> — Havamal

We can gain knowledge through study, wisdom through experiences and practice, and others can offer us guidance, advice, or recommendations but, in the final analysis, only our self can determine what is right or wrong, what is of benefit and what is injurious to the spirit, or how we should live in this life. This is not to say that we should not read the Sagas or study the mythologies and wisdom teachings of our Fólk, nor learn from those further along the Path than we are; on the contrary, all of these are absolutely essential to the Path and as we pursue them we must always be aware that they can only take us so far before we will have to rely upon our self to reach what should be.

To this end then two things are important for anyone wishing to follow the Path of Odhinn: an understanding of *heimliche acht* and the motifs which are inherent in our Fólk-Soul. The primary problem with interpreting theological texts today that were written so long ago, is the impulse to see in lore and legend a single literal meaning, or worse, a universal meaning meant for everyone, which is absurd.

The natural order of our world is threefold, three-dimensional, and the tripartite structure of organizing and ordering this world emanates exclusively from our Fólk-Soul. Georges Dumezil demonstrated this, as have countless others, though there is nothing more profound perhaps than the *heimliche acht* of Guido von List. This concept embodies the notion that all knowledge and wisdom generated by our distant ancestors and handed down to us for untold millennia, has a threefold aspect to it: the esoteric or higher symbolism, the exoteric or lower symbolism, and the mundane or worldly understanding. Contemporary culture is based almost exclusively on this last; thus is the reason for the moral and spiritual decay and decadence of our Fólk.

Von List understood the *heimliche acht* as arising, being, and passing away, though this seems a bit simplistic. The Trimurti of the Aryans is Brahma, Vishnu, and Shiva or creator, preserver, and destroyer respectively; their counterparts in Odhinism are Odhinn, Hoenir, and Lodhurr, and these too can be seen as creation, preservation, and destruction. This seems to be a better way to view *heimliche acht*. Along the same lines the *heimliche acht* is the esoteric that gazes down from above, the exoteric that looks up from below, and the mundane that sees only what is before the eyes. It is through this lens that we must view the world around us as well as that within; this unlocks a door to a *Weltanschauung* based not on books alone, but an internal inheritance as well, an inherent character rather than one obtained externally. This worldview derives not from any one individual, but from the Fólk-Soul and is our ordered and organic spiritual development, expressed as existential framework from which will and power derive; it is not reliant upon purely psychic, rational, or theoretical thought or conceptions, but a balanced approach to life, an attitude that includes Intellect, Impulse, and Instinct in a holistic and harmonious whole.

> *"As there are three divine concepts and three intelligible realms, so is there a triple word, because hierarchic order is ever manifested by the triad. There are (a) simple speech, (b) hieroglyphic speech, and (c) symbolic speech. In other terms there is the word which expresses, there is the concealing, and finally, there is the word that signifies. All hieratic intelligence is in the perfect science of these three degrees."*
>
> – Pythagoras

It is not merely the way in which we perceive the world that is important, however, but what we see as sacred and spiritual, the motifs made manifest by the Fólk-Soul, as well as how we relate these to one another and the world at large. Since the dawn of consciousness some of the more significant symbols and ideals for Fólk include:

The Sun: our Fólk are and always have been solar worshippers in the truest sense of the term. The sun is life itself and what emanates from it is considered sacred; the *fylfót* and swastika symbolized this. All of the oldest solar observatories are in Europe, demonstrating the importance of the sun for our Fólk. The sowilo rune represents the sun as well.

The Circle/Spiral: to our Fólk the circle symbolizes Eternity and completion, while the spiral represents cyclical time and evolution. There are hundreds of known henges spread across Europe that evince just how sacred the circle is to our Fólk. Within this are the notions of caste, the four Ages, the seasons, etc. corresponding to the jera rune.

The Cow: our most distant ancestors considered the cow sacred and it is the first living thing in our cosmogony. The cow represented wealth and the aurochs was central to our belief system from its beginning. The cow is one of the few animals we know from our proto-language in the word **gwous*. The concept of the cow and its primal origins is found in the uruz rune.

The Horse: another animal known from Aryan is the horse or **èkwos*. The horse was both spiritually significant and practical, in that it is found all through our mythology since before we first domesticated it. The importance of the horse is found in the numerous rituals and ritual burials involving it and this is represented in the ehwaz rune.

Ancestor Worship: reverence for the Fólk who came before is and has always been a key component of our spirituality; it is this more than anything else that impeaches the universalist agenda. We have likewise long understood how important the blood is as evinced by Blót and blood rituals. The significance of our heritage, culture, and inheritance can be found in the othala rune.

The Tree: perhaps the most sacred of all our motifs, the tree represents all of existence, as well as our Fólk itself as we are descended from trees. In addition, all of our rituals are ideally performed in groves and most henges were made of wood as it represented life. The tree is found as a sacred symbol throughout our mythology and is represented by the berkano rune.

The Hammer: exclusive to our Fólk, the Hammer is the ultimate symbol of balance, as it is capable of both creation and destruction, depending solely on how it is utilized by the individual; the Hammer can and is used by the blacksmith as well as the warrior. Additionally the sign of the Hammer is known to predate that of the cross and represents the four gifts given us by the Gods: *óð, önd, lá,* and *litu goða.*

It is this archegnosis that Odhinism has reclaimed, embodies, and seeks to realize as Sovereignty. Many Fólk today attempt to emulate the Víkings not realizing that the Norse were but the last of the great large-scale Heathen cultures that stretched back to Tacitus' Germania, Homer's Trojans, the Aryans of the Rig Veda, and even further back into prehistory. As more and more Fólk awaken to our ancestral traditions and wisdom teachings, heeding the call of their blood, it becomes necessary to prepare a path for these Fólk to follow.

It is long past time to reclaim our birthright (from the *óðhal* lands to the Sovereignty of the Fólk-Soul), to liberate our spirituality from the misunderstanding and misappropriation of the masses. If we are to succeed, the Sovereign, that nomad of the spirit, must step forward and lead the way. The Path first forged for Fólk by Odhinn is Empirical, a journey of becoming that begins with what is and leads to what should be; it is not fixed for all Fólk, but is a form found in the individual Intellect, Impulse, and Instinct. This Path is akin to a map and like any good map is not the territory to be traversed nor the journey itself, but simply directions to a destination; in this instance from *óð* to Odhinn, or self to Sovereign Self. This Path has been cleared of detritus and debris and leads to the edge of history.

ODHINISM: RELIGION VS. SPIRITUALITY

"I wonder how many of you know that the earliest unquestionable evidence of mythology and ritual has been found precisely in this part of the world: Switzerland and the German Alps."

– Joseph Campbell

Embodying the wisdom and inspiration drawn primarily from the written sources of Sagas and Eddas as well as the inherent instincts in our blood, Odhinism is the Path for whom true spirituality is a way of life rather than a religion as defined and understood by modern standards. Odhinism is the purest form of spiritual practice found in the world today, though the Timeless Truths it is predicated upon predate any known organized religious system and are based upon the eldest spirituality to be found anywhere: the first known worship, the oldest altars or figurative art, the earliest statuettes, figurines, and pendants, even the eldest script or hieroglyphic symbols, all of which date to c35,000 BCE in Europe. In addition, these are the oldest solar observatories, used to monitor and measure the skies, aligned to the Summer and Winter solstices, spread across the European landscape, from the British Isles, Shetlands, to the mainland, dating to as early as c5,000 BCE. All of these are emanations of the Fólk-Soul, reflections of Absolute Law, and the inherent order of the multiverse. Odhinism is at the same time atavistic and eternal, exemplified in the customs, practices, lore, legend, traditions, and culture of Pan-Aryan Fólk, their ancestors and descendants exclusively; in a word, Odhinism is gestaltic, a Path for the eclectic European of today.

Manifestly the philogenesis is the consanguineous unconscious, the Fólk-Soul that connects us to one another and the Gods, that Breath of Life wherein the spirit resides and through which we are bound by blood not borders nor base beliefs. The soul is incorporeal, has no body or material form as such, though is the foundation upon which all life is built; it is drawn from the collective unconscious of our Fólk (often symbolized by a cauldron or well in our mythology) when we are born and contains the aggregate knowledge of our ancestors from the dawn of consciousness. During our existence each of us accumulate experiences and understanding that nourish our soul and upon our death this accumulation returns to the well to add to this great fountain of wisdom known as genetic memory, that "mens' certain knowledge" of Mimir's Well. Ultimately this soul of our Fólk can and will attain the state described by Nietzsche as the *übermensch* as a whole people, by each of us achieving Sovereignty as individuals. Odhinism then is the Path to this state of supraconsciousness through which we transcend the mundane, unnatural, and inferior quality of the masses (the temporal) towards the Sovereignty of Eternal Existence.

It is in the contemporary cultural climate, wherein monotheism and materialism reign supreme (what we would call the Wolf Age) that the Heathen way of life requires a name, though for thousands of years all who walked the Path, from Achilles and Leonidas to Beowulf and Egil Skallagrimson, Roman, Celt, Víking, and Aryan alike could each be considered Odhinist and yet none were compelled to give their way of life an appellation, let alone a label. Most modern adherents are satisfied simply being referred to as Heathen, even in the sense that it is widely given today: those who do not accept or acknowledge the "one true god" of monotheism. Others feel it necessary to distinguish themselves further, thus we have everything from Asatru, Theodism, and Wotanist, to Vanatru, Norse Paganism, Neo-Druidic, and even some obscure fringe types who mistakenly attempt to blend elements of Wicca or Satanism into the Heathen belief system, all ranging from the unnecessary to the ridiculous.

Worse yet are those who create confusion by foolishly claiming that ours is not a Folkish way of life that is unique to and emanates from the Fólk-Soul of those we refer to as a whole as European today. This idiocy stems first from fear of being branded a racist or tied to the actions of World War II Germany and secondly from the guilt (especially in America) our Fólk are supposed to feel for what occurred during World War II and all the associated atrocities we are allegedly directly responsible for today and which demonstrate how inherently evil our Fólk must be. This fear and guilt are unequivocally misplaced, however, first and foremost because we are not responsible for any of the incidents so often cited as examples of what we should feel guilty for; this mindset comes from monotheistic notions of original sin, whereas Odhinists believe in personal accountability and meritocracy. All of the worst atrocities this world has ever known were committed by monotheists whose actions were supported by their holy book and perpetuated in the name of their one true god: from forced conversions to being burned at the stake for being different or simply disagreeing; from the Inquisitions to the Crusades; from the Catholic and Protestant conflict in Ireland to the jihad of the Muslims that continues to wage war on the world. Monotheism is responsible for more death and destruction than anything else in history put together, something that cannot be said of Odhinism, nor any Heathen.

As to the charge of racism, this remains among the most absurd accusations lodged against Fólk who firmly believe Odhinism to be exclusive to Europeans, their ancestors, and descendants alone and attempt to ensure it remains that way. Recognizing a difference or distinction between two things is not discrimination in and of itself; it is only when a value judgment is placed upon differentiation that it becomes something susceptible to measurement. As two examples we can look at Judaism and Shinto: on the one hand Hebrews declared themselves the chosen people of their one true god which is inherently racist by today's standards, while Shinto is the indigenous religion of Japan marked by reverence of the spirits of natural forces and ancestors (virtually identical to Odhinism) and is considered exclusive to Japanese people alone; both are accorded the proper respect as religions, not racist ideologies, and

Odhinists demand the same regard. Thus is the final word on the charge of racism.

It is under Odhinism that truly Folkish Heathens find spiritual nourishment through our culture, tradition, heritage, and worship of the Gods, Ancestors, and Self. With this in mind it only remains to explain exactly what Odhinism is to those of us who actually walk this Path, rather than relying on the reconstructions of supposed scholars who have absolutely no clue about our Gods or how to experience the exchange of divine energies with them.

Many often mistakenly view Odhinism as an attempt at Heathen monotheism with Odhinn in the role of the one true god, however, nothing could be further from the truth. While Odhinn may have revealed the Path of Wisdom that leads to Sovereignty, it takes all types to make a tribe thrive, and all of the Gods and Goddesses are equally worthy of respect and reverence, as are our Fólk as their descendants.

There can be no doubt that Odhinn was not the first Allfather, nor was his worship widespread; rather he represents a concept for our Fólk that empowers each of us to realize that we too can be Sovereign; this can be found in the very roots of his name, which was likely a title or tribal designation akin to shaman initially. The Old Norse *Óð* (Germanic *wit*, archaic *wot*; akin to skt. veda) can best be defined as "to know," thus Odhinn would be "one who knows." *Óð* however has been variously translated as ecstasy, the stuff of poetry, possession, understanding, inspiration, movement, frenzied, sense of mobility, power, divinity, and fury (to name but a few), all of which can be found in what we have come to understand as the shamanistic structure, yet the extant mythology would seem to place Odhinn somewhere between a shaman, sorcerer, and ascetic. The similarities between the stories surrounding Odhinn and known shamanistic practices are too striking to be mere coincidence; his predominant attributes, however, would appear to be of a more ascetic nature, in that pursuit of knowledge, wisdom, and the mysteries of life, death, the runes, spells, etc. along with their subsequent preservation seem to be of primary importance rather than a sole concern for the spiritual nourishment and health of Tribal members which was the exclusive domain of the shaman.

The Old Norse *Óð* seems to have taken on the totality of the Old English *wod* (meaning rage, fury, wild, madness, etc.) and *wot* ("to know" or understand, mind, thought, etc.) which makes sense when one examines *óðr* in the context of having both *hugr* and *munr* (Intellect and Impulse) inherent in it. Odhinn is the ultimate example of how the two are properly balanced. Because the Intellect discriminates as part of its natural function and is an active part of the psyche, it is directly analogous to consciousness, thus linked to Impulse and Instinct. Subconsciousness is simply Impulse-Intellect while unconsciousness is Instinct-Intellect. This interconnectedness demonstrates the importance of the three aspects of the soul: Instinct influences both Intellect and Impulse, Intellect monitors Impulse and Instinct to separate need from desire, while Impulse allows for the Will to Power to fulfill Intellect or Instinct.

Those who would claim that our ancestors did not have this depth of comprehension or understand consciousness as such need look no further than Skaldskaparmal 70 where "thought" is described first as the act of thinking, but second as emotion, referring to the Intellect and Impulse-Intellect dynamic respectively. Initially it makes mention of a metaphysical way of viewing the Instinct-Intellect as the "wind of troll-wives" or "whichever one you like," i.e. "wind of Odhinn" would refer to divine thought and emotion.

With this in mind it is imperative to those seeking Sovereignty to gain a spiritual understanding of Odhinn's ravens and their relation to him. Just as *óð* is the self of Intellect and Impulse and Odhinn is the Sovereign Self balancing these two aspects, Huginn and Munnin represent the perfected state of Thought and Emotion.

Many mistakenly translate Muninn as "memory" or some related notion of remembrance, though the etymology does not support this interpretation. The Old Norse *mimir* means memory, while *minni* translates as "my" or remembrance, implying the act of remembering rather than memory itself or even a memory. On the other hand, just as Huginn derives from the Old Norse *hugr* ("thought" or "mind") Muninn stems from *munr* ("desire" or "delight") suggesting something longed for, sought after, a wish, or what one takes great pleasure in, all of which is appropriate to sensibility. The Old Norse suffix *-inn* is used to form the superlative degree and can be translated as "leader of" or "first in" (equivalent to modern English *-est* denoting the highest degree of a quality or attribute, or the most and highest) implying THE, as in THE Self (Odhinn), THE Intellect (Huginn), and THE Impulse (Muninn); it should be noted that the feminine equivalent is *-yn*.

Sovereignty: The Empirical Path of Odhinn

In this we see a strong correlation with left-brain logic and right-brain intuition: Huginn represents that Higher Intellect of strong mental faculties, the capacity for reason, logical deduction, and the contemplation of Higher Thought; conversely, Muninn symbolizes Higher Impulse, Will to Power, desire as aspiration, and action towards something specific, often indecipherable and subconscious, and stresses the strength of a feeling, especially the intentions and intuitions of Higher Desire.

Huginn ok Muninn	Sovereign Intellect and Sovereign Impulse
fljuga hverian dag	fly every day
jormungrund yfir;	over earth's wide ground;
oumc ek of Huginn	I worry about Sovereign Intellect
at hann aptr ne comith	that after he not return
tho siamc meirr um Muninn	more though fear for Sovereign Impulse

Etymology often holds an integral key to spiritual concepts that can be missed or overlooked if not examined closely and such is the case here. When put into proper context it is easy to see how Odhinn's Intellect and Impulse could be personified as ravens and it is this that connects the shamanistic elements of Odhinism to that of the psyche: Huginn and Muninn are Odhinn's totems, his tutelary spirits, what we refer to as *fylgjur* today, though they also represent wisdom, wherewithal, and Will to Power.

Each day Odhinn must balance the Intellect and Impulse to tap into the collective unconscious and maintain his Sovereignty, thus his ravens "fly" over the earth each day, likely alluding to Odhinn contemplating and intuiting daily through meditation, trance, *staða*, etc. seeking ever more knowledge. Odhinn fears the loss of his ability to think, reason, rationalize, and analyze, as the capacity for contemplation is essential for higher states of consciousness. Whether due to old age or some other cause he feels a sense of dread at the possibility of "losing" his mind as it were, which in an age of Alzheimer's we can certainly understand today. Conversely, he seems more concerned at the possibility of "losing" his ability to feel, his passion for life, drive, and desire, with intuition being likewise essential for higher states of consciousness. Emotion compels us, is our Will to Power and desire to accomplish ever more and without Impulse we could not live; if one DOES nothing then they ARE nothing.

Odhinism: Religion vs. Spirituality

This is certainly a genuine concern as can be seen in Havamal 95: "No sickness is worse to one who is wise than to lose the longing for life."

Accepting that Odhinism evolved from shamanism it then becomes necessary to examine this evolution, so as to fully understand what Odhinism is today and where it will be tomorrow. Ultimately the study of the past should and must be undertaken in an effort to pinpoint why and precisely where the sacred and spiritual became profane, so as to incorporate the relevant remnants into modern philosophy and practice; at the same time we must focus on the future as the only way we will grow, thrive, and evolve naturally once more, never stagnating nor becoming fixed and rigid in our spirituality.

The term shaman is said to be derived from the Evenki *saman* (sa- "to know") which, while it has an interesting correlation to Odhinn as "one who knows," is not likely where it originates for our Fólk. In the so-called Proto-Indo-European reconstruction can be found *kaman or "man who desires," while others claim shaman comes from the Sanskrit *sram* "to heal oneself" or "practice asceticism." Either way it is likely that Odhinn is the Old Norse equivalent of shaman and served initially to designate the individual who took this role for the Tribe; Wotan would be the Germanic counterpart.

Shamanism is defined as a religious system practiced by the indigenous peoples of Northern Europe and Siberia and can be characterized by belief in an unseen world of gods, demons, and ancestral spirits responsive only to the shaman; a definition that could equally apply to Odhinism. Also like Odhinism, shamanism is empirical, not determined by doctrine or dogma. Even today we have no guru, rather *goðar* who act as guides and intermediaries between the Fólk and Gods in spiritual matters only until such time as the individual is able to communicate with them on their own.

In support of Odhinn as shaman and Odhinism being rooted in shamanism, we see in the Ynglinga Saga:

> *"Odhinn often changed himself; at those times his body lay as though he were asleep or dead, and he then became a bird or a beast, a fish or a dragon, and went in an instant to far-off lands on his own or other men's errands."*

Some Fólk claim that Snorri's account of Odhinn in the Ynglinga Saga is merely a Christian attempt at euhemerism, though this is unlikely for many reasons. First, his apparent desire to record the truth as best he could from the poems of skalds and "old wise men," both of which he had a great amount of respect for, as his introduction makes clear. He likewise states that lies and loose talk would be considered "mockery, but not praise." Lastly, much of what Snorri wrote throughout the Heimskringla has been substantiated by other sources, so it makes no logical sense that he would intentionally euhemerize the "mythological" beginnings if they were believed to be true during his time.

Nevertheless, a few of the more prominent shamanistic elements include Odhinn hanging from the tree of knowledge, Yggdrasil, "Ygg's horse"; the shaman's drum often being referred to as a horse and used for divination, and we know Odhinn gained knowledge of runes from this ritual. He likewise would journey to the underworld on behalf of himself or others such as Baldr, seeking answers, cures, resolutions, etc. We also find fasting and mutilation, along with necromancy, and the use of symbols to cast magical spells and charms. This is by no means an exhaustive list of shamanistic practices Odhinn was said to partake in, but a few examples to demonstrate the connection between the two.

It should also be noted that, much like the South American shamans who utilize Ayahuasca as a "hallucinatory" entrance to the "other world," Odhinn is said to survive on mead alone, though this mead, like Soma (or Haoma) was likely not merely an alcoholic one but included ingredients that have since been lost, perhaps the leaves of a Yew tree properly prepared or even some form of cannabis to give it a hallucinatory quality. A familiar entheogen to our ancestors was *Amanita Muscara*, native throughout the temperate and boreal regions of the Northern hemisphere only; it could not be cultivated, thus had to be found and likely kept on hand by the shaman of the tribe.

Before being recognized as the spiritual leader of the tribe, a shaman had to go through a series of initiation rites culminating in his or her "death" and "dismemberment," at which point they would journey to the underworld to undergo a trial that ultimately led to the initiate being measured (worthed) by the Gods and Ancestral spirits. Upon being found worthy (or not as the case may be—these latter were said to never return from the underworld) the shaman would return to their body "resurrected" and "reborn" with an ancestral tutelary spirit to guide their work in the world. In the case of a particularly powerful shaman there would likely be any number of supporting spirits, as with Odhinn's Valkyries, ravens, wolves, etc.

This "rebirth" was the only means by which the shaman could be initiated into the mysteries of the underworld, much the same way Odhinn, from his place upon the tree, looked down and grasped the runes. According to Mircae Eliade, the *Axis Mundi* (a central pillar most commonly referred to as a World-Tree) allows access to the underworld and the subsequent knowledge gained from those inhabiting it; this Path is one normally reserved for the dead, however, becomes accessible to the shaman while alive through their worth and "rebirth." Eliade further asserts that shamanism itself consists of a collection of techniques allowing one to negotiate the bridge between this world and the next, collect the knowledge and wisdom associated with it and bring it back for the betterment of the Tribe. Among these techniques are rhythmic beating of the drum, dreams, fasting, trance, hypnosis, isolation in remote regions, the use of hallucinatory intoxicants, or some combination of these. Most often, however, it is a "near-death" experience that leads to the more profound attainment.

Shamans reach into their unconscious (where the Ancestral memory exists) through these techniques to bring information contained therein to conscious awareness; in this, we see the symbology behind the shaman's journey from "this world" (consciousness) to the "underworld" of unconsciousness. The "death" of the shaman and subsequent "rebirth" can be explained by the *Betawellen* and *Alphawellen* described by German physician Hans Berger as the two fundamental biorhythms of man: the first is a pattern of normal frequency in the brain waves for a conscious person, while the second is a pattern of brain wave activity much slower, associated with an alert but daydreaming mind akin to a trancelike or meditative state. It is in this latter defocalized condition that the shaman is able to tap into the stream of unconsciousness where "mens' certain knowledge" is contained. Connecting all existence is the DNA of life itself, which is matter, thus to attune oneself to this uniting principle one must (like a resistor) slow the flow of energy into or through the body. Matter relies on a slow rate of vibration, thus conducts and utilizes less energy while spirit itself exists at a level far beyond the capacity of most to even comprehend, likely at what is known as the harmonic frequency, said to vibrate at 144,000 hertz, a very suspicious number. Sometime later the terms Delta and Theta rhythms were coined to describe the lower levels of the subconscious, which could seemingly mimic "death" in their pattern of slow brain wave frequency.

A shaman is one who alters their consciousness in a manner consistent with metaphysical methods—a chief concern to modern Odhinists as well. Ecstasy can be defined as the uninhibited display of unconsciousness that pours forth from an individual attuned to their inherent nature, primarily through the stream of genetic memory completely unfettered by egotistic control. When Instinct overrides and drowns out convention, conscious control and contemporary limitations, the result is a powerful display of unlimited potential and unbridled godliness. Odhinism, like shamanism, was at one time frenetic and frenzied, a sublime state of completely free unconscious projection realized consciously.

As *óðr* suggests, shamanic techniques were ecstatic and yet unconsciously psychological; rhythmic drumming, dance, song, etc. assist the shaman in entering the alternative reality of the unconscious, where all potentiality exists, where time and space are not limited by the three dimensions of Midgardh. While the actual methods of the shaman and psychologist are different, their results remain the same: overcoming and "curing" mental disorders (chaos) and psychological deficiencies that have their origin in the psyche. In elder times these imbalances were attributed to "evil spirits" (much the same way the extant mythologies depict *hrímthursar*) which, of necessity had to be banished by the shaman as the sole link between the Tribe and the world of Gods and spirits; conversely, psychologists are members of society specially trained to assist those mentally unbalanced and make them "whole" again.

Perhaps ironically, shamans are said to have been selected based upon their mental instability in the earliest times and most, if not all, would likely be considered unstable by today's standards. It is interesting to note that the past several generations of Fólk have seen a growth and prevalence of "psychological disorders" such as schizophrenia, ADHD, manic-depression, neurosis, etc. which may indicate an imminent paradigm shift in consciousness. Nevertheless, the shaman was the prototypical psychologist whose function was that of defender of the psyche and spirit of the entire Tribe.

The overriding belief in a decadence of contemporary shamanism is due in large part to enlightenment: the more we learn about our psychological processes and abilities (whether manifest or not) the less amazed we become by what we are capable of achieving, nor are the apparently incomprehensible feats of extraordinary accomplishments our ancestors are said to have practiced on a regular basis unbelievable to us any longer. The same has been said of Odhinism, that it is antiquated and no longer serves as spiritual nourishment for our Fólk, though those who could or would make such an assertion have a myopic view of what Odhinism is, not realizing that true Odhinism stretches from the earliest shamanistic practices to the supraconscious state of Sovereignty.

It seems likely that the remnants of early European spirituality found in Veda and Edda alike could be the result of shamanistic elements clashing with the more magical rituals of a related Fólk, such as the "first Fólk war in the world," presumably fought between the *Aesir*/Asuras and *Vanir*/Devas (sky and terrestrial deities respectively) for their share of worship. This war represents an actual battle between Celtic tribes which were spread across Europe west of the river Don at the time, and Aryan tribes that migrated west from "Asia" bringing with them a belief in the Aether. In this we find a unique dynamic and period of paradigm shift: the evolution of psycho-spiritual practice to a more magico-religious impulse. The natural progression this demonstrates, from ecstatic techniques to asceticism would appear to culminate in the Individuation of Jung: the self-realization of supraconsciousness that derives from a synthesis of the soul as Instinct, Intellect, and Impulse, the perfect harmony of the Sovereign Self or Odhinn.

Spirituality, philosophy, and science are but reflections of Instinct, Impulse, and Intellect; separating the three former in the physical realm has resulted in the latter being at odds with one another as well, and chaos has ensued because such a split is unnatural. Only by bringing them back into a cohesive whole can we find a spiritual balance again and regain the true spirituality that serves as sustenance for the Fólk-Soul; such is the purpose of Odhinism.

Odhinism, much like the shamanism of our Ancestors is at its core a psychological schema, deriving its power from the very depths of the psyche itself, here used to include the subconscious, unconscious, and conscious collectively. This likewise explains many modern Heathens affinity for Carl Jung's psychoanalytical thought and its application to our way of life. Indeed, Jung's Individuation would seem to be the next logical step in our spiritual evolution towards the *Übermensch* and in fact the Path of Odhinn is marked out in Grimnismal:

Sovereignty: The Empirical Path of Odhinn

> *"Now I am known as Odhinn*
> *Before that was I Yggr*
> *Though first was I Thund."*

Thund comes from the same Old Norse root as *ðandi* meaning "becoming" and is related to the Old English *thunian*, meaning "swell," implying growth, increase, and a rising up, supported in the Edda by "...thus did Thund write before the world began, when up he rose in aftertime." This root word is the base of many words meaning "to rise," and is likewise related to semantic notions of breath.

Yggr signifies "the terrifier" or "terrible one" and marks the awe-inspiring ability of those who impose their will upon the world, individuals whose deeds are recognized as inspirational or worthy of emulation and through which a noble reputation is developed. Yggr is etymologically connected to the Sanskrit *yogi* and *yuga* meaning yoke or bring together/bind and an age of time respectively.

It is the winning of *Oðroerir* and its contents (which Odhinn subsequently gifted to Mimir for a draught of his Well, i.e. the genetic memory) that was the initiatory act that elevated Thund to Yggr, while it is this latter's sacrifice on *Mimameith* (later nicknamed Yggdrasil in his honor) to learn the runes and gain knowledge of the mysteries of life and death that transcended the temporal Yggr to the Sovereign Self of Odhinn. In the recounting of Odhinn's sacrifice upon the World-Tree, however, we find a unique paradigm: unlike earlier examples of shamanistic initiation where the initiate was "sacrificed" by others to the Gods and Ancestors of the underworld, Odhinn sacrificed his self to himself, implying that he embodied both the shaman and the God of the "underworld," which of course he is. Here we find the Path down which others could attain Sovereignty if their desire, dedication, and discipline be firm.

Perhaps the most profound understanding of this comes from Else Brita-Tichenell in her masterful "Masks of Odin":

> *"Yggdrasil is Odin's steed, or with equal logic, his gallows, the implication being of a divine sacrifice, a crucifixion of the silent guardian whose body is a world. In this thinking any Tree of Life, large or small, constitutes a cross whereon its ruling deity remains transfixed for the duration of its material presence. While Yggdrasil may refer to a whole universe, with*

all its worlds, each human being is an Yggrasil in its own measure, a miniature of the cosmic ash tree. Each is rooted in the divine ground of All-Being and bears its Odinn-omnipresent spirit which is the root and reason of all living things."

As each of us are world-trees in our own right, individual universes, it is the *óð* within that gives us the ability to achieve Odhinn, the Sovereign Self. With this we also see the evolution of spirituality from a somewhat superstitious practice allowing outside forces to play a role in the shaman's initiation and guidance to the self-realizing and self-sustaining individual ability to attain Sovereignty on one's own through manifesting their inherent divinity. Odhinn as Sovereign Self speaks to the self-realization of the supraconscious state of Godhead, that point marked by the "second birth" as spiritual fulfillment. The significance of the designation "twice-born" (Aryan, Odhling, Atheling, etc.) to describe spiritual attainment likely originally derives from the very act of becoming a shaman.

There are a plethora of philosophical concepts in Carl Jung's writings that compare to far older Heathen wisdom, far too many for coincidence to be within the realm of probability. The great Swiss psychoanalyst is an example of allowing one's genetic memory to manifest itself through Instinct, his Intellect and Impulse apparent in his studies and publications. Among the more significant concepts to Odhinism are:

Anima/Animus = *fylgja/fetch* specifically, though likely applies to the *Dísir* or *Idisi* (*siðe* of the Celts) in general.
Archetype = An ancestral God or Goddess; Instinct
God-image = Odhinn as Sovereign Self
Individuation = Path of Odhinn (self-realization) as seen in the "thrice-great" evolution of Thund, Yggr, Odhinn.
Mandala = Sunwheel/Eye of Odhinn
Persona = Masks of Odhinn as manifestations of individual will in the physical realm.
Quaternity = Three plus one as the Four Ages and Caste.
Self = Óð/ego/consciousness as Intellect and Impulse.
Synchronicity = *Hamingja*; "guided fortune" or meaningful coincidence.

These are but a small sampling of the similarities between Odhinism and Jungian philosophies, though it is likely that he never made the conscious connections himself, as most of the extant mythology and wisdom contained in the Old Norse texts had yet to be fully explored or developed in relation to the Sanskrit of which he was more familiar. Jung seems to have some knowledge of the Germanic mythologies, for in his influential work "Wotan" he describes a concept he terms *Ergriffenheit* ("the state of being seized") which on the one hand is reminiscent of shamanistic techniques of ecstasy, while on the other is an accurate description of the legendary Berserkr and the claims that they seemed to be possessed by the fury that was beyond their control. Today the concept of *Ergriffenheit* would apply to the call of the blood that more and more Fólk are starting to heed, that state of being seized by the Gods and Goddesses and called upon to walk the Path for a Higher Purpose.

When understood according to a strictly psychological construct the Gods and Goddesses are not merely personified archetypes, but projected instincts from the collective unconscious. In this way they are individual aspects of our inherent nature, while the God-image itself is one of wholeness and completion, that which each of us is striving to realize. Odhinn is the God-image Archetype, the perfected state of man known as Sovereignty.

This by no means is meant to suggest, nor imply, that Allfather Odhinn does not exist, nor that he is a deity of divine origin in his own right; to the contrary, as the God-image of our Fólk-Soul, Odhinn has far too many attributes for most to keep track of, from a God to Shaman, Ancestor to Archetype, and everything in between. Thus the reason so much is ascribed to him in our mythologies. Else Brita-Tichenell simplifies this somewhat:

> *"As Allfather he is the divine root of every being in all the worlds, the essence of divinity present in all life forms, in the smallest particle as well as in the cosmos itself."*

Odhinn is the Ultimate Reality underlying phenomenal existence, imperishable, and macrocosmic infinite soul which is reflected by the microcosmic *Laeti* of man. It is only through the consanguineous unconscious of this Ultimate Reality that all potential and potential for all exists. Our reality only consists of what is known, while the unknown is at best unrealized potential, though at worst illusion. Similarly, only that which is natural can be real, while all that is unnatural is illusory or not manifest. Reality cannot exist beyond the known boundaries of *óð*, our individual conscious awareness, except in Odhinn or Ultimate Reality itself; it is here that the illusion of the material physical world, the unknown universe of limited consciousness becomes reality through the manifestation of *óð*.

It has been suggested that the origin of a deity often derives from phenomena which occurred beyond the contemporary comprehension of those witnessing it and their exemplary effort at describing it and this seems appropriate to our earliest Ancestors. Furthermore, the designations given these deities often became separate, thus distinct, from the divinity or phenomena originally described, evolving into general terms. With this in mind then one must wonder where exactly worship of Odhinn began: as a God, the role of shaman, simply an ancestor who achieved great deeds, or to describe the phenomena of the self-existent consciousness of the cosmos? What we know for sure is that his presence in the Fólk-Soul has been constant since before the dawn of consciousness and will continue in one form or another eternally. There can be no doubt as well that his worship goes back before the madness of monotheism stained the Fólk-Soul.

> *"Odhinn died in his bed in Sweden, and when he was near death he marked himself with a spear point and dedicated to himself all men who died through weapons; he said he should now fare to the Godheims and there welcome his friends. The Swedes now believed that he had gone to the Old Asgarth and would live there forever. Then began anew the belief in Odhinn and prayers to him arose afresh."*

This one simple passage from the Ynglinga Saga contains so much significant information for modern seekers that it is necessary to explore it fully.

First and foremost is the distinction between the Odhinn mentioned at the beginning and that mentioned at the end: it is clear that the former was a person, likely a chieftan of some sort and what we would refer to as a *goði* today, but what's more he was also a religious reformer, while the latter is the God we know as Allfather Odhinn.

Sovereignty: The Empirical Path of Odhinn

This historical Odhinn clearly brought about the resurgence of Odhinism as the last sentence makes obvious where prayers to and belief in Odhinn were renewed, but he also brought about a new belief: that those who died through weapons would be dedicated to him. This implies that it wasn't the belief before that period in time which is interesting on many levels. This Odhinn instituted the practice by marking himself with a spear point and dedicating these warriors to himself just as the Allfather won the runes upon Yggdrasil; after which he ascended to the Home of the Gods, presumably to the Hall of the Slain, to welcome those dedicated to him. It is likely that he marked himself with a Valknot as do all who dedicate themselves to Odhinn to stand among the Einherjar at the Ragnarokr, but further it was this reformer who had to have foreseen the coming of the Ragnarokr and instituted this practice and belief to prepare for the eventual battle; it could be argued that it is this Odhinn who is swallowed by the Fenris wolf. Either way, Torfaeus asserts that the historical Odhinn in the Ynglinga Saga entered Europe c70 BCE, while Thomas Carlysle in his lectures on heroes says that Odhinn's existence goes back "unknown thousands of years" before the common era and both are correct, in that there are and have been many historical Odhinns (in addition to the divine Allfather), which has created confusion for many Fólk over the years.

The last thing to note about this passage is that the Swedes believed this historical Odhinn would live forever (i.e. Eternal Existence) in Old Asgardh; this last mentioned by Snorri as both a place and a language in the Prose Edda. This Old Asgardh then is synonymous with the Godheims on a metaphysical level, while on the physical points to the area in which the language originated: just east of the river Don where the *Aesir*, the Aryans, come from initially.

It is said that no person who is not themselves divine can successfully worship a divinity and Odhinism bears this out from the earliest times. As descendants of the Gods we recognize that Odhinism is at once mystical, magical and metaphysical, both physical and spiritual, and it is this way of life that the sincere among us endeavor to emulate and see evolve. Sovereignty is the next step in that evolution, a spiritual system of self-realization rather than a religion as such.

Religion is and has always been man's attempt to categorize and rationalize those forces he knew existed within himself, as well as those he saw reflected in nature, determined to define and label these seemingly ambiguous energies which appeared inexplicable and ultimately failing to do so with any certainty. This gave life to analogy, allegory, symbolism, and what we've come to know as mythology, as the only means of expressing these mysteries with some semblance of reason and insight. Metaphor goes beyond the mundane meaning of a thing to a more meaningful understanding; rather than a literal definition that is too readily accepted blindly, the intent of the metaphor is to make one contemplate a thing carefully, considering all possibilities so as to draw a definite conclusion for oneself.

The use of symbol and metaphor through time has remained paradigmatic and while understanding of these seemingly vague descriptions during the period of their origin is likely, their interpretation becomes more elusive with each subsequent generation, often leaving modern seekers confused to the point that the principle concepts become impractical, meaningless or misleading. This became especially difficult after the Fólk of the West adopted rational thought almost exclusively. Traditional man held no delusions that "pure thought" alone could reveal Truth, nor offer the meaning of life; instead this latter was innate and contemplation merely clarified what already existed within.

To add to the confusion for the contemporary spiritual seeker is the predominance of spoken lore and metered verse in elder times, as the accuracy of these teachings can never fully be ascertained, leading some to question their veracity and applicability. Once the conversion from an oral tradition to a written one occurred, much of the wisdom of our ancestors was lost, either through unintentional misinterpretations by those recording the teachings or the capricious and deliberate destruction of classical knowledge at the hands of those who could never hope to fathom or comprehend such omniscient illumination entirely. The result remains the same in either case: the loss of integral information that may have led to complete enlightenment for present day disciples. Sadly, perhaps even the most in-depth study of what pieces have managed to survive could never hope to reconstruct the whole from the written record alone, for far too much has been forfeited to time.

With this in mind it may seem like an overwhelming, if not altogether impossible, task to distinguish reality from illusion amidst all the fallacies and deficiencies permeating modern "religious" beliefs and nowhere does this appear to be more evident than in the current attempts at restoring the elder spiritual systems of the primeval age to their former splendor.

Sovereignty: The Empirical Path of Odhinn

It is not as daunting as some Fólk may believe, for despite much being lost in the physical realm, a great fountain of wisdom remains embedded in the Soul of our Fólk and those who seek answers from within will find them in the collective unconscious, while those who rely exclusively on external sources or influences for guidance will never be fully satisfied. This is the reason the Path of Odhinn is an Empirical one: rather than rely on so-called scholars, or any outsider for that matter, to interpret or define the Heathen way of life, it remains the task of those truly dedicated to the Path to prepare the way for future Fólk through experience and the exchange of energies between Asgardh and Midgardh that will allow us to grow, thrive, and evolve.

Anyone who hopes to understand nature, and through nature the Gods, Goddesses, ancestors, and our self, must first be able to speak the language of nature; many early Fólk spoke it fluently, for nature communicates through signs and symbols and it is through similarities in form that one comprehends this language. The written word is subjective, while images more accurately portray the inherent meaning of a thing. The word "bird" for example is easily envisioned as some type of animal with wings and feathers by those who speak English and perhaps by some who speak a related tongue, however, those who do not will have no clue as to the meaning behind those four letters; a fairly accurate depiction of a bird, however, will be immediately understood by anyone who has ever seen one. This is the language of nature that is reflected in the metaphors of mythology, the kennings of skalds and bards.

Symbolism is likewise the language of the unconscious, metaphor its manifest attempt at realization, poetry its creative reality, and the spoken word its divine manifestation; the written word is but a dilution of divine symbolism, having evolved from the most distant wisdom into the profanity of today. The spoken word still maintains its power and ability to relate symbolic concepts through the vibrations of sound; the spoken word is the purest form of relating ideas and Ideals, as it balances the Intellect and Impulse into a harmony that evinces itself in the greatest orators through history and the most charismatic Fólk the world has ever known. This is also why *galdr* has been essential to Odhinism since the dawn of consciousness.

It is interesting to note that, while our ancestors shared, related, and understood traditional teachings according to kenning and metaphor, modern reconstructionists seem to adhere so completely to a fixed form for the Gods and concepts surrounding them instead of delving deeper into their esoteric natures or how they truly relate to our Fólk. The Gods represent archetypes as much as they do actual ancestors and one does not take anything from the other nor dilute their divinity in the least. The notion behind the word represent itself is illuminating. On the one hand when we speak of representing a thing, we are re-presenting it, or presenting it again, implying that it had already been present once before, likely in its perfected form; on the other hand, we are bringing it into the present, thus marking it as valid once more, even as we redefine it for modern consumption.

It has been proven that our earliest Fólk had a rich oral tradition that encompassed their experiences and beliefs as they grew, changed, and evolved with the Fólk and thus is a truly living spirituality. Nor were these Fólk incapable of writing or relating religious phenomena, as they were highly intelligent and intellectual Fólk with the ability to record any idea or Ideal they desired; this is highlighted best by the early evidence of runes if nothing else, yet they chose not to wrap their experiential wisdom up in a web of written words. It should be remembered that the Rig Veda had existed for hundreds (if not thousands) of years prior to the Aryans descending into the Indus Valley, at which point the indigenous Dravidians put it into fixed form in a syncretism that saw their own deities superimposed on our original wisdom teachings. Likewise the monotheist monks recorded our mythology not because the Norse were unable to do so themselves, but because the former thrive on fixed forms of "religious" doctrine and dogma.

It can be no coincidence that our Fólk held out the longest from recording their lore and legend in written form, of all who had the ability to do so; they believed that doing so would surely suffocate the spiritual aspects of our way of life. We know that at least eight of the runic glyphs painted on the cave walls in the French Dordogne Valley some 17,000 years ago match runes in the Elder Futhark still in use today; these continued to be used as the Old Stone Age shifted to Neolithic times 12,000 years ago, though it grew to include half of the Elder Futhark. In addition, engraved symbols on statuettes, plaques, dishes, and other objects from c5,500 BCE believed to be votive offerings have been interpreted as evidence of an "old European linear script" which includes seventeen ideograms that are identical to still existing runes, so to think that our ancestors could not have recorded their wisdom teachings at any time if they chose to is absurd.

Either way, it is clear from the evidence that, on the one hand, early Fólk had the capability to write and record beliefs, events, etc., while on the other these pictographs were never intended for the profane use of writing, but instead as spiritual signs and symbols that speak to the Soul of our Fólk directly and were meant to mirror the innate language of Nature known as metaphor used to represent something spiritually significant.

The same can be said of idols. Man has a long-standing practice of creating his gods in his own image and erecting effigies that reflect those who worship them, removing what is sacred and replacing it with a demi-divine icon, more human than god. Once they become fixed these images are permanent and come to define religious practice for that particular period rather than being defined by those who glorify them. In the process this displaces the spiritual elements for subsequent generations by allowing spirituality to stagnate, no longer growing or evolving naturally along with the people, but remaining firmly fixed until eventually the entire system is cast aside by distant descendants who find little use, need, or even understanding of the idols themselves and minutely more for the religious practices surrounding them; quite simply they are unable to identify with these images as they did not create them nor define their divinity and are often so far removed from those who did as to make understanding their purpose, symbolism, and usage difficult if not altogether impossible. It should be noted that it is not the image that is inherited but the instinct to manifest a particular archetype.

Interestingly, there is very little evidence of early Heathen creating idols as part of their primary worship beyond the end of the Neolithic period until the time of the forced conversion. In fact, Tacitus is quite clear that he found no idols whatsoever among the Germanic tribes nor any evidence of their ever having been used:

> *"The Germans, however, do not consider it consistent with the grandeur of celestial beings to confine the Gods within walls, or to liken them to the form of any human countenance. They consecrate woods and groves, and they apply the names of the deities to the abstraction which they see only in spiritual worship."*

Odhinism: Religion vs. Spirituality

Attempts to define the divine can be found in the multitude of philosophies, systems, and religions that have been given life throughout time and nowhere is this more readily apparent than in the way man deifies those extraordinary individuals who accomplish amazing feats of strength, courage, intellect, etc. From the dawn of consciousness man has admired and revered that which he recognized as being more profound than himself, be it in nature or among Fólk. Such admiration is natural and inherent in all men, though the truly inspired ones view these paragons as examples to emulate and an impetus to achieve even greater renown for themselves while contributing to the Fólk as a whole. This is the very essence of Effective Evolution in the context of Will to Power, though the inspiration that should be drawn from divinity is today misapprehended as the end all be all to religious practice, used as a crutch to support the status quo of the plebeian perspective and our Fólk need to move beyond this mediocre mindset; as Nietzsche makes abundantly clear in his writing it is time we Good Europeans move beyond good and evil, to shed the shackles of slave morality the monotheistic god has fettered Fólk with and become Gods in our own right.

With the advent of the written word, as such, many of the accounts and anecdotes of heroic deeds, mighty Fólk, interesting incidents, et. al. were recorded in one form or another from memory and oral traditions, constituting the bulk of what is referred to as mythology today. The average person could never hope to attain the recognition of a warrior or priest and so must be content in singing the praises of these great Fólk and keeping alive the memory of their exploits, which ultimately leads to their ascension from mere mortals to Eternal Gods. As tales of mighty deeds were repeated over and over the line between reality and myth blurred and eventually disappeared altogether. There can be no doubt that virtually all of what we call mythology originated from actual events and real people and every organized religion in the world is predicated on some form of ancestor worship and mythology; there are no exceptions to this, and the sooner Fólk recognize this fact and accept it the better equipped we will be as a Fólk to forge forward.

History eventually replaced mythology as the medium of choice for recordkeeping, though largely in context only not content, as evidenced by early history being saturated with mythological references and undercurrents. This demonstrates a natural progression from mythology ("embellished history") to pseudo-history (or mythic history) to a more precise history, just as innocence and wonder gave way to reason and methodology. To deny that mythology has its roots in historical fact is to repudiate history itself, as it was from myth that history developed. Nevertheless, history is a relatively recent invention in the overall scheme of things, an idea foreign to Tradition, one based on the novel notion of the past systematically resolving the present rather than the former being a restricting circumstance on the latter only, an influence; in truth, history as we know it is devoted to "progress," characterized by reliance on reason and rational thought, technological culture, socioeconomics and materialism, all alien to the Absolute. Despite a number of written texts having attained popularity through widespread acceptance, to the point of being canonized, the fact remains that each are merely compilations of myths, parables, and legends deriving from achievements of otherwise ordinary people. No sacred or holy book is more significant than any other except to those who embrace it as such. There is no doubt that sacred texts can and often are guides to proper conduct and pursuing a path that leads to divinity, though they should always be viewed as just that: sources of inspiration for realizing one's inherent potential, not as infallible or absolute.

The thing most worth noting about religion is that it remains merely a fixed form of spirituality, in the same way that monotheism was a result of elevating a single god to prominence and relegating the rest to minor roles (i.e. "saints") or simply disregarding them completely; in doing so the divine becomes profane. Prior to the suppression of polytheistic practice, spirituality was an ever-changing perpetual adaptation that evolved as the Fólk did and grew as the people increased their conscious understanding of life's many mysteries; they devised innovative ways of expressing and putting to practical use the wisdom gleaned along the way and applied it to everyday life. This is what a living, breathing spiritual way of life is and should be, in addition to an incessant striving toward something greater, a higher form of existence both for the individual and Fólk as a whole.

Religion is the subjective desire to pursue divinity externally, while spirituality is the objective reality of living a divine life from the inside out; the former exists for the physical and temporal while the latter is metaphysical and Eternal, the means through which each of us nourish our spirit. Spirit is the core of our essence, the animating principle of who we are both as individuals and as a Fólk, and we should need no external source to substantiate that to us; religion proposes to do just that however, in a dogmatic and domineering manner, one that sets out to create slaves, automatons whose sole purpose is perpetuating the plebeian perspective of the masses.

The separation between spirituality and religion is a thinly veiled one at times and a yawning chasm at others; while spirituality celebrates and embraces the divine in all things, religion attempts to categorize that divinity, creating nice tidy compartments for wonders and phenomena to fit into so that man may understand them on a conscious thought-provoking level. This last is not entirely a bad approach in and of itself, however, it is at the point where religion becomes rigid, dependent upon dogma and doctrine exclusively, that it becomes dangerous. Time and again history has clearly shown that wherever there has been belief in one true god there have been wars fought in his name. The fact is that Truth never need be forced on another as it should be apparent to anyone as answer to any question they may pose. It is this that demonstrates the ephemeral nature of monotheism, as it could not exist in any form without blind faith in a single omnipotent deity to whom adherents relinquish responsibility for, and control of, their own lives.

The danger of transforming spirituality into religion lies in the complete acceptance of religious tenets as absolute truth, based solely upon faith not fact. Not only does this place Fólk at odds with one another (and often Nature) it likewise effectively closes the door to spiritual evolution, as religion resists change instead of embracing it as absolutely necessary to ascension. In addition, that which is widely accepted as religious truth is then often used as a measuring stick to ascertain sacrosanctity according to the narrow, limited view of those who define the divine by their own "truth"; anything that is opposed to their truth, even remotely, does not measure up to its standards, or simply cannot be comprehended properly according to this "truth," is quickly dismissed and discarded, labeled as heresy, and denied to most Fólk.

Furthermore, it has been said that where truth cannot be found men will create it and nowhere is this more readily apparent than in the various religious doctrines of the world; whenever "religious" men have been unable to define some phenomena or philosophy by known and accepted standards it is typically viewed as nonsense or more often as heresy without regard for what is natural or inherent. Therein lay the fundamental difference between religion and spirituality: the latter eternally strives to emulate nature, grow, thrive, and endlessly seeks truth to this end, while the former serves only to substantiate itself, searching for any "truth" that will sustain its own stagnant existence awhile longer and offer comfort to the masses through empty promises and platitudes as a spiritual placebo.

All in all, religion fails by its very nature to satisfy the spirit completely, as it places the emphasis on dogmatic doctrine, in essence shackling its adherents with spiritual stasis instead of accentuating self-realization through the strengthening of the individual spirit, the pursuit of knowledge and the conscious awareness that leads to true transcendence.

Spirituality, at its very core, is synonymous with consciousness, in that both are dependent upon enlightenment for fulfillment and evolution. Spirituality is not predicated on faith as such; it ultimately derives from the spirit that exists in each of us, indwelling and indisputable, an inseparable part of who we are and is natural and innate. So too should be the spiritual practices of a Fólk. Just as the pine tree is inherent in the pinecone, the spirit (and spirituality) of a people is present in their blood; try as one may they cannot produce an oak, ash, or elm tree from a pinecone and neither can the spirit of our Fólk be sustained or strengthened by the customs, culture, or creed of another. A Heathen is unique in that they never seem satisfied for any length of time and is always striving for more, to ever excel, testing the known limits of their own will, and determined to achieve greatness; it are this that Sovereignty captures and encapsulates.

Spirituality is and should be an ever enduring and growing adaptation of the spirit; conversely, religion will always remain fixed, stagnating and ultimately becoming useless in its antiquation, as most are today. Those people and beliefs that do not grow and evolve shall be cast aside as so much slag as the Sword of the Sovereign is forged in the fires of ordeal; what does not develop decays and this deterioration portends the decomposition of man himself in the absence of increase.

In the final analysis, both religion and spirituality propose to answer three questions: how we came to exist, why we are here, and what will happen when we die, if anything at all. These are the fundamental elements of EVERY religion and spiritual system, small or large, though each succeeds in differing ways to varying degrees. Most can be summed up as follows: the world and men came from a self-existent supreme being; we are here to lead virtuous lives according to some sort of divine law; and there's something better awaiting us in the next life, though usually only if one subscribes to a particular system and lives according to its precepts or conversely one could end up somewhere worse. The truth about the cosmology of the world (or the "creation" of man) may never be known, likely having been forfeited to time; what may or may not transpire after death is the ultimate unknown, which leaves only why we exist at all. When everything else is stripped away, philosophy (as Plato observed) is indeed the one true religion, the middle point or balance between theology and science.

Anyone who proposes to undertake a serious study of the history of religion or the evolution of spirituality must first accept that once you remove a religion from its cultural context it loses all spiritual value for succeeding generations, as well as those who hope to recapture its original sacrality. The study of the past must be made in an effort to understand its relevance, relation, and applicability to the present; as man evolves so too must the spirit which guides him and this is natural, for with new understanding and awareness comes fresh ways of applying that knowledge and wisdom.

The shift from spirituality to religion is prominently found in the way knowledge is passed along: in the change from oral to written tradition the teachings themselves altered, from sacred to profane, symbolic to literal, evolving to fixed, spiritual to religious. It is the nature of Fólk to seek out answers and once found, to classify them accordingly, however, once a divine thing of indeterminate character attains a definite and permanent meaning it becomes religious, no longer awe-inspiring and incorporeal, but fixed and rigid. In man's attempt to understand the mystical and metaphysical he began to question and seek out answers, dismantling the intellectual observations until there was nothing left to the imagination or Instinct, until he had completely destroyed the very spirit of what he had set out to understand in the first place by categorizing it into compartments. By doing so he defined dogma, setting limitations upon himself based upon religious tenets: that which he understood and could clearly classify he termed doctrine, while the unknown, mysterious, or magical he labelled blasphemy. Throughout it all the contemporary religious zealots allowed faith to supersede discernment, until we have reached the point of perversion and perpetual spiritual stagnation prevalent today.

The primary distinction between spirituality and religion is that while the former demands discipline to the point that we must each live our convictions, in accord with Nature and her laws (not in spite of them), the latter renders their followers slaves to blind faith, empty promises, and unnecessary guilt. An increasing number of Fólk have begun to seek out answers to questions that faith alone cannot supply, searching for a spiritual identity denied them in the rush to rationalize religion, instinctively knowing there is something more just beyond current conscious awareness, but unable to identify it. It is unfortunate that so many of these have drifted to various oriental systems, new age philosophies, etc. settling for the modicum of truth each contains, while others continue to wander aimlessly, never quite satisfied or fulfilled by what modern religion has to offer. It is for these Fólk, and those to come, that the Empirical Path of Odhinn has been cleared of debris, stands unobstructed and free of impediment; it is for those with the Will to pursue it to be able to do so and gain true spiritual nourishment and understanding. The Path is paved by contemplation, intent, and action through Effective Evolution and is above all else a living, breathing, spiritual way of life. Living a virtuous, noble life, achieving great deeds, earning a good reputation, actively attaining more, striving for knowledge and wisdom, thriving, advancing, these are the means by which we purify the soul, strengthen the spirit, and seek Sovereignty; in the final analysis religion belongs to the lunar, priestly, temporal, southern and oriental cultural polarity, whereas spirituality is an emanation of the solar, sovereign, eternal, Northern, and Occidental worldview. Spirituality is the nourishing of the spirit by the most natural and necessary means, implying that it does and must change to fit the needs of the time, while religion, by its very nature, organizes and categorizes the specific spiritual practices of a particular period to help the people of that specific time to understand the divine; this last will always fail due to the removal of the spiritual from its historical and cultural roots, destroying the divine in the uprooting.

The same can be said of attaching a fixed form to an archetype: once it is removed from the unconscious to conscious mind the sacred principle is removed, for by its very nature the Intellect must distinguish and categorize everything that enters the conscious field of awareness so it can discern between what is useful or necessary to the individual and that which is not needed. The divine then becomes profane by its very definition and the same can be said of disregarding one's Instinct in favor of Intellect or Impulse alone.

Odhinism: Religion vs. Spirituality

Both religion and spirituality are much like a mountain with a variety of paths leading individuals to the peak in search of something greater than themselves, seeking explanations for those mysteries that seem just beyond mortal comprehension and an understanding of life itself. Many of these trails are well-worn, having been traversed by the masses for centuries in the same way that livestock are herded in a particular direction and often with the same result: the hiker is misled or gets lost on paths that wind around in circles without meaning or destination until death mercifully brings a close to their pointless existence, while other paths are more obscure, hard to find, or overgrown with debris from lack of use. Among the maze of confusing courses, aimless paths, and routes whose wayfarers claim that the map they use for direction is the "one true way," the student of spirituality can easily find themselves lost on a labyrinthine pseudo-spiritual journey that leads to a life devoid of reason or resolution. This need not be the case, however, for interspersed throughout the jumble are the Folkways forged by ancestral feet; these paths were pioneered by people who placed an importance upon the Instinct inherent in their very blood, and the only sacred text one need to study or follow is that found in the genetic memory, etched upon the Soul of the Fólk. Odhinism is one such Path.

Odhinism is not for everyone as it is the true spiritual askesis of twice-born Fólk and demands dedication, discipline, and the desire to attain ascension to the realm of the Gods, not merely with the Gods but as a God. As Snorri so succinctly said almost a millennium ago, "The frost-giants and mountain-trolls would go up into heaven if Bifrost were crossable by everyone that wanted to go." To that end Sovereignty is simply the new orientation and adaptation mentioned by Jung as necessary to reawaken the sleeping spirit of our Fólk-Soul.

> *"Our consciousness only imagines that it has lost its Gods; in reality they are still there and it only needs a certain general condition in order to bring them back to full force. This condition is a situation in which a new orientation and adaptation is needed."*
> - C.G. Jung

The shift from the spiritual and sacred to the religious rigidity required by material monotheism was the factor that found Fólk lost, leading to the dormancy of Odhinism, its stagnation and inability to naturally

Sovereignty: The Empirical Path of Odhinn

evolve; we recognize the importance of evolution today however, though it should be noted that Odhinism is not a tree-hugging, nature-based way of life. While we do live in tune with Nature, Odhinism is founded upon natural Primal Law not the nature around us; a focus on the material is not in accord with true spirituality, rather the spirit and soul are the primary factors to our way of life. Nature, as such, merely provides the backdrop from which we nourish the spirit.

Along these same lines Odhinism cannot coexist with contemporary society; the only environment in which Odhinism can thrive is one in which each of us is allowed to realize our potential for perfection. Most of modern monotheistic society stands in opposition to our way of life, to the point that even Heathens compromise our culture and collective principles in an attempt to find cohesiveness with the community at large. Odhinism today is a mere phantom of what it could and should be simply because we live in a world where we cannot reconcile our spirituality with society; until we reclaim the *Óðal* land and create a community committed to culture, heritage, and the proper nourishment of the Fólk-Soul any hope for a real reawakening will ultimately fail. Any society not conducive to the spiritual sovereignty of its citizens is diseased, for progress cannot be measured by material advancement or technology, but only through Effective Evolution.

This last is of particular importance to those who tread the Path of Odhinn, simply because each of us consciously strive for greatness in all we do; as such, we are Creators in our own right: only in creating the future through Will to Power and inspiration (the in-spirit of *önd*) can one even find the Path let alone have the fortitude to step foot upon it. Unlike our composite cousins to the Southeast, we do not subscribe to the universalist or inclusionist philosophy of welcoming all who would claim to feel an affinity for our way of life, nor are we world renouncers in the sense that we deny the physical completely or seek to destroy the individual self; instead, we strive to bring into balance the physical and spiritual with the ego in an effort to elevate our self to the Sovereign Self. Renunciation rests on the notion that the sacrifice of all superficialities is a declaration that nothing is needed beyond one's self, their inherent nature alone; an Odhinist believes that through the ascetic affirmation of *AT TRUA A MATT SIN OK MEGINN* and its subsequent manifestation in Sovereignty, true power can be directed to all possibility and potential, a power incomparable to any other.

Odhinism: Religion vs. Spirituality

Likewise the notion of egalitarianism is equally absurd, an artificial idea invented by inferior individuals to shackle the superior into the servitude of socioeconomic enslavement; instead, each of us must accept our Self as exactly who we are supposed to be, that we have a proper place in the evolutionary chain, and do our duty according to our inherent nature. The ash tree cannot exist as a rose and neither can the wolf act as though he were an eagle; man should revel in his diversity instead of denying its existence in a futile attempt at forging an illusive bond of "brotherhood, equality, and love" that merely seeks the unjustifiable elevation of the inferior and ignoble, while simultaneously stifling the superior, relegating all into a mundane mass of mediocrity. This is involution, the process of something folding in on itself, and opposes evolution, for in removing the superior qualities and strong characteristics from any society, stasis and stagnation is the only possible result; instead of advancing and evolving according to Nature this society will deteriorate to the point of becoming a mere phantom of their former glory and every spiritual element will eventually perish. One need only look at Greece today or the future of America.

Spirituality is a natural evolutionary process that has continued since the dawn of consciousness, from the origin of the self-existent embodied in the very spirit of our Fólk and which has never died out but simply sought expression through various (often obscure) means and only needs to be brought back to the forefront once more. The early ecstatic practices of primitive Odhinism expanded to include asceticism and the magical, mystical, and metaphysical elements necessary to the growth of spirituality and spiritual nourishment. Odhinism now stands upon the brink of another great paradigm shift in which we will see the realization of the "great Godhead" (Seeress' Prophecy), the Sovereign that Nietzsche foresees as the *Übermensch*.

The time for manifesting our deities to represent the unknown and mysterious has long since passed; now is the time to recognize our own divine nature, our inherent ability to achieve Sovereignty. While the symbology and mythology of the past is just as relevant today as it was millennia ago, we as a Fólk have evolved to a point where we can better understand and embrace the concepts that were so abstract to our Ancestors and all that is required is a reawakening of the spirit that once made us the envy of the known world.

Sovereignty: The Empirical Path of Odhinn

All who set out consciously committing themselves towards achieving ascension will be aided in their quest should their intent be pure and no obstacle will be placed upon the Path that each individual does not have the fortitude or wherewithal to surmount; failure can only result from a deviation or disregard for the signposts, as success is assured those with the discipline and dedication to seek Sovereignty. The Path of Odhinn is Empirical, ever existing and has eternal patience; it awaits all Fólk with the Will to Power and worth to step foot upon it.

ØRLAG: PRIMAL LAW

"That a principle flowing from itself must always act in conformity with the laws responsible for its own existence is undeniable."

— Manly P. Hall

This world and the universe it inhabits are governed by a set of principles and patterns present since they came into existence; we refer to these as laws because they are at their core absolute, in the sense that they always work the same way under similar circumstances. This law is capable at the same time of substantiating scientific speculations and systematic approaches to accumulating accurate evidence of the innate order of nature. When we understand this natural law as the fundamental framework for all of existence in the universe, we can then use this knowledge to validate the natural philosopher's perspective of mystical and metaphysical realities in our own individual universe. Everywhere one searches for evidence in the natural world, seeking scientific explanations, they find an order that substantiates both science and spirituality, be they biological, chemical, atomic, or otherwise.

Sovereignty: The Empirical Path of Odhinn

The primary problem with contemporary spiritual, even religious, belief (as well as scientific methods) is that few Fólk believe the universe to be a living, breathing entity in its own right, existing apart from man, nor that what we term nature is the universal manifestation of this existence. The first step upon the Path comes in accepting that the universe is a mental construction, founded in consciousness, and that *oðic* energy is the exchange of power in the natural world: thoughts, ideas, emotions, actions, etc. all contribute to the well-being and existence of this universe, both internally and externally, in a ceaseless state of synergism. Life and mind are the *önd* and *óð* of the soul on the microcosmic and macrocosmic levels and all existence is energy; matter, our physical being, is merely a conductor of energy at various rates of vibration.

As we exist and are conscious of our existence, so too must the universe and nature be alive and aware for both are our Source, the origin from whence we sprung and the cause of which we are the effect; in simply contemplating this it is substantiated, for without the ability to ponder, let alone comprehend such a notion, it could not exist at all. Once one accepts the universe as mental creation, that it is conscious and capable of creation and that each of us are able to alter our own awareness and psychic state, then we must likewise accept that each of us create our own reality as well; ours is the microcosmic potential which influences macrocosmic realization. Within this consciousness persist a number of principles, perhaps neurological pathways, that regulate life, laws that allow for an exchange between *óð* and Odhinn and it is these one must master to become Sovereign.

When one fully comprehends law to the extent that everything is connected by a concerted effort via a logical and rational framework that forms all of existence, they must also come to the conclusion that random chance does not fit into the pattern. The equilibrium necessary to support life is far too precise to sustain the notion that the organizing principles we call law could possibly have arisen by blind chance; in fact, the circumstances required to exhibit random examples do not even exist in our universe. Order comes from organization, thus the interconnectedness of the patterns that govern the framework for all existence, the organized and organizing fields (gravitational, *oðic*, electromagnetic, morphogenetic, etc.) which regulate all substantial and sustainable systems. These fields are considered universal for the simple fact that they form the foundation for every facet of our universe, and collectively these *a priori* patterns are absolute and referred to as Primal Law.

Primal Law recognizes the order of nature and this symmetry precludes random chance or haphazard happenstance. Logic leads the rational observer to the conclusion that there can be no pure randomness and what is regarded as random is merely innately indeterminate or imperceptible, requiring empirical evidence to discern effectively. Once one acknowledges and accepts that there can be no chance, the only logical explanation to be found for the perfect balance of our universe is *oðic* force, the source of *önd*, the energy of which permeates all of existence, saturating life completely and embodying the animating principle behind Primal Law.

This primordial pattern must be infinite as nothing can restrain, restrict, or control it; there is no other power which it is subject to and nothing can confine nor define it except itself; it is not changeable and cannot be diminished or increased, as it is immutable, immortal, and immaterial; it is Eternal, is and will always be, as everything is created, preserved, and destroyed according to the Absolute. Eternal Existence is the state from which one reaches the perfect balance and harmony that then polarizes any progress as unnecessary, neutralizing their momentum, and creating a cessation of all rhythm as necessary to the realization of that perfect balance.

Either way, this Law is no less dynamic or dependable by simply becoming aware of it. The universe is subject to laws and that fact precludes our escaping them or ascending beyond them so long as we remain in time; the rarest of individuals may come to master Primal Law to the point of giving the illusion they have moved beyond them, however, true ascension requires attaining Eternal Existence above time. The essence of Primal Law is that the universe is made up of matter, has conscious awareness, and an animating principle, and so it is for man as well. For our Fólk, this Primal Law is referred to in Old Norse as *ørlag*.

Ørlag is perhaps the most misinterpreted concept among Fólk today, as many have perpetuated the misapprehension that *ørlag* means fate or destiny, an interpretation that is completely inaccurate: *or-* means "out of," "primal," or "earliest," while *-lag* literally translates as "law," from "layer" or "laying in order," thus *ørlag* is "earliest layers" or Primal Law, neither of which even remotely relates to fate or destiny. The mistranslation likely derives from misunderstanding the Norn Urdhr, whose Well serves to collect the layers of Worth, as her function is that

Sovereignty: The Empirical Path of Odhinn

of "what is," the unchangeable that acts upon and influences what is becoming and what should be. If there were a concept of fate or destiny in Old Norse it would be *dómr*, meaning "doom"; rather than the purely negative connotation it holds today, doom means "to set" or "to place" as in irrevocable lot. In this sense *dómr* is what is laid in the Well and took on the context of judgment of one's lot at the end of their life. That said, our Fólk never believed in any form of fixed fate, as it would remove free will and individuality; instead, we have long known the Law of Cause and Consequence rather than a predetermined destiny as such. Skuld does represent what should be, however, this is not definitive, but dependent upon different decisions we make, acts we undertake, etc.

Ørlag seems to encompass aspects of law, duty, justice, right action, spirituality, and custom, way, or manner; more than anything, however, *ørlag* represents original order. The best possible explanation for *ørlag* can be garnered from two of the most significant stanzas in all of our wisdom teachings:

Unz thriar kuamu	Until three came
or thui lidhi,	of those gathered,
oflgir ok astkir	great and kind
Aesir at husi;	Aesir from home;
fundu a landi	found on land
litt megandi	seeming to lack meginn
Askr ok Embla	Askr and Embla
orlaglausa.	without ørlag.
önd thau ne attu;	their race had not önd;
óð thau ne hofðu,	their head had not óð,
lá ne laeti	lá nor laeti
ne litu goða.	nor litu goða.
önd gaf Odhinn,	breath gave Odhinn,
óð gaf Hoenir,	consciousness gave Hoenir,
lá gaf Loðurr	blood gave Loðurr
ok litu goða.	and Godlike appearance.

This is a literal translation of the improperly named "creation" stanzas in the Edda; order from chaos is not creation, but change, in the Eternal sense of evolution. The Gods did not create Askr and Embla per se, but found them without *ørlag*, and, taking the ashes and embers of a lower race, transformed them into a divine Fólk; they consecrated these remnants by giving them law and order, as they were powerless and chaotic. The notion of creation is a false narrative intended to ingratiate the created to the creator. The Sovereign first and foremost knows eternal freedom, for if we lack liberty we are not capable of creation and find our independence and free will fettered to false foundations. To acknowledge creation as such is to accept a beginning and allow also the ambiguity of linear time; this last leads to an eventual end rather than Eternal Existence. Conversely, cyclical time embraces no notion of creation, but rather that all is as it ever was and will ever be on the grand scale of things: there is no beginning or end, but only Eternity; return, resurgence, renaissance, revival, renewal. In other words, the wheel will turn time and again for eternity.

There are times when translating from one language to another that it becomes difficult to discern the definition of a specific concept, when one word will simply not suffice for another and such is the case with the above stanzas. In instances such as these the concept must be explained instead, to give a complete comprehension to Fólk seeking such.

Meginn means might or power, plus the potential of possibility. The word potential is the key to understanding *meginn* as it first means capable of becoming, but also characterized by power (potent-ial), both of which are significant to the state in which Askr and Embla were found: they were *megandi*, without might, powerless, or lacking potential, which was remedied with *ørlag*, the four gifts given them by the Gods, the potential to pursue Will to Power and the ability to assess all possibilities. Power is the aptitude to act, though more than this, we find two types of *meginn*, both of which correspond to the four gifts given Askr and Embla as well. First is the *meginjörð*, the power of the earth or physical potential; the second is *ásmeginn*, the divine power of plenary possibility present in our self and spirit. The former is blood and body, while the latter is the soul; together the *ørlag* that set in motion man becoming. The *meginn* to fulfill one's potential comes from an absolute liberty: Sovereignty.

It needs to be noted that the Gods used the ashes and embers of the "logs" they found to fertilize our Fólk. Many today still adhere to the mistranslation of Embla as elm despite there being absolutely no etymological tie to any tree in Old Norse. Instead, embers as a symbol of stored solar energy, hidden power, and a reservoir of heat, completely self-contained, with all the potential of a full-blown blaze nestled within itself seems a more likely understanding of Embla; conversely, ashes represent a static principle, that of the residue of life, without value or worth, and together they symbolize the dual energies of the universe: the passive and active, masculine and feminine, et. al. From ashes and embers we are born to return to ashes and embers on the pyre. This understanding of Askr and Embla is supported and substantiated by *líf* and *lífthrasir* as well, life and longing for life.

Ørlag as Primal Law (or original layers of our well) is comprised of the four gifts given us by the Gods, the container and contents that correspond to *oðroerir*: *önd*, the Breath of Life and animating principle we refer to as spirit; *óð*, the self of Intellect and Impulse or conscious awareness; *lá*, the blood that sustains; and *litu goða*, literally "godlike appearance" that alludes to the body. These four gifts likewise correspond to the four elements as well: air is the Breath of Life, fire is self, water is blood, and earth as body, all of which held a prominent place for Fólk from the earliest time. These four gifts combine to collectively make up our very nature, the initial layers of life and without this Law Askr and Embla would have had no potential, not worthy of power or *meginn*.

Önd is vitality, the drive and desire to be divine and as the nucleus of the soul comprises the Instinct of archetype found in our Fólk's phylogenesis, the collective unconscious symbolized by Mimir's Well. The cauldron of Inspiration (*Oðroerir*) which Odhinn is said to have given the men of Midgardh contains the mead of poetry, a kenning for inspiration or in-spirit, the equivalent of *önd*. Inspire means to fill with an animating, quickening, or exalting influence, however, its archaic meaning was literally to infuse life by breathing into; Odhinn inspires each of us to emulate his example both through his gift of inherent Instinct, as well as the Path he forged for Fólk to follow and it is this Instinct that is the potential for Sovereignty.

Óð is consciousness, the knowing and perceiving within one's self, motivating us to motion or action as the exertion of energy and influence to accomplish a specific act; this self is our potential for Individuation found in Intellect and Impulse. Where *önd* is the nucleus of the soul, *óð* is the neutron and proton. The inherent ability to elevate the self derives directly from awareness and the capacity to call forth consciousness, as well as the innate aptitude to achieve the supraconscious state of Sovereignty by invoking in-spirit, its manifestation the ever-present *oðic* energy exchanged between *óð* and Odhinn.

Laeti is the collective *óð* and *önd* in our universe, thus represents the soul to individuals and the Fólk-Soul as a whole. *Laeti* likewise refers to our disposition, character, and persona, who we are as individuals, and to the action of ordering or regulating by especially divine right or power; it also applies to being set in order, spatial arrangement, or relative position, notably of constituent parts, which relates it to *ørlag*. *Lá ok Litu Goða* are so inseparably integrant that they must be taken together to truly comprehend. At the base level these are blood and body, though they represent something more signficant in the genetic memory and godlike appearance respectively; this latter is not limited to look alone, but to both being distinct and becoming. Blood is the vehicle of oxygen, the element essential to the Breath of Life, while the body houses the mental and sensational faculties of the self, thus both blood and body are integral to Instinct, Intellect, and Impulse. Lodhurr is an obscure figure not mentioned anywhere else except the single stanza of Voluspa, however, it is likely that this is simply a scribal error and this deity is Hlodhyn, the feminine creative counterpart of Odhinn and chthonic deity. Either way, the Old Norse *loð* means fruitful or yield, referring to prolificity, while *ljoðr* is people or community, as in Fólk, and both apply to blood and body. If the Fólk are to exist at all, let alone evolve spiritually and substantially, we must be fruitful, prolific, and productive in not only procreating to carry on our genetic legacy, but pursuing physical perfection as well; the substance is essential to sustain the soul, as it cannot exist without matter.

With these contributions to Askr and Embla, *ørlag* originated as the Primal Law of our existence and these layers form the foundation of *Urð*, which means "worth" in this context; the three Norns are those who weave the Tapestry of Time:

VERDHANDI
(space/simultaneity)

URDHR   SKULD
(time/before)   (time/after)

Physics posit that you can prove events either happen before, after, or simultaneously, this last being an absolute, an observer independent fact, and these three correspond to Urdhr, Skuld, and Verdhandi respectively; in addition, these three can be considered cause, consequence, and acausal as well. It is Urdhr and Verdhandi combined that create the Tapestry, manifesting in Skuld; once an act has been committed the thread of that deed is woven to our *Urð* and cannot be undone without destroying the weave. It can, however, be compensated with another act that produces a better picture. Urdhr and Verdhandi are inseparably linked in that the former represents value, character, and quality as it is, not as any would want it to be, while the latter betokens becoming, the deeds and actions that allow one to Worth their self; Skuld represents the realization of that Worth, with Sovereignty being what should be.

Urð is an accumulation of every individual's deeds, the aggregate actions that make us who we are; *Urð* is our Worth. Worthing is the root of the Old Norse Verdhandi and it literally means "man becoming"; each of our deeds have an active influence on the present moment and the future simultaneously. The Norn Urdhr is said to collect what is, was, or will ever be into her Well, to nourish the world-tree, and this Worth is where *Urð* derives its distinctive nature. Interestingly, *Urð* is said to carry over to an individual's next life and this belief is expressed in the extant wisdom teachings that offer examples of money or other material wealth being borrowed from one with an oath to repay it in the next life by the other.

Each of us is directly responsible for our own *Urð* and cannot change it without altering our lives first: how we act, what we think, the emotions we feel, etc. We are our Worth. Whatever is in the Well is indelible, however, all we add in the absolute now is a conscious choice and can contribute to the clarity of the contents that affect what should be. In seeking Sovereignty we consciously strive for greatness through Effective Evolution by acting with honor in harmony with our Skuld and soul, and achieve accomplishments that will allow ascension above time to Eternal Existence; what makes *Urð* so unique to our Fólk-Soul is the inherent sense of duty and obligation each of us is born with: be it family, Fólk, or faith, we know we owe a debt to those who came before, for our very existence, and attempt to live accordingly. As descendants of the Gods our *ørlag* is the original layer of Worth from which we become *einherjar*, the Inheritors of a divine legacy.

Urð can also be seen as having the power to control destiny, what we would refer to today as Will to Power. At its core the concept of *Urð* is a function of the Law of Cause and Consequence, wherein all actions bring forth positive and negative effects in relation to the deeds done; while *hamingja* is acausal, *Urð* is unequivocally linked to specific acts. Skuld can only be attained through active achievements and accomplishments, through performance and merit, not simply effort or intent; what should be is Sovereignty, the objective of the Path of Odhinn.

Each of us is bound by our *Urð*, be it from a previous existence or our own current one, and the only way to escape time is to realize our Skuld; we must embrace our *ørlag*, contemplate and comprehend our self, and balance this with the Instinct of spirit to become Sovereign. Skuld can be seen as either fixed, as a sequence of subsequent events that follow a particular pattern, or determined by the decisions we make, though the truth is that the balance between these two is the more certain connotation: there is a particular Path each of us SHOULD follow, though it is left to us to choose our own course. While the Norns weave the Tapestry of Time they must use the threads of our actions and deeds to do so.

In psychology it is well known that every deed plants a seed in the mind that begins to blossom at some point in the future, under certain circumstances, as the consequence from the cause; *Urð* is neither retribution nor reward, but an expression of natural actions that are not fated, only able to be mitigated through subsequent deeds. Worth is founded upon the framework that the results of deeds are returned to the individual instigating them initially and in this way each of us are solely responsible for reaping the rewards or consequences of our action, as well as becoming who we are meant to be.

Ørlag as Primal Law presents two important principles to all who seek Sovereignty: duality and balance. Urdhr as being and Skuld as what should be are the duality balanced by becoming in Verdhandi. This is likewise seen in the Gods of Asgardh and giants of Utgardh being balanced by man in Midgardh. There are many precepts and principles which influence our world and existence, but there is only one true Absolute: the perfect point of balance between two polarities that allows for all potential and possibilities, the equilibrium amid thesis and antithesis where synthesis is situated. While it remains necessary to avoid stagnation at all costs, stasis as a state of equilibrium, not of inaction, is to be striven for in all things.

Sovereignty: The Empirical Path of Odhinn

In order to grow, thrive, or evolve, an organism must first bring into balance its inherent nature; encroaching on either extreme enables the organism to be inflexible and less likely to attain or maintain equilibrium. It is this balance between *önd* and *óð*, as well as that of the *laeti* and *lá/litu goða*, that creates a bridge that connects the self and Sovereign Self, Midgardh and Asgardh. Harmony is sought through the synthesis of substance and soul through empiricism, as Sovereigns are among the most extreme existentialists.

Perhaps one of the most important concepts for Heathen is *Hamingja* (guided fortune or spiritual momentum), which represents the belief that one's fortune is inextricably tied to their actions and accomplishments; in this way it is believed that leading a virtuous life, maintaining a good reputation, achieving noble deeds, etc. are all interwoven into one's own *hamingja*. Long before Carl Jung coined the term synchronicity to describe seemingly chance occurrences that had a significant connection to causal events, our Fólk knew *hamingja*; as synchronicity is not truly understood by most, they are unable to explain it with any exactitude, thus the reliance on the spurious explanation of "luck" for *hamingja*. It seems far easier for Fólk to simply dismiss a significant event than to take the time to contemplate or comprehend it; this is the reason most will attribute good or bad luck to an important incident.

Hamingja as luck is arbitrary and ambiguous and actually has nothing to do with chance or happenstance at all, as these imply a sense of vague or indeterminate significance, neither of which come close to a comprehension of this concept; a more accurate means by which to understand *hamingja* is as guided fortune, Fólk receiving direction from *fylgjur*, though this too falls short of a sufficient interpretation. *Hamingjar* are acausal experiences that may seem coincidental or fortuitous, but in fact are meaningful in some manner; far from being random, these events are connected by a conscious and logical pattern that often eludes the casual observer. *Hamingja* can best be described as signposts on the Path of what should be informing the seeker they are headed in the right direction. *Hamingja* embraces and enhances the understanding of cyclical time and evolution as it reveals the pervasive pattern underlying the foundation and framework of all existence.

Hamingja stands alone and apart from cause and consequence, in that the two occur simultaneously in synchronicity as spiritual momentum; it is the synchronicity of the absolute in Verdhandi, wherein the relationship between two people, places, minds, ideas, incidents, et. al. are formed in a rational manner all its own. *Hamingja* is a logical form of association between parallel events unexplained by causation; it is empirical, in that it cannot be measured by mechanistic means or duplicated with precision as science demands.

Hamingja requires recognition of a significant event and contemplation into its significance; only in this way can we consciously comprehend the framework of life and our role in it. Synchronicity is a signpost on the Path that guides each of us from what is to what should be and only comprehensive comprehension of our inherent nature and embracing it entirely as it is (rather than how we want it to be) can lead to true Sovereignty. *Hamingja* allows the awareness that we are pursuing the proper Path, wending the way we should. Anyone who has ever consciously experienced synchronicity can easily understand this, for when we are following the Path, prosperity and pleasure result, though once we deviate from it, even slightly, irregularities start manifesting in our lives. The increase of meaningful coincidence becomes more significant and observable when our *hamingja* is good, thus is the realization of synchronicity and the recognition of natural occurrences. In the final analysis synchronicity is Instinct made manifest in our lives.

Many Fólk will smile with satisfaction at the mere mention of good luck, while in the same breath grumbling about bad luck, never taking the time to contemplate that both must originate from the same source to exist at all: what should be. These events are only good or bad based solely upon the perspective of the individual: those that are positive or have a beneficial outcome beyond the norm are classified as good, while those considered negative or have some sort of disadvantageous end outside of the status quo are bad, though both are relative. These same Fólk will instinctively claim that they either "happen for a reason" without bothering to consciously consider what that cause might be or simply disregard the significance of it altogether. By taking time to contemplate these events, however, we take a more active role in our lives and *hamingja* becomes spiritual momentum, the impetus impelling us along the Path to perfection.

By intentionally seeking out synchronicity and recognizing it when it occurs we will experience it more, it will increase in intensity, and a paradigm shift will take place allowing us to access the collective unconscious at will. Reality consists of what we consciously recognize and contemplate, and *hamingja* is a means by which subconscious and conscious elements may realize themselves: one has a sudden urge to speak to their mother when the phone rings and it is their mother on the other end; a person is walking into a store and finds a quarter on the ground before entering and upon returning to their vehicle they find a ticket because the parking meter had run out while they were shopping. The possibilities are endless, but the one common theme is that, while these seem coincidental or causally unrelated, upon further reflection one can clearly comprehend the significance of what they experience and perhaps prevent deviating from the Path. Most Fólk do not bother to take time to think or simply overlook synchronicity altogether, being completely oblivious to the world around them, content to drift along without direction; worse are those who simply dismiss *hamingja* as some sort of random chance despite overwhelming evidence that this does not exist in our universe. Everything that has a consequence has a cause, whether we consciously comprehend that cause or not and negates any notion of luck.

All Fólk must actively participate in the progression of their lives, the development of their own potential through Effective Evolution and all who seek self-realization will be assisted as necessary. Our *fylgjur*, or tutelary spirits, are the personification of *hamingja*; the two meet in the *hamr*, or aura, which sensitives can observe, discern, and even explain to some degree. Our *fylgjur* exist to guide us along the Path and *hamingja* is the visible manifestation of this, the cosmic ordering of our universe.

Hamingja then is synchronicity, accepted as guided fortune, the directing principle of *Urð* leading each of us towards our Skuld, the spiritual momentum necessary to achieving Sovereignty. The Old Norse *hamingja* comes from *hamr* (shape or aura) and *gengr*, which means walking, thus it is our walking aura, referring to the unconscious interaction between our *hamr* and the outside world; *hamingja* is the spiritual link to Eternity, while the *fylgjur* are our physically manifest connections to the world of the *hamr*, all three being inextricably tied to our individual Skuld. *Fylgjur* follow us throughout our lives to assist us and assure our persistence along the Path; these are likely the souls of Fólk who have attained an Eternal Existence, the Einherjar that Freya select to take the field of Fólk (Folkvangr), a kenning for our world. As Alfheim was given to Frey as a tooth-gift, it is likely that the ability to fill it with Einherjar was bestowed upon Freya as a complimentary gift; the *álfar* are known to be spirits and sprites, so it is from among these that our *fylgjur* come: the archetypes of noble Fólk who were not to join the Allfather at the Ragnarok.

The *fetch* and *fylgja* correspond to Carl Jung's *animus* and *anima* respectively, the envoy between unconscious and conscious awareness; the Old Norse *fylgja* literally means "follow" and as such are those who accompany us along the Path, personal companions believed to represent an individual's *hamingja*. Such things as auras, nicknames, divine intervention, etc. are all said to be derived from the *fylgja*, though it is believed that the only time we will actually see our *fylgjur* is when we are *fey*, or doomed to die. *Fylgjur* can and often do manifest in animal form as well, while a particularly powerful person may have a number of tutelary spirits that accompany them, such as Odhin with wolves, ravens, Valkyries, etc.

The *fylgjur* have common psychological roots from which they spring: the shared image of the opposite sex an individual acquires, the empirical data one accumulates about the opposite sex through their interactions, and the inherent principle of the opposite sex latent in each of us. Most notably, men acquire an understanding of their *fylgja* from the experiences they have with women, primarily their mother, while women form a foundation for their *fetch* from their father. Next to tapping into and accepting our Shadow, getting in touch with our *fylgjur* is the most important part of the Individuation process. Many men today have heard that they need to get in touch with their feminine side and most believe this to be the product of a new age sensitive society, the misanthropic mass endeavoring to eradicate individuality, culture, and the superior elements through role reversal in gender, however, this is simply another example of usurping and abusing a far older Heathen belief by modern mediocre minds. For men the recognition of their *fylgja* and contact with her allows the balancing of Impulse with Intellect and Instinct that causes a paradigm shift in consciousness that strengthens their intuition, imagination, and intense creativity, what the Greeks referred to as our Muses; for women the *fetch* can bring into harmony their Intellect with Impulse and Instinct to allow her belief system to become firm, her resolve steadfast, and add conviction to her feelings and emotions. When a woman needs courage and aggression to deal with a particularly perilous situation it is her *fetch* that supports her and stiffens the spine. Our *fylgjur* are the direct connection between conscious awareness and unconscious urges, and as such, link us to Instinct, genetic memory, and our Shadow.

Sovereignty: The Empirical Path of Odhinn

Anima and *animus* come from **ane-* meaning "to breathe," thus are related to the Old Norse *önd*; it is likely that this derives from the fact that we acquire our *fylgjur* at birth, when we take that first breath. Where the concepts of *anima/animus* and *fylgjur* begin to diverge is in their spiritual significance: while Jung viewed the former in a purely psychological context, the latter is literally the breath which accompanies each of us throughout our lives, following us to guide and guard the self as spiritual momentum, moving us along the Path towards Sovereignty.

The *fylgjur* act as mediators between Asgardh and Utgardh, there to guide us in how we interact with the outside world, what of our inherent divinity we reveal or reflect; one's *fylgjur* will abandon them if they live a particularly ignoble life or participate in unnatural acts that will lead to their Extinction.

The *hamr* is the spiritual emanation of the physical body; it is luminous, often emitting a particular color corresponding to the character of the individual. The body has a biofield which is the equivalent of the *odic* field of our universe; both are immeasurable, but meaningful nevertheless. The *hamr* is an abstruse vivifying energy radiating around animate objects, invisible except to the enlightened, as only the truly illuminated are capable of seeing beyond the profane to the metaphysical.

The Old Norse *dómr*, or doom, is a force implied in nature: it is the indifferent, irrational, and irrevocable power that weaves and shapes all realities using the *urð* of everything in existence. *Dómr* is fixed only insofar as what has already transpired cannot be changed or altered, thus the consequences or benefits of that *urð* must be realized in some form or fashion, but beyond this, man becoming is open to individual will and the pursuit of what should be; our Fólk, like the Gods, implement our will through struggle, not fiat, through action rather than stasis and stagnation, seeking Sovereignty through Effective Evolution.

Time is an endless cycle in which all possibilities are repeated for all eternity; all that will happen has occurred before and all that has occurred before will happen again in time. Thus is the foundation of Primal Law. The only way to truly understand *ørlag* is as rhythm and vibration, through the absolute laws of nature and the supernatural.

It is by shedding the shroud of illusion that opposes absolute law that each of us may realize our potential and venture along the Path towards Sovereignty. Everything in our universe which is natural acts according to absolutes, allowing for natural law in as much as law is the only absolute. From this we must draw the conclusion that it takes a capacity for reason and rationality to recognize, understand, and apply absolute law; irrationality precludes any notion of law, order, principle, etc. for in its unstable condition can be found only chaos and imbalance. Since intentional action requires reason, man himself must be rational by nature to even exist (at least to some degree), let alone realize the relationship between causality and consequence, marking irrationality as unnatural. Absolute law contains myriad concepts with the same point of origin and in seeking Sovereignty we do our best to discern these and conform to them so as to comfortably fit into the whole rather than being at odds with nature. Absolute law also contains universal principles and processes for manifestation and realization; when we accept that absolute law exists, we can then begin to live a life that does not interfere with nor resist the existence of an ever-evolving whole, but compliments and contributes to it, bringing about self-realization in the process.

Pythagoras taught that what gave life to the unlimited was the limited; only through laws, or limitations, of the universe could all potential exist. This could not be chaos, but only true power, the potent-ial to bring into being or create. As creators, law and order is essential to our Fólk, for one must know the law to create any possibility. That said, no living thing has rights, only responsibilities; determinism nourishes the garden. None may be Sovereign without first moving beyond the illusion that they have some type of right; instead, we understand that each of us has a responsibility to that which gave us life, to live it in a manner that reflects divinity and guard the garden within from the chaotic forces without. The biggest fallacy being disseminated today is the right to life: no individual has a right to exist unless they consciously and continually protect that existence. Nothing in nature, nor absolute law, allows a right to life; to the contrary, every moment we draw breath is fraught with struggle, the balance between life and death at the forefront at all times, scoffing at the absurd and unnatural notion that someone has the right to exist simply because they were born or even conceived.

In the same way, morality, ethics, virtue, etc. *ad nauseum*, are experiential; all codes and commandments are but another's empirical reality, the crystallization of experiences had by another put into fixed form according to their personal predilection. Good and evil are subjective. Everywhere one looks in the natural world they find examples of this simple truth: what is good for one is often evil to another. Therefore, no moral code can be universally applied to all, as each of us is Sovereign over our own inner sanctum and only we can know for sure what is good and evil in our universe. The objectiveness of order and chaos, however, must be balanced in a way that allows free will to exist at all. Without this complete balance man's demeanor would be inherently good or naturally evil, with no ability for the opposite to exist. Life then is about balance, Will to Power, and through this, absolute self-realization: if the will be good, virtue will shine brightly like the sun, illuminating the world with the individual's luminescence, but if the Will be evil, darkness will surround the individual, ignorance, ignobility, and immorality blocking brilliance like an eclipse, casting shadows upon everything in their path. In the absence of light darkness prevails; the weak masses use morals to subdue the strong and superior.

Absolute law, like Primal Law itself, balances order and chaos so precisely that the Path is paved with potential and possibility, while Will to Power pursues perfection, and the Sovereign strides with pride and purpose. *Ørlag* as the Primal Law of nature can be comprehended as:

EMBODIMENT
All phenomena can be considered alive, containing a persona of its own, thus an entity in its own right. Within this, however, there are two polarities that are consistent with the Path of Odhinn:

INTROVERSION
As we create our own reality so too do we have the ability to summon any reality from within; the conscious stream is overwhelmed by the macrocosmos becoming unconscious awareness.

EXTRAVERSION
As reality exists beyond our physical body, so too do we have the ability to summon any of these realities to ourselves; the sorcerer embodies the Source itself and becomes the Creator. In altering the manner of viewing the world around us, the world around us is altered.

OSCILLATION

Everything moves and no living thing is ever at rest; life itself is vibration and these biorhythms are determined by cycles: ebb and flow, rise and fall, etc., the pendulum swing expressing the rhythm of life. All of existence consistently remains in a state of constant change and this modification is not random or accidental. Both development and disintegration are necessary to evolution and all change comes about through cycles, like a spiral. All organisms remain at a constant velocity unless an external force exercises influence over them and for every force acting thus the organism exerts energy in equal measure to the source. According to wave theory, light is conveyed from a luminous body such as the sun, stars, and moon to the eye by an undulatory movement and this corresponds to the *oðic* force, its influence on man and the rainbow bridge connecting Asgardh and Midgardh.

DUALITY

All existence is sustained in duality, the designation of degrees between two points of the same thing. Everything has its polar opposite, though opposites are identical in nature, only different by degree. All energies are dualistic, having polarities from which to measure one another: male and female, order and chaos, love and hate, etc. These polarities can be powerful when fully understood in their proper context, as each ultimately contains the essence of the other within itself. The nature of light and darkness is as the medium of visibility or lack thereof, wherein, the latter is merely the absence of the former. Duality can be seen as the rate at which an object vibrates, as it is possible to alter the vibrations of one polarity to any point along the plane to the opposite extreme.

EVOLUTION

Just as all phenomena are alive according to EMBODIMENT and no living thing is ever at rest, all life strives to grow and life itself indicates the natural imperative to achieve a Higher state. Evolution presupposes death, in that, there can be no recreation or increase without decrease and destruction; no inferior entity can survive a superior element and the very nature of evolution is such that it demands the disintegration of the lesser and unneeded in favor of the greater and necessary.

SOVEREIGNTY: THE EMPIRICAL PATH OF ODHINN

EQUILIBRIUM

There are many precepts and principles which influence our world, but there is only one true Absolute: the perfect point of balance between two polarities that allows for all possibilities and potential to exist; the equilibrium between thesis and antithesis wherein synthesis lay. While it remains necessary to avoid stagnation, stasis as a state of equilibrium, not of inaction, is to be sought in all things. In order to grow or thrive an organism must first bring into balance its inherent nature; encroaching on either extreme enables the organism to be inflexible and less likely to attain or maintain equilibrium and it is this balance between *önd* and *óð* that creates the Bifrost Bridge. The ascetic, in seeking balance and harmony, restricts the vibrations of a thing to the point from which they aspire to find stillness and silence, thereby attuning themselves to the nature of the desired state before subduing the motion which would carry them to one extreme or the other like a pendulum. This type of discipline can be used unconsciously, though only the dedicated can accomplish this with full awareness of their actions; doing so is true Will to Power. Most Fólk today simply drift along as the sea of life carries them back then forth and it is only those capable of self-mastery who can take rudder in hand and navigate the Path they choose to follow. Only through equilibrium can this be achieved.

INFLUENCE

An organism having some connection in common with another can concede control to the other and the extent of that commonality determines the influence the two have upon each other; the pinnacle of possible association between two organisms is the exchange of energies to which one may become the other and wield its power. What at one time created a connection maintains a reciprocal exchange of energies even after separation, as with *óð* and Odhinn. No thing can elevate itself above its source of origin; neither can it evolve properly without first being involved.

SENSIBILITY

Sensibility is empirical reality: none can know or prove that the information gleaned from our senses is all that exists, as they are limited in the range and type of information available to them. There are as many ways to experience and perceive the world as there are people in it and no living thing can be omnipotent, nor omniscient, to know all there is to know; no individual will ever run out of things to discover, learn, or imagine. All that assists an organism can be classified as true or good, while anything that hinders the organism is seen as false or bad according to the particular organism's sensations, be they physical or metaphysical, therefore, sensibility is experiential reality.

ERUDITION
The more an individual knows about someone, some thing, or the self, the more complete is the control they have over it and themselves. Knowledge of an organism, object, or phenomenon provides power; this is expressed in the very name of things, as it has long been held that in knowing some thing or someone's true name, sway can be exerted over that which has been identified. Words have power and like linguistic alchemy can change and even influence reality. Many words exhibit potency simply through sound, as evidenced in *galdr*, mantras, and chanting, while others gain power from meaning or the emotion behind them.

CONSEQUENCE
In every facet of life there is cause and consequence, for neither could exist without the other. Likewise there are those who are agents of activity and others affected only by the aftermath; the former are Fólk who consciously make things happen, while the latter allow things to happen to or around them. In neither case is chance or happenstance the guiding principle, as it is the mere illusion created by those who do not comprehend why a thing occurred; random chance is the belief of the mediocre masses that they are victims of an indecipherable and unjust unknown force of luck.

Our ancestors lived in accord with nature and her laws, not at odds with either, and this was clearly effective for countless centuries prior to our Fólk losing touch with their Instinct and inherent nature; it can only be through a return to this that we will move forward once more. The influence of nature on every aspect of life, from survival to spirituality is evident to anyone with eyes to see, everyone who elects to consciously recognize it and can best be summed up in the words of the sixteenth century physician and alchemist Paracelsus:

"The first man who learned anything useful was taught by nature; let nature teach us as she taught him."

History exhibits endless examples of the consequences of a disregard for nature and her dictates, or worse, putting oneself at odds with either; though these standards can be demanding, they are in place for a purpose: to guide Fólk along the appropriate avenues of advancement and evolution. To this end, nature could be seen as the protective mother who instructs her children in the ways of life, steering them clear of danger and instilling the morals and values held in high regard by her, those characteristics and qualities inherited by her parents, passed down by theirs before them *ad infinitum*, as life develops and the lessons are learned for survival and perpetuation of the species; this last being nature's primary Instinct. Every peoples on this planet have a set of natural innate tendencies, traits, and predispositions encoded in their genetic structure, as unique to their racial group as the blood that binds them and this Instinct is the spirit of that people, what distinguishes them from one another more than any kind of superficial appearance ever could. In this there are only three types of Instinct: chaos, order, and balance, corresponding to Emotive, Cognitive, and Equimotive respectively. Our Fólk recognize the timeless truths of Primal Law as essential to our evolution and take an active role in sustaining our spirituality by seeking Sovereignty; this can be accomplished through understanding and utilizing the Primal Law to bring into harmony the self and spirit of the soul.

In conclusion, just as the oak is latent in the acorn, the potential for perfection, that of the Sovereign Self, is inherent in the soul of our Fólk and in the same way that an ash cannot sprout from an acorn, neither can the seed of a particular people be anything else without disregarding that inherent nature and existing in contradistinction to it. The three phases of the Path of Odhinn are essentially spiritual evolution, as we are each born with the spirit of divinity within us and must develop that deity consciously; we are the blades forged in the fires of ordeal, tried through trial and tribulation, and worthed in the weal and woe of this world.

ÖND OK ÓÐ:
INSTINCT, INTELLECT, IMPULSE

"What lies behind us and what lay before us are tiny matters compared to what lies within us."

– Ralph Waldo Emerson

Men are composite creatures consisting of an animal nature and inherent soul, marking him or her as capable of either a base existence or that of the divine, depending solely upon the Will to Power of the individual. This Will to Power comes from the self which itself is, or should be, a reflection of the Self in the same way the moon reflects the light of the sun. Physically and spiritually there is constant and perpetual interplay between this *óð* and Odhinn, with the microcosm mirroring the macrocosm, having been patterned according to its intrinsic nature. This self is the consciousness of Intellect and Impulse.

Spirit on the other hand is that Instinct inherited from the Gods through the gift of *önd*, that Breath of Life which carries the whispers of wisdom and inspiration through our blood. The term spirituality itself is derived from the Latin *spirare* (meaning "to breathe") and can be defined as anything pertaining to the spirit, the principle of life, the vital essence of living beings. The Old Norse *önd* is likewise translated as "spirit" or Breath of Life and has the same sacred quality as the Sanskrit *prana*: the spirit is the very essence (or breath) of life without which we could not even exist. This gift from the Gods is what makes each of us divine, separating man from the rest of the animal kingdom and allows us to attain Sovereignty. For this gift we owe a debt or obligation to the Gods: as their descendants we are required to reflect their nature in all we do and leave undone so as to honor and pay respect to the legacy endowed us. This *önd*, our spirit as Instinct, is the nucleus of the soul, around which the *óð* as Intellect and Impulse (the self), gathers. The self and spirit are intertwined to the point of being indistinguishable from one another, only deviating by degree in that the former is or should be conscious of itself, its nature and purpose, while the latter remains unconscious, indecipherable, though integral to the self and soul.

The Old Norse *Laeti* is often translated as our disposition, though should likely refer to the soul; it is only mentioned in the Edda one time: in Voluspa as one of the things Askr and Embla lacked, however, is not one of the four gifts given them by the Gods. This leads to the conclusion that *Laeti* is in fact the combined *önd* and *óð* (Instinct along with Intellect and Impulse) that is carried by the *Lá* or blood. This *Laeti* is the essence of existence without which a divine life would not be possible; conversely, the soul could not exist without the blood or body (*Lá ok Litu Goða*), marking the reliance of the physical body and the soul upon one another as equally integral. The soul shapes and integrates the body, insisting that it pursue Higher Ideals, while the body depends almost exclusively on stimuli; today more than any other time in history our Fólk deny the divine and focus on the base materialism of the body, completely ignoring the soul's requests to participate in a lofty life.

In the purest pan-Aryan spiritual systems the significance of the soul comprises the core of sacred teachings, from the Old Norse *önd* and *óð* to the Sanskrit *prana* and *atman* (Germanic *athem*) representing the Breath of Life and self respectively. *Óð* is the substance of the soul while *önd* is the spirit that animates it and together comprise our *Laeti*.

The soul, however, is not an aggregate of elements to be distinguished one from another and analyzed apart from each other, despite their being three distinct components which comprise its whole. The existence of these constituents does not precede that of the soul, for this latter is a form, a pattern from which the parts neither come before, nor after, and do not determine the design, but fixes the fragments according to the inherent nature of the whole, its morphogenetic field. Knowledge of this pattern, of its laws and structure, could not possibly be derived from discrete discernment of the individual elements exclusively, but only through their relation to one another and the integrity of the whole. That said, to truly comprehend the soul, we must first examine the various aspects that make it the sun of our personal universe, those characteristics, traits, and features that distinguish it from all others as unique to a particular people or person.

The soul is Eternal, indestructible, and only found in physical form as it seeks out perfection, divine consciousness and the individuality of Sovereignty. Every soul engages in lengthy cycles of reincarnation and transmigration; through gaining spiritual nourishment and enlightenment during the life of its mortal existence, the periods in which the soul inhabits a body, one can eventually break this cycle and achieve Sovereignty over the self. Reincarnation requires each individual to return to Midgardh, to be reborn, and live out their Skuldic debt, and this Path of duty is the way to Sovereignty as it leads directly to divinity through the destruction of the cycle of time binding the soul to temporal existence. Upon the death of the body the soul passes to Hel, the realm of entropy, where it awaits one of three possible destinations: rebirth into another body, extinction in Niflhel, or (if one has attained Sovereignty over the self) into the realm of the Gods, that of Eternal Existence.

Laeti is likewise the center of our *verald*, literally "man-age" and what we refer to as our world, the framework from which our internal as well as external existence is structured, an outlook emanating from within that we strive to realize beyond ourselves; creating, in effect, a situation in which we both act and react according to this *Laeti* with certainty, knowing without a doubt that this is truth. Many modern Heathen speak of this as a way of life rather than a religion and it is reliance on this *Laeti* that guides each of us along that Path. Our individual *verald* has at its center its own sun, just as the universe we see when we look into the sky, and this sun is our soul. This world is Midgardh, our individual middle garden between Asgardh (the garden of the Gods within) and Utgardh (the garden of giants outside ourselves), the three corresponding to balance, order, and chaos respectively.

Sovereignty: The Empirical Path of Odhinn

Óð as the primary matter of the *Laeti* should be understood as our Intellect and Impulse in the same way Odhinn has the dual aspect of Huginn and Muninn. *Óð* as potential is the ability to become, the power to actualize all that lay dormant within. In its simplest context *óð* can be seen as the self, understood in Jungian terms as the ego; Odhinn then can literally be translated as "one who knows" themself, or the Sovereign Self. To exist is to actively pursue potential and purpose, thus is consciousness sprung, while realization comes through the development and revelation of the inherent nature of each individual, our *ørlag*.

To this end then, *óð* is the acorn within which exists all potential for the oak tree; each branch, root, leaf, etc. is latent and must become the stout oak through proper nourishment. Whatever is not present in the acorn cannot possibly become manifest by nature in the tree; likewise the supraconscious state of Sovereignty that Odhinn represents is inherent in our individual *óð* and simply requires the proper conditions to bring to fruition. Growth and evolution in particular are the eternal struggles of that within to manifest itself without, the striving of potential to realize itself in final form and the Path from *óð* to Odhinn is defined by Verdhandi as "man becoming".

From *óð* comes everything and everything is nourished through *óð*: it creates but does not control, oversees but is not overbearing, exists in all and all exists because of it. All of existence then rests upon Will to Power: the eye realizes the will to see, the legs and feet the will to walk, etc. True Will to Power then is not the destruction of the self, nor its subjugation as some would have it, but its complete balance and harmony with Instinct, the complimentary relationship between the self of Intellect and Impulse and the collective unconscious that elevates this self to the Sovereign Self.

Óð is at its most harmonious and powerful when it is manifest in the individual who accepts their inherent nature (or *ørlag*), embraces the synchronicity or *Hamingja* present in their lives, and understands what should be, their Skuld, as the guiding principle along the Path; in so doing we can comprehend our *óð* completely and the pursuit of Odhinn becomes much more spontaneous and natural.

Óð is Intellect and Impulse, two concepts that seem to be easily identifiable for most Fólk, though rarely understood completely in either their individual capacity nor combined context. First, it should be clear that the Old Norse root words *hugr* and *munr* literally mean Intellect and Impulse and combine to make up our *óð* as consciousness or self (even our individual ego), which is influenced by, experiences, and reacts to the physical world and environment. The self is meant to be a mediator between external effects and internal instincts, the intermediary of the outer and indwelling influences that ultimately guide each of our lives, monitors, and filters our field of consciousness.

This self is the "I" of Intellect and Impulse, our persona, and as such is primarily a product of nurture; its development depends almost exclusively upon education, experience, and sensory stimulus in contrast to the nature of inherent instincts. This is why culture and tradition play such an important role in the evolution of the self and Fólk as a whole. This persona is the means by which we interact with and perceive the world according to our individual *Weltanschauung*, as well as that of the communal conscious; in this way, the self is a reflection of everything we are told and taught, mirroring the reality we consciously create for ourselves.

Consciousness itself has two aspects from which all awareness arises: Impulse or emotion is the state of experiential conscious and sensational feeling not directly attributable to a particular stimulus stemming from the five physical senses and generally becomes manifest as impulsive or reactionary responses; Intellect is the complex cognitive capacity of thought, reason, and understanding from which rational realization emanates. The Intellect monitors urges, the impulse aspects of the self, ensuring a proper balance between desire and necessity; it is definite, relying on precision to perform properly, while emotion remains equivocal and involuntary, impulsively reacting to outside influences, though both are essential to our individuality.

Plato referred to the Intellect as the *nous* and believed it to be the first and purest emanation in the universe, regarded as the self-contemplating order of our universe and to this should be added the very urge to exist at all, that Impulse to give life to such an emanation, showing that both are inseparably intertwined. In much the same way many elder traditions refer to a "self-existent" or "self-created" one, often identified with a Sovereign such as Brahma or Odhinn, marking the intellectual pursuit of knowledge and wisdom as one path to supraconsciousness, while asceticism is seen in the complete control of one's emotions as the other. The balance of these two, however, is the true Path to Sovereignty.

The Intellect discriminates, divides, and opposes, processing information from the environment, emotions, Instinct, etc. and interpreting this input ideally to resolve issues and decide upon the most rational response to a given situation. Problem-solving, goal setting, strategic planning, etc. are all results of intellectual integration and rationality. The Intellect is naturally inclined to coherency and consistency, which predisposes it to maintaining a single position on a particular issue, reflecting one's opinions, views, beliefs, convictions, prejudices, et. al. from an individual perspective according to one's own perception; it makes assessments that determine whether one is an advocate for something or in opposition to it and the very definition of "keeping an open mind" is allowing the Intellect to properly process input without becoming mired in a myopic or narrow-minded view of the world around it. Such limitations lead to stagnation and stasis in the growth and nourishment of the soul, such as we find prevalent since the predominance of monotheism over the natural spirituality of henotheism.

The Intellect depends upon discursive knowledge, dreaming, imagination, differentiation, judgment, correlation, and memory, through which it simultaneously holds both past and future, to function properly. The Intellect can never know objective truth as it is not the true "knower"; it can evaluate, prognosticate, assume associations, cite authority, form hypothesis, even contemplate the creation of the cosmos, but it is unable to view things objectively, from the inside, as they actually are inherently. The only way in which the Intellect can see things directly is to still itself, to stop itself from reconciling the subject and object as its innate disposition demands it to do. Only when the Intellect is completely quiet and vigilant can the actual object and subject be present simultaneously, thus be aware of both at the same time, opening the "third eye" of the mystics in the process to reconcile them. Discernment is essential to one's development, as it allows the separation of the useful from the unnecessary, while at the same time the Intellect is the ultimate uniter, bringing together the Impulse and Instinct into conscious awareness, allowing one to act in a reasonable and rational manner, according to their inherent nature, in any given situation.

Emotion on the other hand is essential to spiritual nourishment, for without feeling and sensation the Intellect would lack integral input from which to base its beliefs and the physical body would remain free from pleasure, pain, love, lust, hate, sorrow, etc. necessary not only for surviving but thriving as an individual as well. Impulse is the act or action imparting motion, thus the very foundation for emotion to spring forth, a strong mental feeling as distinguished from knowledge, usually stemming from sensational stimuli. Emotion comes from the Latin *emouvoir*, to "excite or move the feelings of" and Impulse is the impetus behind this movement (meaning "inner life force" or "inner energy") as it stems from *önd* or Instinct (the drive and desire to act or impel) and is a force in its own right. Impulse is undoubtedly connected to memory, in that we tend to retain memories of incidents or events to which we have an emotional link, such as traumatic experiences, sexual stimulation, near-death encounters, etc. Emotion is the aspect of *óð* that is the most difficult to control as it is dependent upon movement, either from within or outside of ourselves and that movement can often be the hardest to slow, stop, or speed up.

Óð, like consciousness itself, can best be summed up with Rene Descartes' declaration *Cogito ergo Sum* ("I think therefore I am") as it was at the point when Askr and Embla were imbued with *ørlag* that true consciousness began for Fólk: when self (*óð*) arose from the depths of unconscious Instinct (*önd*), an archetype most commonly referred to as the Breath of Life. *Óð* was likewise the gift of independence and individuality, for free will and freedom forge forth from the self of Intellect and Impulse, the Wisdom to Power and Will to Power respectively. Freedom is an emanation of Eternity in everything finite, thus freedom is infinite, possibility immeasurable, and perfection the potential for all.

Önd then, as Breath of Life, is the animating principle of the soul, innate insight, and impulsion; what we know as inspiration or the in-spirit. This Instinct is internal and includes inherent inclinations, tendencies, and predispositions present in particular peoples as a whole; these primal proclivities are phylogenetic at their core, properly referred to as the collective unconscious of our Fólk, and embody the primeval patterns of archetypal constructs found in the soul of specific groups. In Old Norse this would be known as the Fólklaeti or Fólk-Soul: as our individual soul is composed of Intellect, Impulse, and Instinct, so too is the Fólk-Soul made up of these same elements, the archetypes expressed through cultural and conscious awareness of what connects us. The state symbolizing perfection for our Fólk is found in the god-image Odhinn (the Sovereign Self), and his ravens represent Sovereign Intellect and Sovereign Impulse for the Fólk-Soul. Carl Jung believed the archetype to be exclusive to a particular people, a genesis of sorts that embodied the essence of a deified individual and/or deed and all evidence seems to support this conclusion.

Instinct can be defined as the aggregate knowledge and wisdom of our ancestors, our archegnosis. Reflexes are physically manifest instincts and like the former, the latter are protective by nature, ensuring one is safe and their needs are being met, automatically directing the body, Intellect, or Impulse to act or react in a certain way to prevent injury or neglect, to repeat a learned behavior, etc. To ignore or disregard one's instincts can be, and usually is, as detrimental as neglecting to defend oneself when in danger. In this way, reflexes can be seen as the short-term memory that acts in concert with the physical body, while the Instinct is the long-term memory of the Fólk, the collective unconscious which we are given access to through the gift of *önd*, the phylogenesis from which one draws inspiration and intuition. Anyone who understands the concept of cellular memory, what is commonly referred to as muscle memory, can comprehend how genetic memory is imminent and incontrovertible. Just as reflexes and habit can be learned through practice, ritual, and repetition, so too can the genetic memory of Instinct be accessed through contemplation, trance, fasting, etc. In addition, just as short-term memory must be processed into the long-term and can only store limited amounts of information for any length of time, so too are the experiences of one's life assimilated into the collective unconscious of our Fólk prior to being lost upon the death of the physical body, though these are likely only those deeds determined to be worthy of the Fólk-Soul.

Perhaps the best insight on Instinct and the importance of instincts can be found in the words of Carl Jung:

> *"Instincts are highly conservative and of extreme antiquity as regards both their dynamism and their form. Their form, when represented to the mind appears as an image, which expresses the nature of the instinctive impulse visually and concretely, like a picture. Instinct is anything but a blind and indefinite impulse, since it proves to be attuned and adapted to a definite external situation. This latter circumstance gives it its specific and irreducible form. Just as instinct is original and hereditary, so too its form is age-old, that is to say archetypal; it is even older and more conservative than the body's form. These biological considerations naturally apply also to* Homo Sapiens *who still remain within the framework of general biology despite the possession of consciousness, will and reason. The fact that our conscious activity is rooted in instinct and derives from it dynamism as well as the basic features of its ideational forms has the same significance for human psychology as for all other*

members of the animal kingdom. Human knowledge consists essentially in the constant adaptation of the primordial patterns of ideas that were given us a priori. *These need certain modifications because in their original form they are suited to an archaic mode of life but not to the demands of a specifically differentiated environment. If the flow of instinctive dynamism into our life is to be maintained, as is absolutely necessary for our existence, then it is imperative that we should remold these archetypal forms into ideas which are adequate to the challenge of the present."*

It could be said that our instincts are the primordial and ancestral archetypes personified as Gods and Goddesses, making the collective unconscious of our Fólk the pan-Aryan pantheon. Instincts have their origin in necessity and survival, though over time became "second nature" to subsequent generations. This familiarization ultimately leads to the elevation of those qualities and characteristics deemed good and worthy, perpetuated and reinforced through habituation, and deification of individuals who seemingly embodied these aspects or instincts. In the same way that different periods of time necessitate varying degrees or modes of survival, so too do the deities of that particular period represent that need and the contemporary psyche of that people. Religion itself is relevant only to the context of time, appropriate to specific intervals from which it held significance. Spirituality is the reliance on the Instinct inherent in our blood and allowing oneself to be inspired by it, while spiritual nourishment is developing the ability to recognize one's instincts and utilize them for growth, evolution, and achieving greatness; spirituality is likewise the nourishing of the soul by means of necessity, implying that spiritual nourishment does and must change to fit the needs of the time. Thus, Instinct is meant to grow and evolve with the Fólk so that we may be able to attain Sovereignty.

Odhinn signifies Sovereign Self and it is here where we find the ultimate expression and realization of Sovereignty. The pursuit of knowledge and wisdom is, has always been, and will always be, an inherent instinct in our Fólk, since the dawn of consciousness, and Odhinn represents the purest manifestation of this. At the same time most of what was at one time considered mysterious or worthy of pursuing an understanding of during the heyday of Heathen practice has become common knowledge to Fólk today, leading to claims that this way of life is somehow outdated or antiquated; the simple truth is that it was not allowed to naturally evolve as it should have due to the almost total annihilation of Heathen beliefs, values, and practices by zealots bent on imposing their one true god on our Fólk. Had the Heathen way of life continued to grow and evolve it would now stand proudly among any of the world's spiritual systems. As it is, the call of the blood is bringing Fólk back to the Path in droves and Carl Jung's *Ergriffenheit* is spreading. In the final analysis, the pursuit of wisdom at any cost is just one example of an instinct as archetype and is as relevant today as it was thousands of years ago.

The archetype is the initial pattern, the form from which later foundations are laid. With the distinctions of sociobiological differences among the peoples of the world comes an archetypal understanding of these various groups, all readily apparent in the individual and communal instincts, the personal and collective unconscious. It should be noted that it is not the representation that is inherited, but the Instinct to give a particular archetype life, to manifest it in physical form and realize its divine nature. It is only through a conscious effort, even imaginative, that the archetype takes on a definite physical or material form. The true nature of the archetype, however, like the instincts themselves, are incapable of becoming conscious, nor of finding realization in the individual Intellect, for the mere act itself is one of enlightenment and transcends the mundane in achieving awareness. It is religion, not true spirituality, that insists that archetypes have a definite form, no matter how inaccurate or illogical, hence the absurd image of the christ figure in the Western world.

The self is drawn from these archetypes and it is to the degree that each individual integrates these instincts into their lives, realizes their inherent divinity (or lack thereof), and imposes their will upon the world (or not) that determines their place in the phylogenesis. Our Gods reflect the period and place they were popularized in and at the same time attest to the very spirit of our Fólk as a whole by demonstrating the power of the archetype, the Instinct, present in the collective unconscious to continually manifest itself. When we are born and the Instinct influences the self into becoming an individual we are then considered a separate entity, much the same way the newborn babe is from the mother, and just as helpless. The connection between the individual and the collective unconscious is present, though tenuous, at this point and remains so for the duration of one's life if not strengthened and made solid through morphogenetic resonance. In much the same way a child needs guidance and parental nurturing to grow and thrive properly, the individual self requires the Instinct of the collective unconscious for spiritual nourishment to develop and embrace its divine nature; without it the child will suppress their inherent character in favor of reflecting their environment, whether good or bad, as it is much easier to mimic what one sees than emulate what they do not.

Often the link between the self and Instinct can be more easily fortified in childhood simply because the wonder and awe of adolescence is still prevalent; the recognition of the divine in all things is much stronger prior to the cynicism and plebeian perspective of adulthood, which in the modern world leads to the dominance of the individual ego over the Instinct of the unconscious. This has become particularly problematic since the introduction of monotheism into our collective consciousness. Our Fólk have been increasingly led away from their instincts, to the point where we are today, and most are selfish, self-loathing, genophobic, immoral sycophants concerned only with materialism and consumerism, just as the Voluspa predicted we would be during the Wolf Age. This is a direct result of ignoring and disregarding one's Instinct.

Carl Jung made it abundantly clear that instincts, thus archetypes, are unique to a particular people; indeed, instincts can be considered the very phylogenesis of a people, distinctive, defining them through the evolution of their individual archetypes, and to which their spiritual systems are manifest. There are essentially three instincts: order, chaos, and balance. These three instincts, when combined with the Intellect and Impulse, give life to three distinct types:

TYPE A: Cognitives follow the Instinct of order in relation to intellectual pursuits, placing a high regard on intelligence and increasing mental acuity, in addition to that which generally stems from such activities, though often at the cost of emotional numbness. This type, while building advanced machinery, great philosophical schools, technology, even empires, often lack simple feelings, rarely demonstrating emotion in common ways such as music, poetry, humor, dance. etc.

TYPE B: Emotives are those who live according to the Instinct of chaos with an emphasis on emotional experiences such as singing, dancing, sexual license, living in the moment, enjoying the here and now with little regard for tomorrow, and place marginal importance on intellectual ideals or laying the framework for the future by undertaking such endeavors as building civilizations, lasting governments, and societies, or devising firm philosophical systems.

TYPE C: Equimotives rely on the Instinct of balance to produce a proper harmony and are inevitably among the minority the world over, for their sheer spiritual outlook is rare among the planet's population. These Fólk have produced some of the greatest intellects, whose genius manifested in the sciences, philosophy, technological advancements, etc. as well as art, music, poetry, plays, humor, et. al. while maintaining their inherent and instinctual nature.

These types can be seen on both a biologically distinct and individual basis, separated into peoples or persons corresponding to the various degrees of Instinct, Intellect, and Impulse demonstrated in their personal or collective unconscious, culture, traditions, practices, experiences, etc. What's more, the soul of an individual or group is quantifiable according to the degree of energy each element expresses or expends.

Energy is the exchange between two polarities creating the power for activity and potential for animation. The self as Intellect and Impulse is a ball of energy, discharging at a rate of vibration consistent with a particular thought or feeling and congruent with the color spectrum. The soul as a whole is a source of light that emanates outward from within, as the sun does the universe; some have identified this outward emanation as an aura, which in Old Norse would correspond with *hamr*, a transfigured life form. This *hamr* would be the manifestation of an individual's mental and emotional vitality; this is likewise the root of *hamingja*, which is believed to be the personification of fortune and can be either attached to an individual or group. *Hamingja* is not some abstract notion, but has a definite quality as a soul-like protective spirit, which is to be seen as the *hamr* in conjunction with an archetype, i.e. the Intellect and Impulse with the Instinct.

ÖND OK ÓÐH: INSTINCT, INTELLECT, IMPULSE

A strong emotional response, whether positive or negative, will vibrate to the level of that feeling manifesting on the physical plane as adrenaline, sexual arousal, loose bowels, etc. Conversely, a thought consists of electrical energy traversing the neurons of the brain and will emanate outward, often measured as heat around the head. Thus the physiological aspects of Intellect and Impulse are readily apparent and, as mentioned, find correspondence with the color spectrum: just as red has the highest rate of vibration, so too does anger or thoughts of violence (i.e. "he saw red"), in contrast to love or happiness, which correspond to violet, the lowest vibration in the spectrum. The vibration of supraconsciousness or Sovereignty are too rapid for discernment by conscious means, much the same way ultraviolet rays are invisible to the naked eye.

The energy of the soul vibrates at a pace too high to sustain itself on the physical plane without a proper vessel to contain it and become the vehicle for its manifestation. Symbolically, this has been represented as a cauldron or ketil such as *oðroerir*, both the container and contents of inspiration in the same way the *litu goða* (or body) and *laeti* are integral to one another's existence here in this world. In terms of physics the soul could be compared to antimatter, in that, while it is theoretically possible that matter composed of the antiparticles of electrons, protons, and neutrons could be as stable as normal matter, they could only exist in isolation from it. The same can be said of the Fólk-Soul, for while the collective unconscious could manifest itself on the physical plane (in the form of a god perhaps) it is only theoretical, simply because the energy and power that would emanate from this force would be too great to exist in the world without destroying everything around it; thus the "particles" (individual spirits or archetypes) that desire manifestation must be isolated and contained in a physical form capable not only of holding it for a duration of time but keeping the spirit separate from the collective. In this, the body is but a temporary vehicle, as it ultimately erodes and decays from the spirit's desire to return to the collective or attain an Eternal Existence. Understanding the soul as energy in this way can further demonstrate how *önd* as spirit can be considered vitality, the breath that gives life to *óð* as the self.

It is ironic perhaps that Cognitives are often considered "fast" or "quick-witted" whereas Emotives can be seen by some as "slow" or "dull-witted." When we look at the biorhythms of each (the innate rhythmic biological process), they coincide with radio frequencies of 13-30 hertz and 8-13 hertz respectively, far faster for Cognitives than Emotives. This can also explain why these latter are often more in touch with their Instinct: they are closer to the Theta state of unconsciousness (4-8 hertz) that allow one to tap into the genetic memory.

Nevertheless, all of existence requires the balance between two extremes and *oðic* energy is the interchange between *óð* and Odhinn, the gift of a gift wherein man is given life in order to live it. This reality is really quite simple; only man has made it complicated. Odhinism allows an individual to live triumphantly within the bounds of the Absolute Law that is ever-present in *oðic* energy. Instead of denying the existence of this energy Odhinists seek to understand and embrace it and in contrast to those who would combat it, attempt to repel it, or control it, we utilize its power, potential, and properties to attain Sovereignty; this is why Odhinism is a way of life lived spiritually rather than religion as understood by most Fólk today. It is only by shedding the shroud of illusion that disguises this *oðic* energy that each of us can realize our true potential.

In the mid-19th century Karl Ludwig Freiherr von Reichenbach, a great German chemist, metallurgist, and natural philosopher discovered and studied for nearly three decades a phenomena he termed "od energy," in which the light emanating primarily from sun and moon (though other planets, stars, and cosmic objects as well) have a physiological effect upon both inanimate and living things here on our planet, in addition to one another presumably. It is well known that the Baron drew inspiration for his concept from Odhinn, thus from the Old Norse *óð* and it is fascinating that he only had a fleeting familiarity with Norse mythology, yet chose to name the energy he spent most of his life studying after the very essence given Askr and Embla. Far from being a coincidence or an arbitrary designation it would seem to be instinctual, apt, and unconsciously appropriate.

The Baron's research began by investigating somnambulism and the possible side effects the moon could have on these "sleep-walkers"; it quickly developed into an understanding of life and existence itself wherein the sun's rays had a profound impact upon every individual, though those who found themselves walking in their sleep were just more sensitive to what he came to term *óð* energy. The fact that somnambulism almost always followed specific lunar phases, reaching maximum strength at the full moon, likely explains ritual being held at these times by many Fólk; the point where *oðic* energy was at its fullest would seemingly set the ideal spiritual, even shamanic, conditions. In the Voluspa there are a series of stanzas often considered interpolations, referred to by some as the "catalog of dwarves," which begins with the new and full moons, followed by the four directions, which could easily be the remnants of one such ritual that was used to harness this type of *oðic* energy.

Either way, the Baron's research revealed that *oðic* energy has nine distinctive characteristics:

> *Oðic* energy is an active and dynamic quality not related to either electrical or magnetic forces (nor any other known field) though remains as powerful as either.

> *Oðic* energy is not light itself, but is conducted along light beams and generates effects according to the color spectrum.

> *Oðic* energy induces physiological sensations to various degrees dependent upon individual sensitivity.

> *Oðic* energy exhibits penetrating effects aside from direct luminary contact.

> *Oðic* energy has the capacity of being conducted and incorporated by and into animate as well as inanimate constituents, though having more effect on organic than inorganic objects.

> *Oðic* energy can be stored and sustained for an extended duration of time in both animate and inanimate matter.

> *Oðic* energy radiates rays across space, releasing radiant beams over distances determined by dimension and direction.

> *Oðic* energy can be reflected and refracted, retaining its vitality to varying degrees.

> Pure sunlight produces powerful *oðic* energy, while refracted light is less effective; conversely, moonlight being a reflection of the sun produces polar opposite effects.

From these nine characteristics the Baron built his belief in *oðic* energy and the *oðic* "force" that was behind it. *Oðic* energy can be contained in objects and matter to various degrees for myriad periods of time: everything from water to wood, with crystal being the strongest and longest. Travel time for *oðic* energy is fairly slow, being measured at four feet a second, like honey or molasses poured on to pancakes, though many objects would hold their charge for 10 minutes or more, up to an hour with some material. Unlike electrical energy, which travels along conductive surfaces, *oðic* energy suffuses and saturates. Solar *oðic* energy has a cool, soothing effect, while the lunar brought about allergic irritations. The best *oðic* conductors are solid metals such as silver, while loosely woven cloth did not conduct very well at all.

What is interesting, however, is the fact that when diffused into separate colors along the spectrum, the sun's light had a different effect in relation to the specific color upon individual people. For example, red being at one extreme of the *oðic* spectrum produced "irritating" results, while at the other, violet had a "cooling" effect. The *oðic* polarities are as nourishing as nutrients, however, and depending in large part upon an individual's energetic deficiencies, each craved particular colors during experiments conducted by the Baron; likewise this is the same today in our every day lives as well, where the sun has a profound effect upon the energy level of many Fólk. This phenomena came to be termed "photo allergens." The physical body could be said to slow the higher vibration of the pure *oðic* energy like a transformer, the conduit for *önd* and interestingly the archaic meaning of the word conduit literally means "fountain" and would be analogous to the well and/or cauldron.

An *oðic* field surrounding a magnet corresponds to the color spectrum as well, at specific degrees around the circumference of a circle. It always begins at red cycling around to violet to start again at red in a spiral pattern. This is reminiscent of the Bifrost or Rainbow Bridge, said to connect Asgardh and Midgardh. These colors would likewise produce an effect that could be classified as a photoallergen or allergic reaction to *oðic* energy. The Baron's "sick sensitives," those who had a nervous and sickly disposition that allowed their neuro-sensitivity to be at the extreme with the onset of ill health, bring to mind Mircae Eliades shaman apprentices.

The Baron believed that the *oðic* force was omnipresent, though stronger in some regions than others and therefore *oðic* energy is everywhere ever present; this force and energy constitute a "field" when understood together. In physics there are many types of fields (gravitational, magnetic, etc.) which work together according to Absolute Law and along these same lines the Baron's findings would be termed the *oðic* field and, just as the previously mentioned function as formative fields that could be said to have an intelligence that guides and organizes along precise parameters, so too does the *oðic* field act according to Absolute Law.

Far from being a typical field (inert and inactive) according to the scientific definition, however, the energy that emanates from the *oðic* field seemingly links sensation with nature, a vitality that connects individuals directly to divinity. This field, in addition, has its own laws and properties not yet fully deduced by modern scientific methods, thus still unknown to most outside of the natural philosophers such as Baron von Reichenbach who study and understand it, even if only instinctually. For this reason alone science fails to satisfy the spiritual imperative on its own and once again this latter must substantiate itself empirically.

All energies have a point from which they originate, a source, and in this case there can be little doubt that *oðic* energy emanates from the sun; the fact that our Fólk have venerated it for as long as we have existed substantiates this and the study of neutrinos may yet prove both of these scientifically as well. *Oðic* energy is carried along light waves but is not actually light; neutrinos likewise are believed to be conducted along sunlight and are essential to the physics of biology, in that, with neutrons and protons, they make up the basis of life itself. Recent discoveries by eminent physicists have shown that there are in essence three primary types of neutrinos and three subtypes to each, making nine total. Their nature alters numerous times between the sun and the earth, likely pointing to the fact that no neutrino remains constant enough to measure or predict perfectly, much the same as *oðic* energy.

Regardless of how the study of neutrinos turns out or if it does indeed demonstrate a relationship to *oðic* energy, by now the effects of sunlight upon plants is well-known to most people as photosynthesis so it should come as no surprise that the sun's rays have a similarly nourishing impact upon Fólk as well; though the absorption of *oðic* energy can be likened to the process of photosynthesis, however, in reality it is susceptible only to osmosis, wherein it is absorbed naturally and unconsciously.

The energy lines said to span and crisscross certain areas of the earth are likely mineral and ore veins that carry the *oðic* energy to the planet's iron core (possibly neutrinos from the sun) and can be "felt" by sensitives as they are embodied by that energy. These lines are like the veins of the body that carry blood and oxygen or the Breath of Life for the planet.

Pure sunlight produces powerful *oðic* energy, perhaps the reason our Fólk have long recognized the sun as sacred and essential to our very existence; the swastika symbolizes "well-being" and has been used to represent health, vitality, and well-being generated by the nourishment of the sun since the dawn of consciousness and is likely the oldest, most prominent, sun sign in the history of the world.

All of the oldest "solar observatories" in the world are found in Europe; hundreds, if not thousands, of "henges" and other structures all aligned exactly to the winter and summer solstices. Symbolically, these were viewed as death and life respectively and for good reason: in elder times Fólk recognized the importance of the sun as providing the *oðic* energy necessary not only for survival but evolution. In the summer the sun is closest to us, is providing more *oðic* energy; conversely, in winter it is furthest away and we are closer to "death" than at any other point in the year, with the vitality of the *oðic* energy being at its weakest.

It is both amusing and astounding that historians and scholars alike can claim with some semblance of certainty that astrology and astronomy must have originated in the middle east (just as writing, religion, and civilization we are told) despite the evidence to the contrary. The attempt to substantiate the monotheistic myth is obvious, while the implication is that European man (that paragon of the cave) was never supposed to have devised a means by which to measure the rotation of the planets, the stations of the stars, etc. as they were merely barbarians, uncouth, and lacking civilization, though as early as c5000 BCE our Fólk were building henges that aligned perfectly to the solstices. In addition, the Voluspa makes it clear that the first act of the God's assemblage was to mark out the positions of sun, moon, and stars, ensuring that our Fólk were aware of this from the dawn of consciousness.

Either way, it is logical that astrology and astronomy would originate from a solar worshipping Fólk in the area where the most solar observatories can be found and these Fólk were not just stargazers: it would not take long for them to realize that where the sun was positioned at any given time would determine the well-being of the members of the tribe, that there was a definite and distinct pattern, and from this to the effect the sun would have on one's inherent nature at the time of their birth. Thus was astrology born and from this the more precise science of astronomy.

What our ancestors likely did not, or could not, fully comprehend (except perhaps instinctually) was the concept of an *oðic* force and the energy it emanated at all times, let alone the extent that both would have impacted Fólk from the very moment they are born. When a newborn enters this world the very first act he or she undertakes is inhaling the Breath of Life essential for their very survival and this *önd* is the *oðic* energy present at that precise point of time. The Baron clearly demonstrated how *oðic* energy emanates from sun, moon, and planets and this would seem to support the astrologer's belief that where each planet is positioned, what house the sun is in, determines their sign or inherent nature. With that first breath the child completes their *ørlag*; the blood and body develop in the womb (*Lá ok Litu Goða*) and once the child accepts the animating principle of *önd* they become conscious (*óð*) and aware of themselves, their environment, and begin the journey to meld the two into what should be. This Breath of Life animates the *laeti*, the child's soul, at the moment of birth, which is why the natal chart is the most accurate tool used by astrologers. The four gifts of *ørlag* (primal law) are the initial layer of *Urð* in the Well, thus determine that child's future as much as anything can and this *ørlag* is their inherent nature, which would likewise support astrological belief. Seven thousand years after our Fólk built the Gosek henge we are still fascinated by astrology and this is likely due to the fact that we know, if only instinctually, that the sun, moon, planets, and stars affect our very nature as individuals and as a Fólk.

Ancient astrologers, as well as those of today, seem to have neglected to ask nor answer one simple twofold question: WHY and HOW does the sun have such a profound impact upon our nature and development, including each individual's character? Without realizing it, or attempting to do so, the Baron answered this question with his research into *oðic* energy: the sun determines all life and existence through the vivifying and animating principle it emanates and this *oðic* energy is the *önd* given Askr and Embla, energizing *óð* and thus the *laeti* or disposition in the process.

Up to the very day he died the Baron maintained that nature derived its animating principle from an inexplicable illuminating power consisting of experience pervading vitality which so permeated our world as to be indistinguishable by quantitative means. Due to its ephemeral nature, *oðic* energy could only be measured by "sensitives," individuals whose heightened senses allowed feeling to be more easily stimulated and sustained; these Fólk demonstrated intense sensitivity to all types of stimuli, feeling more of the world than the average person, thus were more receptive and aware of *oðic* energy than most. Because the Baron had to utilize these sensitives for his research, most scientists of his day considered his findings subjective, supposedly tainted by the vagaries of his test subjects and so fell into obscurity for more than a century. Ironically perhaps, in America the FDA requires pharmaceutical companies to test drugs on people before they are approved to be marketed and these tests are run according to the same standards the Baron employed in his research; many of the drugs being tested have drastic side effects, some even lethal, and the test subjects are as subjective as those the Baron was accused of using, yet most today trust these pharmaceutical companies, often taking the latest wonder drug without hesitation and it is these same people who would question or condemn the very existence of the *oðic* force.

There can be no doubt that this *oðic* energy exists and our ancestors knew it as *önd*, the counterpart of *óð*; the exchange of *önd* between *óð* and Odhinn is as that of the self and the Self. Never are *önd* and *óð* antagonistic or at odds in any way, but cooperate with one another to create balance between Instinct, Intellect, and Impulse; once the perfect synthesis between these is achieved Bifrost becomes open to the aspirant connecting Midgardh to Asgardh in a direct Path to the divinity of Sovereignty. As the *oðic* energy is the all-encompassing energy that pervades the multiverse, the animating principle that connects sensation in individuals directly to divinity, it is likewise the *önd* which permeates the self, while this *óð* is an organizing principle to man just as Odhinn is the consciousness of this multiverse.

Self-realization requires a conscious connection to the *oðic* force and its maintenance throughout life; one must be willing to live cognizant of the link in order to reciprocate, most notably with contemplation for the gift of Instinct. Our contemplation of the *oðic* force allows us the power and ability to use it, while our intent is interconnected with the Law of Influence. *Oðic* force is always creating and intention is the link between *óð* and Odhinn; it is essential to the cultivation of the capacity to create. One who lives with intent, who recognizes their purpose, their Skuld, and eagerly pursues it with unerring determination and dedication is creating, mirroring the *oðic* force in the process, thus the power of intent is the very creative and animating principle of Will to Power in our universe.

Oðic energy is qualitative, not quantifiable, having a constitution immeasurable by mechanistic means, thus difficult for most to discern, let alone comprehend fully; like consciousness and virtually all of experiential reality, it cannot be measured with any exactitude. Thus is the reason the current approach of proof through repetition with the assistance of surveying devices meant to measure the precise proportions of a particular hypothesis flounders on the shoals of scholarly myopia, as no two points could possibly be the same and it is this that has allowed true spirituality to stagnate.

Ancient texts speak of *oðic* energy in myth and metaphor, giving it an elusive and ethereal quality, one recognized only instinctually. As with most things of an enigmatic nature, that which lay enshrouded in an otherwise occultic cloak, it is by empirical means that the veil is lifted to reveal veracity; experience is the essence of existence. The most amazing thing about mythology, however, is that anything is possible and one need only experience the "myth" for themselves to realize that potential.

As with all creative principles *önd* has a dual aspect and intent: inhalation and exhalation, positive and negative, with the former being the intake of *oðic* energy to nourish the self of *óð*, while the latter expels that which gives life to everything outside of our self. It is the ultimate symbiosis in that nothing is ever wasted or discarded but used to perpetuate existence itself. It is important to remember that thoughts are energy: positive thoughts attract, while negative ones repel. Thus, the former allow *oðic* energy into one's consciousness (as it has an affinity for and with it), while the latter resist *önd*, acting as an opposing power that hinders the connection.

What remains certain is that current scientific analysis founders on the shoals of ineptitude when it attempts to analyze and examine empirical energies such as *önd*. In a concentrated effort to extract knowledge of the natural world from the control of religious zealots determined to enforce the dogmatic ideals of monotheism upon the populace of our planet, early scientists allowed their views and methods to adopt the opposite extreme, positioning science and spirituality at conflicting polarities and this persists today in many ways. The mechanistic methods employed by modern scientists to measure all manner of things has almost completely ignored the natural, empirical world, nor is it capable of qualitative measurement by quantifiable means. Sensations, awareness, and metacognition cannot be described nor measured in a quantifiable manner, as they are empirical realities; the most notable of which is conscious, subconscious, and unconscious energies and elements, all of these being virtually incapable of being measured by mechanistic means. It is for this reason that so much of our most profound wisdom comes from our earliest ancestors, who, like the Baron, were natural philosophers; these Fólk actually studied nature from an empirical perspective, experiencing it themselves, and did so with full knowledge that true philosophy falls in between theology and science, bringing both into balance for a firmly spiritual worldview.

The self-destructive devaluation of consciousness as purely subjective has a tendency towards personal inclination to the detriment of objective reality. Consciousness is the medium through which our ancestors viewed and understood the natural world and they appraised everything they perceived as regular phenomena against the collective unconscious of our Fólk as a whole. In this way the perspective of the world, as well as our place in it, presented infinite potential for empirical possibilities to our ancestors, and through a heightened sense of perception honed through shamanistic practice they were able to properly interpret the language of nature; it is only through consciousness that we may become familiar with the natural world.

The cosmos is a conscious construct, the exchange of energies between microcosm and macrocosm, and it is only through the *oðic* energy that connects *óð* and Odhinn that Sovereignty may be attained. The pillars of perception are settled solidly in symbolism and experiential consciousness, neither of which are recognized as valid, quantifiable, or "scientific" sources of evidence according to contemporary culture. This is not the case, however, for those seeking Sovereignty, as we see *óð* as the consciousness that is idealized and realized in Odhinn as supraconsciousness; *önd* is the all-pervading principle that connects the two, the exchange between the polarities of microcosm and macrocosm that allows all possibilities to exist, as well as the potential for those possibilities to be realized. Thus is the indestructible Path leading from Midgardh to Asgardh.

To understand consciousness in the context of the sacred or holy one must first realize that we only truly become aware of something once it is separate from ourselves, or we recognize it as such. A number of investigations have been conducted into the roots of holy and sacred (proto-Germanic *wihaz and *hailagaz respectively), most notably from Jacob Grimm in his Teutonic Mythology. Essentially *wihaz comes from the root *vík meaning "to separate" or "appear," thus it is likely that this designation originally applied to consciousness itself; that which entered our "conscious field" or awareness was to our earliest ancestors something profound, thus sacred or holy. That it was perceived as something separate from ourselves seems obvious enough and natural in light of the "eureka" moments still prevalent for Fólk today, where a sudden answer, intuition, awareness, or inspiration seems to "appear" in our mind virtually out of nowhere. This phenomena has been variously described as "divine intervention" or genius, among other appellations, though in this way we remove the natural element and attempt to ascribe it to some source outside of (or beyond) our self when, in reality, it is inherent in each of us. That our most distant ancestors would believe the cause of a sudden awareness or consciousness to be divine should come as no surprise to any who have experienced a profound sense of enlightenment or sudden inspiration.

Perhaps initially these "eureka" moments were perceived as "ecstatic," merely significant occurrences that arose at times in or around particular individuals, maybe even perpetuated by these same individuals as a means of harnessing the power that would inevitably result from such incidents. As man's consciousness began to grow, with the evolution of the unconscious, and awareness of his surroundings became more keen, it would be natural for Fólk to learn how to harness this awareness, giving reign to free thought, interpretation, and the primitive form of Will to Power, which likely stunned the rest of the tribe in much the same way supremely intelligent people today still do. The rest of the tribe would have held these individuals in high regard, depending upon them for their insights, clarity, and intuition to guide them in every important way to the existence and survival of the tribe, from weather to hunting, procreation to death. Thus was likely born the first "shaman" from which ecstatic consciousness originated and to whom we owe a debt for the very ability to consciously discern our own nature to consciously discern.

The means by which each of us expresses our spirituality is through our personal self, as the spirit seeks to realize itself in physical reality, to be known and gain recognition, to manifest as Will to Power. Spirituality is first developed through recognition of the divine, contemplation of the mysteries, questioning the deeper aspects of life and actively striving for answers. Due to the complexity of the soul and its lack of visible or physical representation, spirituality has traditionally found life through myth, metaphor, symbol, lore, legend, analogy, and parable in an attempt to explain, understand, or communicate meaning and substance. This is the strongest evidence that true spirituality is empirical and existential: the best way to convey the meaning of something experienced to another who has not is with a good analogy. In this way we also emit spiritual energy by allowing ourselves to remain open to the divine, while nourishing the soul through natural means and methods.

A uniquely relevant motif of Heathen spirituality is the sacred quality of acquiring a good reputation or worthing oneself through noble deeds and actions. This is in contrast to the world-renouncer who declaims individuality, calling for the destruction of the self as the only means by which one may attain absorption into the universal or all-encompassing "one." The Sovereign seeks nothing so absurd as to fade into nothingness, to disappear into a conglomerate of mediocrity, but to distinguish themselves as divine in their own right and achieve an Eternal Existence as such. As a Fólk we have traditionally sought to balance the self with the Instinct of our collective unconscious and reflect this harmony of the soul in the physical world. To be complete the soul must maintain balance between the Instinct, Intellect, and Impulse and this is accomplished through custom, culture, tradition, language, ritual practice, etc. Those instincts that are strongest in each of us are those "memories" in the collective unconscious immediately connecting us to parents and siblings, then extended family, while the further away from this we get the more tenuous the link between the two becomes, though the bond between our blood and the archetypes in that collective unconscious stretches back to the most distant ancestors; it takes a conscious effort to access this morphogenetic field. Unfortunately, these instincts are supported or suppressed based solely upon the individual's experience and environment; this is why culture plays such an important role in our spirituality: societies that nurture and nourish one's inherent instincts are good, while those at odds with those instincts are detrimental to the individual's Sovereignty. This is why the Western world has seen a steady surge of immorality and spiritual stagnation since the reign of monotheism took a firm hold on Fólk: selfishness, sexual deviancy, greed, unnecessary violence, etc.

ÖND OK ÓÐH: INSTINCT, INTELLECT, IMPULSE

Initially, the self operates on a purely survival mode of existence, as it is as yet undeveloped, depending almost exclusively upon Instinct for guidance. Our consciousness is barely aware of its self, like a newborn babe who first opens his eyes, likely curious about where he is and how he arrived there. In this we find the "child-like wonder" that recognizes divinity in all things, for all things are a mystery to be unraveled. It is easy to imagine our most distant ancestors witnessing lightning strike suddenly for the first time and naturally seeing in it a divine act, though over time and through understanding the environment (as well as nature's laws), Fólk began to lose that original sense of wonder to the point that some spirituality became religious, profane rather than divine, and monotheism completely obliterated that natural sense of wonder by instituting dogma and doctrine that forbade our Fólk from questioning, exploring, or seeking anything spiritual beyond their one true god.

Consciousness, like the child himself, is similar to raw clay, in need of molding and form; the innocence of the soul before it is corrupted by the world is what modern man lacks most and it is this purity which we propose to preserve and maintain by following a Heathen Path. Only in this way can the soul properly grow, thrive, and evolve in an environment conducive to cultural and traditional spirituality according to our Fólk-Soul; without proper nurturing the self will become selfish and self-centered, misconstruing the survival instinct to mean "me, my, mine," separating itself from the collective conscious completely and building a center of egotistical emptiness indifferent to their own inherent nature, let alone the divinity of our Fólk as a whole.

On the physical plane of existence the very first act of a newly born child is to take a breath; without it the child cannot survive. This individual must continue breathing throughout their life in order to live and even at the end death is merely the cessation of breath as evidenced in the final act of any life: no matter how one dies, the very last thing they do is expel their breath. The importance of *önd* then cannot be understated: it is the divine spark given us by the Gods, what marks us as their descendants.

Furthermore, remaining in the physical sphere, the air that we breathe is the oxygen necessary to all our vital internal organs and is carried throughout the body by the blood, making these two things the most essential to life itself. It has been proposed that oxygen at higher altitudes and colder climates is more conducive to biological evolution, that the purity of the air one breathes allows their body and mind to develop at a faster rate than those who take in impure and/or hot air; this may explain why our Fólk have evolved so much more than others.

The importance of instincts is likewise revealed the day we are born: the desire to survive and the newborn babe's persistence in doing so stem from a spontaneous instinct to continue to exist. The child quickly learns what needs to be done to receive physical care, nourishment, etc. and though helpless, a baby must rely exclusively on Instinct merely to get a foothold on life, let alone have a chance at living it. As he grows the child's self begins to develop according to both his nature and nurture and this period determines who and what they will become. If one wants to reinforce the instinctual predispositions and cultural practices their Fólk hold in high regard, they will rear their children in an environment conducive to such desires; if, on the other hand, one does not care enough to raise their children properly, carefully nurturing them appropriately, or worse, find themselves enamored with an alien culture, then these young Fólk will struggle both internally and externally to find an identity, let alone a spirituality that nourishes their nature. Instead, they will adopt the empty existence of environmental influences exclusively, neglecting the internal nourishment necessary for spiritual survival.

It is the self as Intellect and Impulse which enables the Will to Power that other living beings lack to manifest itself in individual accomplishments. The rest of the animal kingdom have a limited ability to think and act for themselves beyond the communal construct, thus are dependent on the collective unconscious of their species alone for guidance and survival. This communal consciousness is based solely upon necessity, not desire, whereas man not only considers what is necessary for survival but how to do so with little effort, leaving time for contemplation of the unknown. Many Fólk today have allowed ego alone to guide their lives, with minimal regard for kith and kin, nor the community or Fólk as a whole, and this creates a spiritual imbalance in the soul, which is ultimately reflected in the societies these individuals inhabit and can be seen in the overall decline of Western civilization during the reign of monotheism.

Whenever an importance is placed on striving for supremacy over nature (be it man's attempt to control the forces of the physical world or pushing aside the indwelling) the individual strives to succeed by suppressing Instinct: the collective unconscious can only be a distraction from which nature cannot be mastered. The phylogenetic cocoon of inherent Instinct allows the self to develop properly, to metamorphose into a spiritual being, eventually expressing the self as Sovereign Self provided the individual does not disconnect themselves from their spirit completely.

We all like to convince ourselves that we are somehow above other animals, that we are civilized or superior to them in some way and perhaps there was a time when we were, when Tradition was contemporary throughout the tribes of our Fólk, though now there is much to be learned from the natural world. If animals are to be considered simple because they must rely on their collective Instinct solely for guidance, then where does that leave modern man who virtually ignores that Instinct in favor of personal desires and material gain over spiritual nourishment? At least animals stay true to their species, never abandoning their inherent nature for individual and selfish purposes, whereas we are destroying ourselves with the very thing that separates us from the rest of the animal kingdom: the Intellect and Impulse of self that allows the Will to Power.

In truth, man is semiconscious in that he is aware of the known but the unknown still lay dormant within his unconscious. Many Fólk today do not realize that this unconscious contains potential for perfection in the same way a pine cone is the promise of an ideal pine tree. All knowledge, wisdom, and understanding can be found in the unconscious, symbolized by the cauldron or ketil, as the container from which the contents are available to those worthy of it. It is the conscious awareness of this potential and actively striving to achieve it that leads to Sovereignty; true Sovereignty is not the absorption of the self into the whole, but the knowledge that the whole is subject to the self, at its disposal, and in this realization (and subsequent ability to actualize it) lay Eternal Existence. In addition, it is the willingness to sacrifice to achieve Sovereignty (the sacrifice of the self for the whole in particular) that unveils all potential and possibility along the Path. The cosmic framework is built upon recurring patterns of self-similarity whose differences are of quantity not quality; the microcosm reflects the macrocosm and in the same way the self exists as a reflection of Sovereign Self, the *óð* is but the ultimate potential for Odhinn.

The first step to true transcendence lay in the recognition of *óð* and *önd* as Intellect, Impulse, and Instinct (collectively the *læti* or soul), and embracing one's inherent nature, their *ørlag*, as it is, in contrast to how others would have it be, nor how one would idealize themselves. Each of us is born with an innate disposition and at some point in our life we must either choose to accept or deny it and that decision will ultimately determine the direction our lives take; those who would place a foot upon the Path to Sovereignty must first realize that they are exactly who they are meant to be. This initial phase is, like birth, a conscious act of inception, taking an active role rather than a passive one in pursuing the divine state of supraconsciousness as the self-existent one did.

Throughout our lives we are inundated with sensory input from our environment and those we come into contact with, both consciously and subconsciously, remembering and reflecting all that we see, hear, taste, touch, and feel, as we search for identity, meaning, and purpose here on the physical plane. We are said to be nurturing our individuality by embracing the influences we are surrounded by, allowing them to shape us in the image of society at large so as to help us fit into the community; in an ideal world, one that comprises a common culture, creed, and virtuous conduct of spiritual Fólk, the nurturing of one's environment would be every bit as important as their nature. Unfortunately, we do not live in this ideal world, let alone one conducive to our way of life, thus the second step upon the Path consists of freeing one's Instinct from the shackles of the societal status quo, the plebeian perspective of the mass mediocre mentality, and learning to tap into the collective unconscious to use instincts as a guide in every aspect of one's life. Our instincts, that "inner voice" that most people ignore, are the voices of our forefathers, with the wisdom and experience of innumerable lessons learned from nature laying dormant in our genetic memory.

This evolving phase is the growth process we all go through, both physically and spiritually, to achieve the awareness of who we are and is typically the longest, most arduous stage of development. Some Fólk (too many in today's oppressive spiritual environment) never move beyond this phase of spiritual growth simply because they have completely lost touch with the collective unconscious by focusing exclusively on personal desires, materialistic pursuits, and selfish goals, or merely cannot see beyond their own reflection to find the Instinct, their inherent nature. In either case, the result remains the same: the destruction of the soul along with the death of the physical body, as it cannot attain Eternal Existence in its original nor evolving state, but only Entropy or Extinction. Worse perhaps, the individual will be forgotten, no horn raised for them at Blót or Wassail, which the cruelest of punishments cannot equal.

The final transformation occurs when an individual on the Path brings to complete balance their Instinct, Intellect, and Impulse in both the physical and spiritual realms, becoming not merely one like the Gods, but one with the Gods, a Sovereign that stands among deities and divinity. By forging an unbreakable bond between the self and spirit, *óð* and *önd*, one can attain a level of consciousness few are capable of here in this world, and the Path then becomes the Bifrost bridge connecting Midgardh to Asgardh and leads to Eternal Existence for the Sovereign.

Lá ok Litu Goða: Genetic Memory

"...race dwells in the spirit before being expressed in the blood. If it is true that without racial purity, spirit and Tradition are deprived of their most precious means of expression, then it is also true that pure race deprived of spirit is condemned to be a biological mechanism and in the end doomed to extinction."

– Julius Evola

For as far back as Fólk have been aware of its existence we have recognized and understood on some level the importance of blood, life's very essence, and examples of this can be found in the rituals and sacrifices performed by various peoples around the world throughout time. The fact that it fascinated our Fólk for so long and was considered sacred can be seen in the Old Norse *hlaut*, or sacrificial blood, that was used in Blót. It could be said that in many ways our ancestors were more knowledgeable about the significance of blood, even if only instinctually, than we are today; only in the last few decades, through the study of genetics, have we begun to appreciate altogether the complexities of the blood and of the DNA and RNA it contains, though this was the gift of *lá* given us by the Gods.

The oldest sacred record in existence today is to be found in our blood; no holy book or sacred scripture can possibly be more significant, nor accurate, than this. History can be written or rewritten at the whim of any man, texts have been lost and found over time, created by men and destroyed by others, yet the one record that remains true is the "men's certain knowledge" found in our blood. Truth can have many meanings depending upon the perspective of the individual and this can be categorized and interpreted in endless ways depending upon the inclination of that individual, but blood cannot lie, misconstrue, or misapprehend the truth; it cannot be anything except absolute indisputable truth, and it is this more than anything else that makes it so important.

Today we attempt to fully understand the intricacies and subtleties of the blood and geneticists continue to glean new knowledge regularly as it reveals more and more about the history of the world and its inhabitants. What these geneticists are accumulating, however, are the physical facts the blood bequeaths us, while the metaphysical remains a mystery to man. The Gods gifted us the Breath of Life, consciousness, blood, and a godlike appearance, and these gifts allow us to tap into the genetic memory of our Fólk to harness that inner voice of Instinct, if only we allow ourselves to listen to it; this genetic memory can be both a guide and a map that assists us along the Path from *Urð* to Skuld, permitting us to attain Sovereignty.

Scientifically, a gene is the primary physical unit passed from parent to child through the separation and subsequent recombination of a linear sequence of nucleotides known as deoxyribonucleic acid or DNA; this DNA provides coded instructions for the structure and synthesis of ribonucleic acid (RNA) into inheritable qualities and characteristics. All living things contain DNA, be they bacteria, birds, birch trees, or human beings. RNA takes direction from DNA about how to build the blocks of protein that generate and sustain life. DNA is made up of four chemical components: adenine, cytosine, guanine, and thymine (A, C, G, T), while RNA shares the first three, utilizing uracil in place of thymine. Guanine and cytosine can only pair with one another, while adenine can only pair with either thymine or uracil, these last two unable to pair with any but adenine. Interestingly while two of these fundamental chemicals are hexagonal in shape (thymine and cytosine) adenine and guanine have a nine-sided structure appearing to be a hexagon overlaid with a pentagon.

The four different blood groups (A, B, AB, O) are the expression of three versions of a single gene, a solitary piece of DNA. DNA tells cells which proteins to make and it is proteins that build and operate the body. Proteins are made up of amino acids arranged in a specific linear sequence and it is this sequence of amino acids that give protein its particular properties; no two proteins are the same. Nuclear DNA comes from the father and mother, while mitochondrial DNA (mDNA) is passed along by the mother to the daughter; conversely the y-chromosome is passed along from father to son. Inside the nucleus of every human cell are a total of 46 chromosomes, their complete genetic makeup, 23 of which come from each parent.

It is believed that 95 percent of the mDNA found in Fólk today came from seven women or maternal clans, the oldest of which goes back some 45,000 years to the region around the Black Sea, while the youngest is from what we refer to as the middle east today. On the other hand, there are eight principle paternal clans, the fathers of our Fólk, who passed along a particular y-chromosome, all of which originate in Europe.

An ever-growing knowledge of genetic research has begun to shed light upon the biological evolution of man and one of the most notable for a searching Fólk is that of a mutation said to have occurred some 12,000 years ago, the time this epoch is believed to have begun with the Battleax Age; mutation is the impetus of evolution. This mutation was European man developing light skin pigmentation, lack of melanin, and capable of processing lactose, the sugar found in milk; interestingly, milk and sunlight harvested through the skin are the only two known sources for vitamin D in any significant amount. Vitamin D is essential to almost every function of the body, including the immune system and is responsible for unlocking 2,000 genes, 10 percent of our genome; it affects everything from mood, muscle strength, and bone marrow to energy level. Additionally, the body cannot process vitamin A without D. The importance of vitamin D is indisputable and some claim that it was the ability to take in more vitamin D that allowed early Europeans to evolve faster and further than others.

Baron von Reichenbach's research sheds some light upon the subject of genetic mutation as well, and if in fact our Fólk did become more susceptible to sunlight roughly 12,000 years ago it could explain why we evolved quicker than anyone else; this, coupled with the purer oxygen of high altitudes, would be the perfect grounds upon which to cultivate a great garden. The pineal gland in the center of the frontal lobe is affected by light coming in through the eyes and it is this gland that is linked to what is routinely referred to as the third eye, though its scientific function is that it excretes melatonin and converts serotonin into a number of powerful hallucinogens. Melatonin is necessary for dreaming and psychic states, thus it likewise becomes significant that our Fólk are the only people on this planet naturally capable of having light eyes (blue, green, grey, hazel) as these are able to absorb more light, particularly *oðic* energy, through a process similar to photosynthesis. It must be wondered if this mutation was the *litu goða* given Askr and Embla.

Nevertheless, whether one subscribes to the so-called "common ancestor" theory or not no longer matters, as there can be no doubt that our Fólk are distinct from other peoples on this planet; this is a fact that can be denied but not disputed. In truth, the fact that modern Africans share no genetic markers with Neanderthal man makes the common ancestor theory unlikely. Either way, Fólk need to get past the mental block of being descended from either apes or some common ancestor out of Africa; as absurd as both are it truly does not matter one way or another. The important thing is who and what we are TODAY and reawakening the Fólk-Soul; this last can never be completely accomplished if we are continually distracted by racial questions, concerns, or worse, wasting time defending Folkish beliefs. If we do not regain a truly spiritual perspective we are doomed to perish, for biology pales in comparison to the spirit.

For a long time scientists maintained that life could only have originated in a warm climate, in temperate conditions from which ideal circumstances for contemporary life would seem most comfortable; the only alternative, according to these experts was the boiling heat of volcanic or similar conditions. A relatively recent reversal has occurred, however, with a number of scientists now believing that life may have begun in ice rather than heat, at temperatures only a few living things could survive today and many assert that the laws of chemistry and chemical reaction actually point towards a cold climate for the origin of life. The fact that our wisdom teachings allude to this is remarkable in itself, however, the science is clear: it is far more likely that the chemicals which make life possible coalesced in ice pockets over periods of time than that life sprang from a primordial soup somewhere in the rainforests or desert. Those who believe that volcanic ash played a significant role in creating life need not think that this would be at odds with the glacial origins theory, as the numerous volcanoes in Iceland, Northern Europe, or even the Kamchatka region of Russia could easily have contributed the necessary chemicals and conditions to create life. It could very well be that life began in both warm and cold climates, separate and distinct, the environment influencing mutations that are now similar to people around the world.

Another contemporary theory claims that the first organisms that existed were in fact RNA molecules that acquired the ability to combine proteins on their own, easing the replication process. Later these organisms evolved into more chemically stable forms with a genetic memory made up of DNA. This would seem to show how Sovereigns can utilize various ecstatic techniques to lower their conscious awareness to a molecular level from which they gain entry to this genetic memory and gather wisdom and knowledge.

A recent field of inquiry that is fascinating is epigenetics, which focuses on both the "instructions" (or chemical markers) and "switches" in the DNA that tell the RNA how to form a particular organism and how outside influences can and do alter the fetus in the womb; in essence, how the effects felt by the mother affect some of these switches and whether they are turned on or left off. Even the smallest error during input, say through drug use, stress, smoking, malnutrition, etc. can cause deformities, chemical imbalances, and other disorders that can be seen immediately or remain repressed in a child until much later in life. In this way it becomes obvious that both inherent nature and external influences determine the development of a child. The epigenome is empirical, though creates a memory that lasts into the future, being handed down from generation to generation. Geneticists are now proving through the study of this epigenome that everything we experience in our lives is passed along to our children. Knowledge we learn and all that we are at the moment of conception is encoded in the child's genes whether it is realized or not.

The simplest way to understand DNA and RNA is to view the former as the blueprints from which the latter constructs the biological building. Past generations of a particular species then are the architects (archetypes) which design the plan according to the morphogenetic field, while the RNA interprets these blueprints for the contractors and workers (enzymes and amino acids) who build the structure accordingly, with the materials on hand. DNA is more chemically stable than RNA and is responsible for remembering everything about a distinctive species; this is what is referred to as genetic memory. This DNA and RNA is contained in our blood. Iron is a crucial component in hemoglobin, red blood cells, and is in fact what allows us the ability to breathe: oxygen bonds to the iron and as it is carried through the body it nourishes the organs and tissues. The core of the earth is likewise made up of iron and it is likely this to which the sun's rays are drawn, leading to the conclusion that it is the iron in our blood that draws in *oðic* energy as well.

At an unconscious level DNA supplies a span to biological recollection of all living things much the same way the Bifrost Bridge connects Midgardh to Asgardh. Many Fólk see the spine as the bridge between these realms, which seems logical in light of the fact that the spine plays an integral role in all biological, mental, and physical processes. In point of fact, drastic biological evolution can only take place through genetic mutation. As scientists have demonstrated, the transition between bacteria and nucleated cells is too abrupt to be conclusively construed as having come about through gradual changes over a period of time. Perhaps this is why no "missing link" has ever been found.

It is amazing that, though DNA has remained constant throughout time, our planet's surface, sky, seas, the universe as a whole have all gone through numerous changes, and despite the myriad species in the world today, all life is still made up of those same four chemical markers. This consistency confirms that all biological combinations are possible so long as the letters of DNA are aligned properly; it makes one wonder if the so-called mythical creatures, such as centaur, griffin, phoenix, or even the much-maligned werewolf are actually as far-fetched as some would suggest. Nevertheless, once one understands that all living things contain the same chemicals, but that DNA contains a memory stretching back to the first organism of that species, they can more readily comprehend what the genetic memory is.

Few Fólk would question the fact that we all inherit certain physical attributes from our parents, everything from eye color and facial features, to a smile or even mannerisms, traits, personal quirks, and predispositions; these are all hereditary, part of who we are from birth. There have been a myriad of recorded examples of twins being separated at birth, growing up in completely different environments, even contrasting cultures, yet walking, talking, and acting or even speaking identical to one another, that demonstrate the influence what one inherits has upon them. Besides carrying the inclinations and attributes of one's parents, our genes likewise carry the memories of our Fólk as far back as the origins of the organism that gave us life; these are embedded in the genetic memory and manifest as instincts, inspiration, and intuition, natural tendencies to act or react in particular ways to a given situation or circumstance. All Fólk who accept that a child is the product of the parents' genes merging must extend that acceptance to other relatives along the child's genealogical lineage, from grandparents to the Fólk as a whole whom they share blood with, for these last have likewise contributed to this child's genetic structure.

With this in mind, the genetic memory is not simply a repository or a blueprint of sorts for building and maintaining a virtuous life based upon the lessons of one's ancestors, but also a constantly evolving entity, expanding from generation to generation with the influx of new discoveries, comprehension, and innovations. This genetic memory is the consanguineous unconscious of our Fólk, the gift given us by the Gods in the form of spirit or the Breath of Life.

There has been a long-standing debate over which is more important or has a greater impact on one's development: environment or DNA. This is commonly referred to as nature versus nurture for good reason and while neither side has yet to present an unimpeachable position, it is becoming more readily apparent to empiricists that the essence has the edge on the elements, or so the evidence of sociobiology would seem to suggest.

Nurture can be defined as the sociological factors which influence or determine one's development, personality, worldview, cultural attitude, and overall outlook, though it should be noted that there are two distinct types of culture that shape an individual identity: inherent and social. The first is heredity, passed down from one generation to the next through the genetic memory, while the second are learned behaviors one adopts throughout their lifetime for interaction with the outside world. These latter are effectively influenced exclusively by environment and constitute the sensory input from a variety of sources, including everything from entertainment, public and private gatherings or activities, associations, to a myriad of other interactions in social settings. In essence then, nurture encompasses all outside influences, from family and friends to society at large, everything one sees or is taught, to the experiences that mold each individual, all of which impacts us on a conscious and subconscious level and serves as development of the self. Nature on the other hand is that unchangeable aspect of the spirit that marks a person and people as unique, distinct, or part of a greater whole, the evolution of which depends upon embracing that nature in a manner consistent with its growth and natural differentiation; this is the genetic memory that each of us is capable of consulting through contemplation and consistently striving for Sovereignty.

Memory is a function of the blood and body, thus is only present in the physical realm, not the metaphysical as such, in the sense that most would understand it; this is why we cannot automatically remember past lives or anything before being born as a general rule. Those who are able to recall something of the past are exceptions to this rule, not the norm, and likely strengthened their connection to the genetic memory in some way either knowingly or not. This said, it could become automatic for future Fólk should we make it a part of the genetic memory itself through repetition, ritual, and the realization of Sovereignty.

There are essentially two types of memory: active/functioning and passive/long-term. Conversely, there is explicit memory, what is brought into an individual's conscious awareness (which is flexible and encompasses conscious thought), and implicit memory, which does not necessarily enter consciousness, but consists of the empirical contents of the subconscious that can and do have an effect on an individual's thoughts and actions without their being aware of it. Explicit memories are those which are seen, that we are aware of, while implicit memories are more implied, based on the individual's responses to particular events or stimuli, often on the subconscious, unknown level.

Each and every person's life is indelibly etched into their memory; some memories are faint, while others are quite vivid, though every moment of our existence lay in our memory and can be recalled with enough effort. Memories come in many forms, as varied as the experiences life itself can acquire, and can never be changed as they are unalterably fixed the moment they occur; these are the layers of *urð* in both Urdhr and Mimir's Wells. As individuals we all accumulate these experiences, these layers that ultimately make up our *urð*, however, this same empirical data is encoded into our blood as well and it is this that we call genetic memory: the memories of deeds, decisions, and the entire history of our Fólk as a whole going back to the dawn of consciousness, the moment Askr and Embla were given *óð*. All who accept that our individual memory contains the contents of our lives cannot then reject the notion that there is likewise a genetic memory that accumulates the empirical aggregate of all who share the same blood. Carl Jung referred to this as the collective unconscious and believed it to be unique to a particular people.

Memories are a linear record of time and as such can only contain those things that occur as they unfold, however, time itself is cyclical, often repeating itself over and over, which is what allows spiritually strong individuals to call upon the intuition and Instinct inherent in our blood to seek answers from ancestors when we are confronted with a situation similar to one that may have been experienced at some point in the past.

Science has demonstrated that sleep is a function for the memory to strengthen itself: during sleep the short-term memories of our conscious are "downloaded" to the long-term memory of the unconscious. This is the reason dreams, even visions, connect the conscious to the unconscious, allowing for prophecy, divination, and other insights from past or future to seep through from the genetic memory when we are at our most relaxed and receptive.

The analogy of life being a great sleep and awakening is apt as it parallels all of existence. On a microcosmic scale, when we wake up each morning our dreams do not automatically enter our conscious awareness, unless they are particularly vivid, but must be brought forth with an effort at remembering them. This is likewise reflected in our lives: all of the memories of previous existence or prior experience is there in our genetic memory but requires a conscious effort to bring forth. Memories from a year ago, a month, or even a week, often demand a determined attempt at remembering and so it is the further we get away from the event or experience; the genetic memory then requires a particularly persistent effort to access, but it can be brought forth just like any other memory. The same way it becomes necessary to wake oneself from a bad dream, so too is it imperative that all Fólk awaken from the illusions of a bad life; thus is the task of those seeking Sovereignty in this modern mediocre and misanthropic world: to awaken the spiritually nourishing genetic memory that can lead each of us to the peak of perfection.

We know that memory decreases in strength the farther from our self we get, in contrast to it being strongest with our own memories, however, there are likely degrees to our connection to the genetic memory: from our immediate family to Fólk as a whole, with no connection at all beyond that. While there are examples of Fólk who can connect to horses, dogs, or other animals, even trees, this is atomic rather than genetic and highlights the power of possibility and potential. For example, psychic communication or telepathy is also possible, though not commonly practiced, and is an ability that can be developed. We all broadcast our thoughts and memories, even our experiences, on an open frequency subconsciously and like radio waves, anyone with the proper receiver can tune into any station they choose and listen. In fact, everything is a frequency, from matter and sound, to light, gamma rays, or neutrinos, even our DNA, and if one puts enough energy through a magnetic field it can change genetic matter.

Most Fólk have experienced a situation where we were thinking the same thought or about something similar as someone else at the exact moment they were and it is always someone we are close to or have spent a lot of time with, and this is an example of exactly how our signals can become so intertwined that we start receiving another's or they ours. This is particularly true of empaths and is one reason why culture is so important, as is who we allow into our conscious awareness; it also demonstrates just how powerful the genetic memory is for those able to utilize it. By allowing the chaos from outside to breach the barrier of Asgardh, the archetypes of Instinct are overwhelmed to the point of remaining silent; in particularly strong individuals the Gods within will destroy these giants, and restore order from chaos, though these Fólk are rare in today's materialistic world and the weak ones will take on the characteristics of the common, a plebeian perspective, the ignoble and unnatural mob of mediocrity beyond Midgardh.

A common refrain often absentmindedly parroted by people is that "knowledge is power," though the significance of this simple declaration just as often eludes the same individuals, particularly contemporary Fólk as evidenced by the current decay and decadence of our cultural and spiritual expression and edification. The Path of Odhinn is predicated upon the pursuit of knowledge and the wisdom that comes from putting it into practice; this is the power of potential and possibility that allows us to achieve Sovereignty. Odhinn was willing to sacrifice anything in seeking omniscience and his elevation was eventually effected through *mimisbrunnr*, Memory's Well; if there is any hope for Fólk to survive, let alone become Sovereign, there must be a return to the reliance upon genetic memory, our Instinct as a people, to guide our evolution into the future. We share the same blood as the Gods and this genetic legacy can always be trusted as a faithful fountain of divine wisdom. Because our genetic memory connects us to our ancestors, a Fólk who have always sought to learn all we could, explore, innovate, and test the known limits of life, the instincts that come directly from this connection, when combined with conviction, can accomplish anything; knowledge without inspiration is static, virtually useless, though together they present all potential and possibility and are vital to the evolution of our self and Fólk as a whole.

Instinct is the root of race rather than biology; Intellect and Impulse are its expression and manifestation. Our Instinct, the archetypes of the indwelling and innate, are what qualify as a race and this race is realized through rhythm, species defined by spirit; as a people we have a particular rhythm and it is this rhythm that defines us as a distinct people instead of heredity alone. This heredity, however, is the source of our genetic memory and the racial rhythm inherent in it directs the action or reaction each of us is capable of, our Will to Power. Anything that attacks this rhythm is regarded as an enemy of everything empirical and eminent.

The Old Norse *átt* translates as "race", a general term used to refer to the physical alone; Fólk, however, is something more significant, spiritual as well as physical, correlating well with the way in which Julius Evola understood it. Fólk is mentioned twice in the Voluspa, both times in conjunction with the war between the *Aesir* and *Vanir* and the significance of this cannot be understated. Askr and Embla were elevated from their race to Fólk through the gifts of the Gods; as their descendants we are likewise a Fólk. When the Voluspa speaks of *fólkvíg* it is a war among a likeminded and aware Fólk for a Higher purpose, not the multitudes with their plebeian perspective; conversely, when it mentions *önd thau ne áttu*, ("their race had not Breath of Life") it attests to the masses who were at that point given the ability to become Fólk. Similarly, the Einherjar gather first on Folkvangr, the "field of Fólk" to await Freya's selection.

Race and nation are rooted in nature; Fólk and *Óðal* land are derived directly from divinity. The former exist in time, founded in life, and geared towards survival alone; a consequence of this is the rejection of sacrifice for a noble purpose. The latter are Eternal, above both time and life and not concerned overmuch with a tenuous grasp on either. Fólk is an Ideal, the belief in a Higher culture created by the common customs and traditions of a homogenous whole. Fólk is elite, while race represents the totality of a mass of people with nothing but biology in common. Fólk is a spiritual concept connecting us to our ancestors and the land consecrated to the Gods through blood.

The conclusiveness of Folkish conviction is found in Tradition, the foundation of which is tripartite in nature, composed of these three primary parts: spirit, soul, and body. In this order they were given to Askr and Embla according to their importance and it is in this same vein that we should value them, meaning that physical look is the least important of the four gifts. Those who have descended from this couple are the Inheritors (Einherjar) of a spiritual heritage that allows us to attain a Higher purpose, the most important of which is an Eternal Existence. The fact that all of the earliest kings and many genealogies traced their lineage to the Gods, most to Odhinn, speaks not to a sense of superstition or savagery, but to the certain knowledge that we have long known and recognized: that we are descendants of the Gods in truth, not theory. It is the Fólk that received the Breath of Life from Odhinn, the Instinct of the Gods which separates us from others, especially *etins* and *thursar*, of whom we know are not Gods. Those who would willingly capitulate to contemporary political correctness in denying our divinity or desire to maintain purity of blood and spirit are forsaking the Fólk and Gods alike, rejecting a sacred and spiritual principle in the process.

That said, the notion of a biological imperative is founded in secular scientism, utterly deficient in anything spiritual, simple materialism at its profane best; the ideal behind Effective Evolution on the other hand is not Darwinism, but the conscious striving for spiritual superiority, attempting to achieve a Higher state as an individual and contribute to the whole in the process. Purify the spirit and the physical form will follow; any animal can reproduce its kind indiscriminately, but only a God is capable of creating something greater than its self. A focus on the purely physical attests to the overall decline and decadence of what allowed our Fólk to be counted among the Gods as creators and such a focus is tantamount to totemism. The epitome of excellence is expressed through the spirit of our Fólk-Soul, the Will and Power of potential and possibility that once marked us as explorers, inventors, innovators, conquerors, and creators.

It is but the wavering will of the weak who are content with self-preservation being the primary pursuit of Fólk seeking a state of supremacy; they cling to life tenaciously, precarious though the hold be, as it is the highest hope they have. These same individuals proclaim the past glories of our ancestors to be examples to emulate yet do not do so themselves, declaring their decadence in the process and contributing to our decline; those who truly desire a reawakening of the Fólk-Soul on the other hand seek Sovereignty, the aristocratic intent of the High-minded who will gladly sacrifice whatever is necessary to achieve greatness. The spiritual form determines the physical function and when the spirit is diminished the body becomes susceptible to corruption. A race deteriorates when its spirit begins to decline, when it ignores, neglects, or destroys its inherent Instinct, not necessarily when the biology degenerates or disintegrates. The physical without the metaphysical is doomed to extinction as race must contain spirit to survive the death of the body; it can be held certain that the inner will expresses itself externally, thus the physical form is but a manifestation of spirit.

To make survival the purpose of existence is counterintuitive; one cannot truly live by merely maintaining the state of being alive. Instead, a Sovereign seeks ascension, never satisfied with sustaining themselves on mediocrity, but demanding excellence in existence through Effective Evolution; the Sovereign at all times strives for superior action and contemplation, seeking the superb wherever it is to be found, while simultaneously avoiding the mediocre or inferior lest they take hold like a cancer from which there can be no cure.

The drive and desire to preserve one's culture and heritage is certainly praiseworthy for ALL peoples, however, can often be confused with the most base sort of bias and this last has no place along the Path of Odhinn; while heritage and culture are undoubtedly essential to true spiritual nourishment and growth, no value judgment need be attached to either. The fact is that racism as it is marketed today was a development of those who first proclaimed themselves the "chosen" people and there it belongs; our Fólk have long believed in meritocracy and it is our actions that will determine our place in history's hierarchy.

As is well known by now, at some point a species separates itself from the rest completely, distinguishing itself as distinct, and in doing so severs the link to all living things' memory; it is at this point the particular species can be said to have their own unique genetic memory. For our Fólk this began with *ørlag*, the Primal Law or original laying in order of our *laeti* as it was given to Askr and Embla; this laying in order refers to both the arrangement of the "letters" of our DNA, manifesting the morphogenetic field for our Fólk, and the order in which we were given the Breath of Life, consciousness, blood, and godlike appearance or spirit, soul, and body. Mímir's Well has accumulated all of our ancestral memories since that time; as all living things share the same DNA there must be something more specific that separates one species from another and for all intents and purposes this is Instinct, the inherent predisposition to do or not do something, to see the world in a certain way, etc. Our Fólk are instinctually called to be creators and so we have been since the dawn of consciousness, until we began to ignore that Instinct, to neglect it to the precarious point we find ourselves in today.

There seems to be three primary influences that sever the link individuals have to Instinct: the passage of time, mutation, and, quite simply, loss of innocence. The first is easily understandable, for the more time that passes, the dimmer all memory becomes and recall becomes difficult at best. The second can be biological, though is likely more environmental; either way, this is responsible for the biggest and most drastic changes in history. The last of the three is through taint and losing that sense of wonder each of us is born with; while we may not be consciously aware of the contents of the genetic memory, we are certainly born with the ability to access it. It is this last that needs to be maintained more than anything else. In childhood everything is new and fresh, all potential and possibility is within our grasp, and our connection to the genetic memory is never stronger naturally than at this point; it is only as we lose that innocence, that we become cynical and start to see life as a struggle, that the link is lost. This need not be the case, however, as we can cultivate this in ourselves, and more importantly, in our children, through culture and preservation of particular predispositions.

Love is perhaps the single most significant source responsible for the strongest connections between people, though hate can bind as firmly, being at the opposite end of the emotional spectrum. Most people have experienced these connections firsthand and the power of each: the suddenly superhuman strength of a mother who lifts a car off of her child or the extremist whose hatred of his enemy is so strong that he will strap on a bomb and sacrifice his life to destroy even one of those enemies. The principle remains the same for both and are both equally valid tools at the Sovereign's disposal, as they seek to build a connection to the genetic memory and tap into that fountain of wisdom accumulated by our ancestors since *ørlag* was given to Askr and Embla; emotion can be

Sovereignty: The Empirical Path of Odhinn

considerably more powerful than contemplation though together pave the Path of Odhinn to Sovereignty.

A Sovereign can consistently reduce consciousness to the atomic level, where the genetic memory of our Fólk is found, through various techniques such as *galdr*, *staða*, *seiðr*, *hamgengjar*, and other types of meditation, breath control, fasting, etc. One of the simplest and fastest ways for Fólk to seek inspiration or intuition through their Instinct is utilizing the runes of the elder Futhark; the runes can be used for a variety of purposes, from focal point during contemplation to magic or divination. It is extremely significant that the runes are to be made of wood, a living organism, and to stain or "blood" them after carving the symbols; this blood gives life to the wood in the same way Askr and Embla as "logs" were given *lá*, but more importantly perhaps, doing this connects the individual to the genetic memory through the runes in the same way two people are connected by a blood oath to one another. We know that the language of nature is symbol, never specific, but always metaphorical. It is relevant that the runes represent the foundation and framework of all existence and are archetypal constructs connecting us to Eternity; it is the Instinct inherent in our blood that allows each of us to utilize these symbols to gain knowledge and wisdom from our ancestral stream.

One of the more significant stanzas in our wisdom teachings is not even found in most modern translations of the Edda: "Hidden in Mim's limpid Well, mens certain knowledge." This simple assertion confirms the existence of the genetic memory as a source of certain knowledge, but more importantly that our ancestors were aware of it as well. The strongest evidence we have that our Fólk have always believed in and placed an importance upon the ancestral memory is the widespread belief in Mimir and his Well; everything necessary to transcend time can be found in Mimir's Well, the collective unconscious of our Fólk. The fact that Odhinn gifted Mimir *Oðroerir*, the cauldron of Inspiration is significant as well, as it was the container of Kvasir's blood, said to have been mixed with honey to make the mead of poetry, the drink that inspires Intellect and Impulse. Kvasir was known to be the most knowledgable of all the Gods as a product of the synthesis between *Aesir* and *Vanir* and it was well known as well that there was no question he could not answer; Kvasir ventured out into the world to teach Fólk and was murdered by materialistic frost giants so they could make a profit from his knowledge. As an analogy, Kvasir's blood was said to have been separated into three containers, that of Son (bowl of expiation), Bodhn (bowl of offering), and *Oðroerir*; while all three are significant, only this last is ever really spoken of.

In the Voluspa there are two mentions of *Oðroerir* and two more allusions to it; these last are Odhinn's pledge, from which there pours forth a mighty stream onto the world-tree, and Mimir drinking from it. Both make it clear that *Oðroerir* is container and contents, not just one or the other. Mimir drinks from *Oðroerir* each morning, amassing knowledge through the memories of our Fólk, which are simultaneously used to nourish the world-tree; this kenning is reminiscent of Odhinn sending his ravens out each morning to gather news and knowledge of our Fólk. We know that after Odhinn drank from Mimir's Well he "began to thrive and wisdom gain," one word leading to another, one deed to some other, and this is an allusion to the memories of our Fólk from the beginning of time; it may be that from this he likewise gained the ability to send his ravens aloft and afar. For our purposes, however, the most profound stanza is:

> *"Well-earned wisdom I enjoyed*
> *Little the wise one lacks*
> *Oðroerir has been brought up*
> *Amidst the men of Midgardh"*

This makes it clear that we too have access to the cauldron of Inspiration, this Well of wisdom within which we now know to be the genetic memory or morphogenetic field from which we can gain certain knowledge. The Path is paved with acts and accomplishments that leave an indelible mark on the genetic memory of our Fólk; whenever a significant event occurs in our individual lives, good or bad, we retain a strong memory of it and this is likewise the case with the collective unconscious as well, in that, all words and deeds are etched upon the Fólk-Soul. The primary problem for people today is that they are not properly prepared to make the necessary sacrifice to slip into that stream of spiritual wisdom seeking answers and it is this more than anything else that Fólk must make part of our belief and practice.

One of the most fascinating discoveries by anthropologists is how shamans acquired the knowledge of the hallucinogens used for sacred spiritual journeys. All who were asked gave essentially the same answer: that it was the plant itself that taught them its nature and how it should be prepared and used. Nature herself communicates the essence of all things if we but listen to her; while the language of nature, however, is symbol and metaphor, that of man is DNA. All who share a particular genetic structure likewise share a memory that includes the history of that structure, the processes of their DNA, and the biological imperative for which certain genes must be present and have a specific effect on the organism; there may be variation based on a number of factors that result in the actual growth of the organism and this is referred to as the morphogenetic field. These fields give all animals, atoms, and even instincts their distinctive composition.

The scientific definition of a morphogenetic field is that it consists of a cluster of interacting cells that are capable of responding to biochemical cues which lead to the production of specific structures, organs, etc. Within the human body there are numerous micro morphogenetic fields, as each is constrained to its own type. For example, an ocular field produces an eye, the flesh field becomes skin tissue, et. al. In developmental biology it is believed that these morphogenetic fields consist of a collection of cells rather than individual cells which produce particular organs and that diverse mutations caused malformations alike enough in nature to be considered identical, implying that mutations impact a collection of cells, a field. Eminent experts have proposed that the morphogenetic field is a middle ground between evolution and genetics, where genes act upon fields, which subsequently act upon a developing organism; on both a molecular and cellular level, recombination is the genetic mechanism that plays the key role in morphogen evolution, obtaining similar results in the presence or absence of mutation.

Nevertheless, as all living things have evolved, they have formed a form-creating field and this morphogenetic field guarantees each organism's development; their descendants will take shape according to the pattern long since established by past generations of their own kind. In essence, one's ancestors have created the framework for their respective species and as every individual evolves they add to the morphogenetic blueprint, though is also influenced individually by the form-creating field as well.

Lá ok Litu Goðha: Genetic Memory

More importantly perhaps, these morphogenetic fields permit communication with the genetic memory through a phenomena referred to as morphic resonance; this term alludes to the ability of contemporary creatures to communicate with those most closely resembling them in the past. Morphic resonance not only allows each individual to tune into their past but also to communicate with their forebears directly, to gain the knowledge, wisdom, and experiences of their ancestors. Plato said that "all learning is but a remembering" and morphic resonance is the ability to remember all that is stored in Mimir's Well, the collective memory of our Fólk.

Morphogenetic fields do not carry energy, thus cannot transmit *önd*, the *oðic* energy of the Breath of Life, but only information beyond space and time without losing intensity once they are created; they assist in forming similar species according to the blueprint found in the genetic memory. The organism originating from this field is able to tune into it through reverberations similar to that of echolocation, the radar system used by bats; the newly formed organism has within it the seed of what came before and is able to utilize this to send requests for information that come back, or resonate from the genetic memory. Western man has become a rationalist, which has suppressed morphic resonance for quite some time now; rational thought only allows what is conscious or intellectual to enter the individual universe, thus the impulsive, inspirational, intuitional, and instinctual, all that emanates from the unconscious, is deemed irrational as it cannot be measured by mechanistic means. Conversely, those seeking Sovereignty strive to balance the Instinct, Intellect, and Impulse; limiting any aspect of the *laeti* is like using a single fist in a fight and intentionally leaving the other out, regardless of the opponent or consequences.

In adopting an accurate understanding of morphogenetic fields we also allow for a more serious study of consciousness itself; those who accept these fields as unconscious constructs then have a foundation from which to consider consciousness as well, in the hopes of sustaining supraconscious Sovereignty. The same concepts can and should be applied to investigating and understanding the memory: we do not store memories as though they were being filed alphabetically into cabinets; instead, the exchange between our brains and the morphogenetic field is constant, information and experiences moving back and forth, with the ability to recollect not only our own empirical data, but any other who has contributed to this field.

Each of us resonates more intensely with our own memories or experiences, which is why we can recall them with relative ease, though the further away from ourselves the experience or memory is, the more difficult it becomes to tune in to them, but not altogether impossible. Being a repository for the genetic memory, the morphogenetic field of our Fólk is synonymous with Mimir's Well; the more Fólk who experience a certain thing or learn something new, share the same thoughts, etc. the stronger it will be for future Fólk.

In the 1970s a theory emerged which was said to support the notion of the collective unconscious, known as the Hundredth Monkey Effect; the general principle behind this theory is that after an adequate amount of single organisms accept a paradigm shift of some sort, the whole species will spontaneously adopt it as part of its very existence without need of external experience or concerted effort to share the shift with the others of its kind.

> *"It may be that when enough of us hold something to be true, it becomes true for everyone."*
>
> – Lyall Watson

The theory was first mentioned by Watson, but gained more widespread acceptance through Ken Keyes' book "The Hundredth Monkey." The principal premise was based upon Japanese researchers observing macaques on the island of Koshima in 1952: these scientists observed some of these monkeys begin to wash their sweet potatoes, with younger generations learning to do so through observation; when the practice reached a particular point, however, it is said that it spontaneously spread to other macaques on nearby islands that had no means of communicating with those of Koshima. It was therefore theorized that all macaques developed this ability naturally once a certain number had become consciously aware of it; in this instance a subjective number was set at ninety-nine monkeys who learned to wash the sweet potatoes, causing the hundredth to do this automatically without having to be taught. More than just a single monkey began to wash their sweet potatoes, however:

once the threshold had been reached ALL of the macaques suddenly began to do so, on every island in the area without being taught.

Though the theory has been widely criticized by the mainstream, it nevertheless presents an interesting proposition of whether or not it is possible for a whole generation of Fólk to know something instinctually simply because the previous generation had learned it. There can be no doubt that more than just physical traits are hereditary; it is not only biology that is encoded into our DNA, but something more substantial. Additionally, the more Fólk who experience something particular, or have the same thought, are strengthening that thought or experience, allowing others who are able to tune in to the same channel to pick it up easier; this also allows each subsequent generation to be more advanced than the last in having these memories present at the moment they are born. If nothing else we "who have chosen out ourselves" like Nietzsche's pre-*Übermensch* can consciously strengthen this bond so as to prepare the Path for Fólk to come. The more Fólk who find the Path of Odhinn, follow it faithfully, and become Sovereign, the more likely we are to create the paradigm shift necessary to instinctually instill it in future generations, and from the genetic memory of our Fólk will the Sovereign emerge like a phoenix from the ashes and embers.

Ár ok Aldr: Time and Eternity

"Eternity in this sense [supra-temporal] is not limitless time, but instead, the atemporal, the realm beyond time, where before and after fuse into an absolute present. This timelessness is also the realm in which Tradition in the Evolan sense operates."

Time has fascinated Fólk for as long as we have been consciously aware and will continue to do so into the foreseeable future. Time denotes an individual's experience during a particular period, though in the same way that man is such only through the lack of acceptance of his inherently divine nature, time likewise has meaning only to those who recognize it as a controlling factor. Change is what gives the illusion of time; without noticeable differences between one thing and another over a given period, time would not exist in our consciousness. As it is, time can only be conceptualized through metaphor; this is why past, present, and future (even in tense) are too objective to describe time or its passage.

Time by its very nature is the primary distinction between this realm and that of the Gods: the former is finite, while the latter is infinite, in essence a total negation of time, and those on the Path must likewise live beyond time to attain Sovereignty. To escape time is an utter departure from the cosmic order of this realm and adopting another altogether.

Time and its measurement are the roots of destruction; when last our Fólk lived without its dictates was the Battleaxe Age, the Age of Truth, though since that period there has been a steady degeneration and decline in both the world around us as well as the Fólk-Soul. Thus is the primary distinction between time and evolution, for the latter is an inherent and steady striving upwards, above time and beyond its constraints; in recognizing evolution as natural we likewise accept and acknowledge that the concept of creation is but a particular point in a perpetual series of new beginnings, spanning cyclical time. To escape time, then, we must embrace Effective Evolution as the only means through which we can achieve ascension. Effective Evolution includes the intentional balance of Instinct, Intellect, and Impulse, wherein stasis as a state of harmony makes time insignificant. There are, in essence, four distinct types of time:

$$\text{TEMPORAL} = \text{Within time}$$
$$\text{ATEMPORAL} = \text{Against time}$$
$$\text{METATEMPORAL} = \text{Beyond time}$$
$$\text{SUPRATEMPORAL} = \text{Above time}$$

Within time there are three aspects: before, after, or simultaneous with one another, corresponding to cause, effect, and acausal or synchronistic. Against time is evolution itself, all that grows, changes, creates, and thrives towards a Higher Purpose. Beyond time we find Sovereigns, those who have achieved a state of superiority here in this realm beyond the mere mundane and mediocre. Above time is where the Aldabjarn, those born of Eternity, exist. All of time is bound up in Eternity and one proof of this can be found in mathematics: numbers cannot possibly exist in time as they are Eternal, indestructible (like the soul), and mathematics must remain Eternal as they are not open to interpretation, but firmly founded in Absolute Law.

The Temporal and Atemporal are concerned with the physical and correspond with *Lá ok Litu Goða*, the blood and body respectively, while the Metatemporal and Supratemporal are metaphysical, the *óð ok önd* of the soul seeking Sovereignty beyond and ultimately above the constraints of time. The temporal and atemporal are cyclical in nature, polarities of time itself, wherein the Destroyers and Creators are in constant conflict.

The modern world is consumed by time, the clock controlling all with its domineering demands, and the temporal holds dominion over almost every aspect of contemporary consciousness. The temporal is likewise linear by necessity, unnaturally presenting as past, present, and future; this conception of time cannot satisfy the spiritual needs of our Fólk. In the next Age (as in the first) linear time will no longer be the binding force in this world; the relinquishing of this fetter will free what came before and what is yet to occur to join the immediate instant, where Fólk will have the ability once more to peer into the past through the prism of insight that comes from the genetic memory, while simultaneously seeing what should be in this moment. This timelessness is found in the morphogenetic field that contains the memories (Mimir's Well) of our Fólk. This morphogenetic field is the *oðic* force that stores its contents in our blood by inscribing memories into our very DNA, likely using the sun's rays. This sounds fantastic until one considers how memory is stored in microchips or that information can be sent at high speeds through fiber optic lines of light.

Nevertheless, to focus on or live one's life within time is self-defeating, a linear progression without purpose, perpetuated by the mindless masses of Utgardh; instead it is cyclical time, where the atemporal and metatemporal meet, that needs to be the focal point for Fólk seeking Sovereignty.

The most significant difference between the Traditional notion of time and that of modern man, is that the former was understood as a vertical movement toward the Gods, while the latter is horizontal to an eventual end. Many modern methods of reckoning time are almost completely arbitrary, having little connection to the natural world aside from the obvious rising and setting of the sun, let alone any spiritual value, and this is true even among those who profess to live their lives according to Tradition.

All life is cyclical, having a finite number of patterns that can be depended upon for a particular outcome. This can be seen in the law of Consequence, where cause and effect appear in all aspects of life: if one does this then that will happen; if that occurs this is likely to follow. The intuitive person can more readily recognize these patterns as they have the benefit of their Instinct to draw on.

As such, cyclical time can best be illustrated by looking to the moon. The moon starts its cycle in the new phase, absent of light and unseen by the naked eye; it proceeds into its waxing phase, increasing incrementally in area of illumination to the point of being "full" or completely luminescent, easily viewed by all, at which time it begins to wane, or extinguish its expanse of incandescence to its new phase once more. The moon repeats this process perpetually and the recognition of this cycle allows Fólk to track the passage of time with accuracy in the same way that perceiving life's patterns permits people to predict with precision imminent or impending incidents. While the cycle of the moon may appear to us as a repetition of exactly the same occurrence over and over, subtle changes in the atmosphere, the sun's intensity, or lack thereof, proximity or actual position of the sun and moon in relation to one another (as well as the earth), an asteroid or comet passing, or countless other influences that can and do affect a particular cycle at any given point prevent any two cycles from being exactly the same, only similar in form. The same is true of cyclical time: patterns can and do repeat themselves to varying degrees, though never precisely, and in recognizing these patterns we can each gain true understanding.

Conversely, the linear measurement of time denotes a beginning, middle, and end, which would imply that the moon (extending the example above) should begin "new," grow to "full," then simply "wink out" instead of gradually disappearing from view according to the cyclical model. This demonstrates the unnatural conception of time prevalent in this plebeian perspective, as it presses ever onward to an end; the monotheistic model of past, present, and future lacks the spiritually significant truth of cyclical time.

The fact that cyclical time is so prominent and prevalent throughout the traditions of our Fólk is significant in many regards, most notably in that of birth, life, death, and rebirth (creation, preservation, destruction, and recreation) as the means by which evolution is achieved. Cycle would seem to imply repetition as identical recurrence, which would not support evolution, as this latter clearly connotes change and growth, however, cyclical here is used primarily to describe selfsame similarities that repeat themselves to some degree throughout time as a pattern: never quite the same, but alike enough in form to be recognized as such.

Cyclical time is evolutionary and evolution is best represented by the spiral; the circle is the symbol of Eternity, the center of which is regarded as the motionless aspect of existence, the pivot allowing the motion of existence to be possible. While the circle is a closed loop, an unbroken and unchangeable fixed form, the spiral continues indefinitely

Sovereignty: The Empirical Path of Odhinn

in a circular pattern, often returning to the same cardinal points endlessly and each time it does, it deviates just enough to alter the composition of the design; if we see the center as the start then each time it comes full circle the spiral gets a little bit wider and it is this change that represents the growth of evolution. The circle symbolizes Eternity as it has no beginning nor end, but exists as a whole; conversely, the spiral signifies the cyclical patterns of this wholeness and harmony as it evolves to higher forms. Even a minute amount of growth will prevent the cycle from returning to its starting point or repeating the same Path perpetually, let alone retrace its steps through involution.

Circles and spirals are found in a sacred context all across the continent of Europe, as well as every island in close proximity to it (or wherever our Fólk have settled), and this includes everything from henges to brochs and chambered tombs, burial mounds, or standing stones to spiral designs in abundance. One of the most significant of these last is Newgrange, a burial mound covered in spiral designs to signify cyclical time and evolution. Inside this burial mound is a chamber deep within its center that contains a small niche, likely where an urn and/or statue would rest, and this niche can only naturally be lit up at one single point of the year: the Winter Solstice, that point when the veil between this realm and that of the Gods is said to be thinnest; for approximately 17 minutes a beam of sunlight can pass through a small hole carved above the cave entrance and one can easily see this beam of light being the Bifrost bridge connecting Asgardh and Midgardh.

It is now a certainty that the megalithic tradition began in the far North before moving South and the circle has been held sacred by our Fólk for as far back as we have inhabited the Óðal lands; all of the most sacred structures spread across the European landscape are circular constructs, with almost a thousand stone and wooden henges in the British Isles alone.

> *"Yes, there are hundreds of 'megalithic' monuments or henges in the world, which we find only in Europe—we don't find them in India, or in Egypt, even the Mesopotamian ziggurats were not built in this way..."*
>
> – Elma Parsamian, astral physicist

Henges were likely the early Hofs of Europe. Most fólk are familiar with Stonehenge, but lesser known and older henges are scattered from

Germany to Croatia, the Carpathians to the Atlantic Ocean, and every place in between; some 200 or more which predate any other known architectural design or structure. These henges are not only unique to our Fólk, but were similar in build to one another as well: a circular enclosure, originally made of wooden posts buried in the ground, having two to four openings (most often three) spaced around the perimeter, always aligned to the Winter and Summer Solstices, with a ditch surrounding the outside of the henge. There is some variation, but not a significant amount, leading to the conclusion that these henges were used universally by our Fólk for a specific purpose. There are not any buildings, homes, or evidence of habitation within these henges (neither human nor animal), precluding their use as pens or shelters of some sort and in at least one instance (that of the Gosek henge) there is clear evidence of ritualistic use, in the form of a headless skeleton being buried feet up in the center. These henges were always near a center of civilization, implying that they were sacred to an entire tribe, perhaps many, and likely used for communal rituals and rites.

It is a long-standing practice among Fólk to set aside and sanctify a space in which to worship, and this continued into the Heathen Era in the *ve*. Dr. Joseph Roder proposed that the function of the circular enclosure known as Goloring was to "cut out a piece of land from the profane and make it holy," thus creating the separation between every day existence outside and sacred space within. There can be no doubt that these henges were hofs or temples to our distant ancestors, which raises a significant question for those seeking Sovereignty: are we required to recreate these sanctified spaces the same as our ancestors did, in groves and other outside areas to receive spiritual nourishment? The answer is a resounding no, at least not exactly; instead, we allow ancestors to enlighten us and inform modern practice.

The word "contemplate" is an interesting one, as it can be translated as "to create a temple" (presumably in the mind), through which to think with intent; this is literally a space marked out for the observation of auguries, and, as such, is sacred and spiritual. Many Fólk absentmindedly refer to the side of their head as their temple without consciously considering the significance of this being a place devoted to exalted purposes. Language is the way in which we relate culture, yet so often we neglect to delve deeper than the surface in today's society, despite the fact that our ancestors were known to wrap words in both exoteric and esoteric significance. In fact, one of the least defined or perhaps most misunderstood concepts today is that of *Heimliche Acht* or the "hidden tribunal," a threefold understanding that underlies all of our mythology. The way in which many Odhinists perceive it, as mundane, exoteric, and esoteric is important: mundane being superficial or just plain obvious, exoteric is just below the surface, and esoteric as the deeper occultic meaning. To the Sovereign these correspond with Impulse, Intellect, and Instinct.

To put this into proper context one need only look at Odhinn. When many Fólk hear his name they think of the Norse God, perhaps picturing him flying through the air on his eight-legged steed, the stuff of lore, legend, and comic books; unfortunately most people live at this level of existence today, not able to see what is beyond themselves, only grasping the thing that seems rather than what is or what should be. This image of Odhinn is purely intellectual and it persists even among a number of Odhinists because of the scholarly works that are incapable of delving below the surface; from almost every translation of the Edda to H.R. Ellis Davidson these remain superficial scholarly works with no feeling or depth quite simply because they are not those of actual Odhinists who believe and practice this way of life.

Conversely, those such as Víktor Rydberg and F. Max Muller (despite his overemphasis on solar interpretation) do delve below the surface, though not quite deep enough, and this is the exoteric or Impulse understanding. In continuing our example of Odhinn, it is what he evokes in Fólk, the *Ergriffenheit* or "state of being seized" that lay just below the surface. Odhinn is known as the ecstatic God, emotional, thus it is how we <u>feel</u> when we hear or invoke his name.

The best example of the esoteric is given us by Carl Jung, as it comes from Instinct, from the collective unconscious: Odhinn as archetype, the god-image every Sovereign seeks to emulate and become unconsciously. This instinct is without thought or emotion, does not even have an image, but is the most powerful of the three as it is the overwhelming urge emanating from the Fólk-Soul to be, not just to exist, but to become a God.

The Old Norse word for head is *höfuð*, the root of which (*hof-*) literally means "temple", demonstrating the importance of contemplation. Aristotle asserted that "Contemplation is the highest form of activity" and this is true to Fólk who strive for spiritual nourishment in particular.

Ár ok Aldr: Time and Eternity

Contemplation is the intentional cultivation of consciousness and Sovereignty is set specifically on self-cultivation, to grow and improve through culture; to cultivate, one needs to nourish and nurture a seed until it sprouts, blossoms, and bears fruit for Fólk to proliferate from. The Old Norse *ár* means year and refers to the harvest, however, likewise represents cyclical time in contrast to *aldr* or Eternity; the connection lay in cultivation, the determined development of something for a specific purpose. On the physical plane cultivation is concerned with crops, while on the metaphysical it refers to Effective Evolution, with culture combining the two. There are likewise two types of places set aside to cultivate these: the garden and field, such as Asgardh and Folkvang.

Today, we are less involved in agriculture, thus have little concern for husbandry or farming except perhaps on a personal level; culture on the other hand, is important to our way of life as it contributes to our customs, beliefs, traditions, and traits. The importance of language, boundaries, and culture cannot be emphasized enough, and our ancestors understood this better than most Fólk give them credit for; this is why there was a tripartite distinction between the gardens that were marked out to cultivate all of existence: seen in the simplest terms they are "mine," "ours," and "theirs" or Asgardh, Midgardh, and Utgardh respectively.

The Old Norse *garð* literally means garden (from the root **gher*, "enclsoure") and is both figuratively and literally a space set aside for cultivation, a place parceled out according to a particular plan, affording consideration to culture; the soil in this sacred enclosure is set to a specific purpose: to nurture in a natural way that which is within its confines. In Odhinism the universe is divided into three gardens: Asgardh, Midgardh, and Utgardh. These three realms are the framework of all existence, the three roots of the world-tree that are found in the wells of *urðar brunnr* (Urð's Well), *Mimis brunnr* (Mimir's Well), and *jötun brunnr* (giant's well; also known as *hvergelmir*) respectively, in addition to the distinction of time itself: Eternity, cyclical, and linear. These three realms vibrate at different frequencies, as well as emanating differing degrees of light; sound, motion, and light are key to knowing these realms, understanding them completely, and comprehending all experience according to each individually and collectively. The three gardens are part and parcel of the world-tree, which itself is existence as all of empirical reality.

Asgardh (from **ansugher*, "spirit enclosure") is the Garden of the Gods, the Eternal Abode of our ancestors, where all divinity dwells,

Sovereignty: The Empirical Path of Odhinn

and is likewise the inner realm of Instinct. Asgardh is the archetypal pantheon, though this is not to say that the Gods are simply psychological constructs; to the contrary, the archetypal perspective and that of living, breathing Gods are not mutually exclusive, but two sides of the same coin that describes a particular phenomenon, namely the esoteric and exoteric. As the god-image, Odhinn is the Allfather of Asgardh and is the Sovereign Self each of us strive to attain, though all of the Gods embody to differing degrees; even Thor pursued the Path of Odhinn. Asgardh is above time and explains why we have always viewed our Gods as being "up there"; at the same time this garden is the universe within each of us, where the soul is the sun illuminating our individual inner sanctum. Asgardh then is also to be considered the unconscious, the source of all Instinct, intuition, and inspiration.

Midgardh (from *meðyogher*, "middle enclosure") is the Middle Garden, the border between Gods and giants where man dwells as physical matter; our body is not merely the vessel of the soul, but also protects our divinity from the inhabitants of Utgardh, the outside world where chaos reigns supreme. Just as all within us is order and Eternity, outside of our self is chaos and time, while Midgardh represents the balance that is essential to existence, and each of us is capable of the atemporal or metatemporal; ours is the cosmos of consciousness, while Asgardh is the macrocosmos and Utgardh the microcosmos outside of our conscious awareness. This is the realm of Will to Power as the potential for all possibilities; the *etins* of ignorance, ignobility, and destruction are always attempting to breach the barrier of Midgardh to get to Asgardh. Thor is the ruler of this realm; he is the defender of man, a protector who ever seeks the destruction of the giants and thus is the warrior to Odhinn's Sovereignty. Thor's Hammer is the ultimate symbol, capable of creation and consecration, as well as destruction and death; this is why many Fólk wear a Thorshammer and make the sign of the Hammer: to protect ourselves from Utgardh and for sanctification respectively. Midgardh is where the self of Intellect and Impulse exist for each of us and from where we seek ascension across the Bifrost Bridge.

Utgardh (from *udgher*, "outer enclosure") is the Outer Garden, even perhaps the Garden of *Etins*, the exterior where everything else exists; this realm extends to the ends of all existence, encompassing anything not set aside as Asgardh or Midgardh. In this realm is illusion, influenced by disintegration, decadence, and decay, the terrestrial and temporal, where all is manifest through time and materialism; Utgardh is governed by the subconscious in the sense of a lack of consciousness. Asgardh and Utgardh are polar opposites, the thing that is versus the thing that seems to be, and act on one another at the point of equilibrium: Midgardh, which is the product of spirit and matter, both divine and animal natures, from which we must choose to pursue only one.

The Valknot is the ultimate symbol of the Sovereign Self, showing as it does, these three gardens; Asgardh above, Midgardh below, and Utgardh outside of the two. These three realms likewise contain three *veraldir* (worlds or dimensions) to demonstrate the nine of the world-tree as mirroring that of divine man.

To truly understand man's purpose for existing, examining the existence of the universe around us becomes necessary, as the macrocosmos acts on and is influenced by both the cosmos and microcosmos; this is a symbiotic relationship, held together by the world-tree or *axis mundi*. One thing of importance to our Fólk, for as far back as we can determine, is that we have long personified the processes of the cosmos as a conscious construct, alive and animated, and it is the same with the world-tree. The very first thing mentioned in the Voluspa is the world-tree, even before Ymir or Ginnungagap, demonstrating that it is indeed the framework of all existence and within this there are nine *veraldir*; some have seen in this everything from the nine planets of our solar system to the chakras with the tree representing the spine and Nidhogg the kundalini. The truth, however, is that these likely represent the dimensions of the universe.

Scientists seem to agree that there are nine dimensions of which most Fólk are aware of only three, and it is likely that the tripartite structure sacred to our Fólk for so long derives from these three known dimensions and equate to the realms as well. Nevertheless, it remains to identify these dimensions as best we can:

1. JOTUNHEIM — Line/height
2. HELHEIM — Plane/width
3. SVARTALFHEIM — Space/depth
4. NIFLHEIM — Sound/potential
5. FOLKHEIM — Cyclical time/evolution
6. MUSPELLHEIM — Oscillation/rhythm
7. LJOSSALFHEIM — Light/source
8. VANAHEIM — Unity/harmony
9. ASAHEIM — Eternity/infinity

These are thoroughly theoretical, however, they do help focus the mind to enable the entrance to other dimensions and realms. The first three are obvious to most and the home of "dark elves" seems appropriate to space. *Hvergelmir* ("the roarer") is indeed in Helheim, while cyclical time and evolution do seem to govern Fólk. Muspellheim would seem to imply movement and energy through fire. Light is certainly applicable to Ljossalfheim, just as unity is to Vanaheim, this last of which did seek balance with the *Aesir*. Asaheim is obviously the home of Eternity, though all of these require study and experience to fully comprehend. One interesting note is that through oscillation acting on light a "rainbow bridge" could be created to connect Asgardh and Midgardh.

In support of cyclical time is cyclical cosmology, the latter being a macrocosmic mirror of the former and proposes to explain how our universe came into being. Contemporary research has discovered that the so-called Big Bang theory may no longer make clear the origins of this universe and the competing theory maintains that our universe constantly generates and regenerates itself in a perpetual cycle of creation and recreation. The key concept to this particular hypothesis derives its foundation from string theory, the basis of which is that our universe is a three-dimensional membrane freely floating inside a four-dimensional "bulk" or background commonly called "space"; there are an infinite number of membranes in this bulk, all of which contain quantities of energy bound up in them. Each of these membranes can exert powerful effects on one another in close proximity and a collision between two of them would release their respective energies, causing what would appear to be an enormous explosion, thus creating matter that would eventually evolve into stars, planets, galaxies, etc. Space in these membranes would begin to expand then and the distance between the two increase until that space were essentially empty, at which point they begin to draw together again involuntarily, at some point colliding to create a new cycle. Each of these cycles are said to last almost a trillion years, thus we have only just begun this one. This explanation for the origins of our universe would seem to support and coincide with the cosmology of our Fólk.

According to Old Norse cosmology nothing existed except the Ginnungagap, an empty space, until Niflheim (static negative energy) and Muspellheim (active positive energy) drifted together to the point that their close proximity combined those energies and created matter. In this case the creation of Audhumbla (*óð*-embla) and Ymir, representing the forces of order and chaos respectively, though the fact that this describes cyclical cosmology is undeniable.

Physicists have been developing a gravity-wave detector to measure the gravitational waves believed to pervade space like ripples that remain from the last collision between membranes and once this is complete researchers will be able to prove the cyclical model. Furthermore scientists have now demonstrated that our universe has many galaxies and in fact that there are an unknown amount of universes in existence; it is believed that each of these universes have their own distinct set of laws that govern them the same way each of our Fólk have their own individual *ørlag* from which their personal *Urð* and *dómr* derive. We know that our self is a universe unto itself, unique in its own right, and that we are Sovereign over it; in fact, it is the complete Sovereignty over the self that is the foundation of life. This is just another example of how the microcosm mirrors the macrocosm and the fact that the earliest Fólk recognized it as such. Either way, the cyclical model itself supports the wisdom teachings of our earliest ancestors, in that we have always believed time to be cyclical and if the universe itself is cyclical then so too is all it encompasses, from our world, galaxy, and the passage of time to the seasons and life itself; everything then has a span of existence that can only be measured by creation, preservation, destruction, and recreation, so this is the standard by which all should be assessed, appraised, and appreciated.

In the eldest Tradition we find the celebration of cyclical time most prominently displayed in the recognition of the seasons of the solar year, as the Voluspa tells us, and this is even more notable in the recognition of the Solstices, when the "sun stands still"; these two particular points of the year take on a sacred context not just in the way they mark the passage of time, however, but by reflecting the growth and expansion of time as well, what we call evolution. As time evolves so too we as a Fólk evolve, and in this way evolution is improvement with an intent at perfection. Evolution is an emanation of Eternity; when Primal Law was set in motion it made possible the perfected state and the importance of the sun to this cannot be overstated, as it is essential to every element of life. Herein lay the key that unlocks the gate to the Path.

The sun is the soul of our universe, both internally and externally, and as such emanates the very essence of existence; each and every planet or star receives this at various rates of vibration, consistent with their proximity to the sun, just as man's soul influences every atom of the body, from blood to bone, depending on how close we are to it. It is the synergy between the sun and our soul that makes Sovereignty possible, and those on the Path need to nurture and nourish this interaction. The essence emanating from the sun has likely been known by numerous names throughout time, though in Old Norse is referred to as *önd* or *oðic* energy, the all-encompassing energy that pervades the universe, the animating principle which connects sensation in individuals directly to Ultimate Reality; behind all of nature's laws, illusions, and anomalies stands this Ultimate Reality, unknowable and unfathomable for most, manifesting itself perpetually, existing as an indestructible and Eternal Source known as *oðic* force.

Self-realization requires a conscious connection to this *oðic* force and maintaining this bond throughout life, as one must live cognizant of the link to achieve Sovereignty, contemplating *oðic* force allows us this power and the ability to use it, while our intent is interconnected with the Law of Influence. The *oðic* force is constantly creating and intention is the link between it and us, as intent is essential to the cultivation of the capacity to create. One who lives with intent, who recognizes their purpose and eagerly pursues it with unerring determination is creating, mirroring the *oðic* force in the process, thus the power of intent can be considered the very creative and animating principle in our universe. From *oðic* force comes everything and everything is nourished through *oðic* force; it creates, but does not control, oversees, but is not overbearing, exists in all and all exists because of it. It is our individual Will to Power in our own universe.

True Will to Power is not the destruction of the self, nor its subjugation, but the balance of Instinct, Intellect, and Impulse, the complimentary relationship between the self and spirit that manifests as Sovereignty. Will to Power is the recognition that the self is Sovereign, "I Will" rather than "god wills" or some other such external source; it is the honest and acceptable notion that one's Highest desire is the guiding principle behind all they are, were, or will ever be. Further, it is the acknowledgement that this Highest desire is what SHOULD be pursued, with wholehearted conviction and unwavering dedication.

Energy is the exchange between two polarities, creating power for activity and potential for animation. All of existence requires the balance between two extremes and *oðic* energy is the interaction connecting the self and *oðic* force on the microcosmic and macrocosmic; instead of denying the existence of this energy, each of us need to truly understand and embrace it, utilize its power, potential, and properties to achieve complete Sovereignty. Many experts claim that there are currents of energy that crisscross most of the henges our ancestors erected, as though these circles marked a sacred site where two polarities or energies were strongest; the sunwheel likely symbolizes this selfsame power: the coming together of two energies inside of a circle, the latter representing Eternity. Together they represent the earth and sky: a horizontal line for *meginjörð*, the power of the earth and the vertical line is the *Ásmeginn*, the power of the Gods/sky, divine power, though together is the very Will to Power.

The fact that our ancestors always chose to worship outdoors, holding rituals in groves and likely henges before this, is also telling to Heathen of today: we did not build temples as they are understood now, but would worship among the trees and stones of our Fólk and ancestors. At the same time we were recognizing the cyclical nature of time through the turning of the seasons, which relied on sun and moon, thus in these groves and henges our Fólk came together to connect to the energies of earth and sky. The sunwheel likewise represents this as well, in our recognition of the *oðic* force acting upon all of the universe through *oðic* energy, having a profound effect on what would come to be called Europe, the *óðal* lands, our inheritance and birthright as descendants of the Gods.

The very first act of the advisors, the *reginn*, was to name and recognize cyclical time through sun, stars, and moon; with the concept of cycles comes the realization of the patterns that govern life, as these blueprints are the basis of all that exists in Eternity, guiding even the most inconsequential aspects of evolution with the symbiosis of existence, wherein all is dependent upon everything. Knowledge of the pattern, understanding Absolute law, allows one the ability to transcend the mundane and mediocre to a state of supraconscious awareness. Despite the fact that cycle seems to indicate a repetition, the patterns evident in evolution should instead be seen as examples to emulate.

A more comprehensive way of viewing cyclical time and even evolution perhaps, is to perceive it as a spider's web. Woven into similar patterns according to species, no two spider webs are ever exactly the same, though the general geometric shape stays constant, as is the purpose for which each is woven. At creation, the web follows a certain set predetermined pattern (as do our Fólk according to our morphogenetic field, our philogenesis), though over the life of this web, things may occur that alter its overall composition and appearance: a fly may get caught in its viscid gossamer and through its struggle to survive and free itself, could destroy part of the web, heavy rain could affect the texture or effectiveness in snaring insects, the spider may abandon the web in its desire to design a new one, possibly in a safer location; the possibilities are endless, though the one constant is that the web will exist and it will be created according to a predetermined pattern each and every time, based upon the instinct of the spider. The same can be said of time and existence: much the same as the spider, who instinctively weaves its web in a particular pattern, our Instinct guides each of us along certain paths of proper action that are appropriate first to our species, then to our individual purpose, our Skuld, and the recognition of this is imperative to the growth and evolution of our Fólk, as well as those striving to attain Sovereignty.

To make time the focal point of existence would be self-defeating and in particular linear time as contemporary society does; we do not view time in a linear, predetermined, or fixed fashion, with a beginning and an end, nor have we ever, as evidenced by the concept of *Urð* embodied by the three Norns Urdhr, Verdhandi, and Skuld. Despite those who would attempt to correlate the Norns with the past, present, and future, their actual functions are far more significant than these simple designations would seem to imply. Urdhr, "that which is," represents the unchangeable, those layers that have already been added to the well, though continue to influence and affect all areas of life. Verdhandi, "man becoming," symbolizes growth, evolution, and all that is occurring in the imminent now, thus is not fixed or static. Skuld, "what should be," embodies the belief that each of us has an inherent nature all our own, an *Ørlag*, and a Path that we should follow to validate our very existence, to achieve Sovereignty, though this does not occur automatically, nor according to some divine plan, but must be consciously sought out utilizing our Will to Power, and embracing the self as it is. This likewise allows for rebirth, in that, those who do not follow their individual Path to Sovereignty (what should be), will get as many opportunities as they need to get it right. Nevertheless, this view of cyclical time is a far more natural, rational, and logical perspective for Fólk to perceive the passage of time than that of the linear. Balance and harmony have always been at the heart of everything, as equilibrium divides this from that, before and after, etc. and it is at the point of perfect equilibrium that all things become possible, in the same way Verdhandi (as man becoming) represents the balance between what is and what should be, allowing for all potentiality. The Norns are the ultimate representation of not only the cyclical evolution of time, but of nourishing the very soul of existence as well.

While the Old Norse *Ár* refers to time, specifically cyclical time, *Aldr* at its root means Eternity, though it also represents an Age and can even symbolize the soul in the sense of being the Eternally existing. The most significant reference to *Aldr* comes from the Voluspa: *alda bornum Ørlag seggja*; which translates as "Eternal born ones set in motion Primal Law." The Norns are those born of Eternity, and the *Ørlag* here, the first layers in *urðar brunnr*, were the runes of the Elder Futhark, the framework for all existence, which "on wood they carved." We know that Urdhr's well is below the world-tree and it was into this that Odhinn peered as he hung on the tree; in so doing he gained knowledge of the runes. Those born of Eternity, like those who attain Eternal Existence, are only above time, and the Norns set *Ørlag* into motion on a grand scale, where Odhinn, Hoenir, and Lodhurr did the same for Fólk. On the macrocosmic level this *Ørlag* is the four Ages spoken of in the wisdom teachings of our Fólk.

In the same way there are four types of time, four seasons with which to measure its passage, and four gifts given to Askr and Embla, the four Ages represent all of these and so much more besides. The primary differences between the Ages is about the energy saturating the world, the *önd*; in the same way certain characteristics are present in the world when a child takes their first breath, so too is there a distinct character to an Age. The four Ages of man can be defined as harmonic digression, wherein a particular sequence of time periods flow into one another in a prearranged pattern of aesthetic decline.

Battleaxe Age, governed by Tyr as *Dyas Pitar, Dis Pater, Dio Pitar*, etc. the *deus otiosis*, and Zisa, the mother Goddess; characterized by truth, balance, law, and spirituality, an Age when all was right, natural, and instinctual. The Gods did not need to involve themselves in the affairs of men during this time, as it was the Age of Truth, the Golden Age of living life according to the Absolute, nature, and the natural order. The Battleaxe culture of anthropologists coincides with this Age, as the battleaxe has long been considered a symbol of power, nobility, and kingship to our Fólk and it was Sovereignty as the balance of Instinct, Intellect, and Impulse that distinguished this Age.

Sword Age, governed by Heimdall, who descended to Midgardh as an avatar, in the form of Rigr, to give our Fólk culture, consciousness, and caste; characterized by the rise of civilization. During this period the Gods made their first attempt at assisting men, as this latter began to lose touch with their Instinct and rely more upon self alone. Heimdall's sword is called *höfuð*, which is a kenning for the head, marking this Age as that where Fólk saw the rise of ego through Intellect and Impulse alone. Of note is the fact that the Greeks understood Apollo to be an import from the North, said to have been worshipped by the Hyperboreans long before his emigration South, and this was undoubtedly Heimdall.

Wind Age, governed by Odhinn as Sovereign Self, the personification of supraconscious thought and emotion; characterized by the first civil wars and philosophical and spiritual foundations being laid. Wind being a kenning for thought and emotion, this Age embodied both until the end of the Heathen Era, which ushered in the reign of monotheism and their self-asserted "thousand year" dominance. It is during this period that a paradigm shift occurred, wherein our Fólk ultimately misapprehended the desire for knowledge as a reliance on left brain logic alone. In our mythology it says "then will the Wolf swallow Valfather" and this denotes Odhinn's time, the Wind Age giving way to that of the Wolf.

Wolf Age, governed by Angrbodha and her evil progeny; characterized by chaos, immorality, darkness, destruction, ignorance, and overall decline. Over the last thousand years, during the reign of monotheism, more murders have been committed in the name of the One True God than anything else, morality has disappeared and the violence of World Wars I and II, as well as the war in Ireland, provide but a few examples of "brother fighting brother, sisters sons betray." Destruction always precedes recreation, however, and while the Wolf Age embodies this like nothing else could, it also prepares the way for the Fridhr Age.

Fridhr Age will be governed by Baldr, the purest of Gods and that of light and illumination, an elevation of everything noble, necessary, and spiritual: Sovereignty. This Age will follow the Ragnarokr, wherein we will find both Baldr and Hodhr reborn to make peace with one another and dwell in Hropt's hall; this, more than anything else, embodies the coming Age of man and Gods.

Fridhr has been explained as reciprocal inviolability among one's own Fólk, and this is definitely part of its meaning; it also has connotations of freedom from chaotic thoughts and emotions that can be found in true contemplation. With this latter, the term *ár ok friðr* takes on a new meaning when considered the peace of mind that comes from spiritual balance and Sovereignty.

More than anything else, the four gifts given us at "creation" characterize the Ages, as they were given us in order of importance, and we were to lose them in the same way: *önd* (our Instinct) as inspiration is the purest of the gifts and represents the Truth of the first Age; *óð* (the self of Intellect and Impulse) that sees life in the Sword Age of Heimdall who gives man culture and philosophy; *lá* (blood) characterizes the Wind Age as both the realization of man as biological being or race, and the shedding of blood in warfare; the last Age being of the body, all that is physical, material, and destructive. The four Ages seem to correspond to caste as well, each period descending according to Kon, Jarl, Karl, and Thrall; this likewise correlates well with what we know as traditional tribalism: leader/chieftain, hunter/warrior, shaman/priest, and trickster, which all evolved into the plebeian perspective of today's society.

In the final analysis, the importance of *Ár* can be found in the fact that it is a rune, an eternally existing symbol of the very framework of life, and together, the significance of *Ár* and *Aldr* is found near the very beginning of the Voluspa: *ár vas alda thar er ymir bygdhi*, or "time was Eternal when Ymir lived." It is this Eternal Existence the Sovereign seeks.

Ragnarokr: Death and Eternal Existence

"The last complete triumph over egoism, the demonstration of his full ascension to immortality, a man can only show us by his death; and that not by his accidental, but by his NECESSARY death, the logical sequel to his actions, the last fulfillment of his being. The celebration of such a death is the noblest thing that men can enter on. It reveals to us in the nature of this one man laid bare by death the whole content of our nature. But we fix this revelation in surest hold of memory by the conscious representation of that death itself, and in order to make its purport clear to us by the representation of those actions which found their necessary conclusion in that death."

– Richard Wagner.

Death is the ultimate unknown, elusive and imperceptible, yet the highest state one can strive for or attain in this realm, provided it is a necessary and noble one. Throughout time many Fólk have attempted to explain death in countless ways, tried to improve its image through subjective hypothesis and hyperbole, and given it significance

Ragnarokr: Death and Eternal Existence

in a plethora of ways, though the fact remains that none can KNOW with any certainty what, if anything, occurs when we die. It could very well be that death is the end, literally, and means absolutely nothing, has no point, and is just simply ceasing to exist. Those with strong spiritual beliefs do not believe this to be the case, but it takes trust and faith in the form of what feels right to one's inherent Instinct to accede to any belief in the afterlife.

For the Sovereign, death is but the sun setting in the soul, a normal and natural relinquishing of ego, allowing spirit to separate from body and return to the collective from whence it came, to either exist eternally with the Gods or be reborn; the third option being that of Extinction. The sun, being the center of the universe, emanates the very essence of existence, externally and internally, thus is the soul of both as well. In the same way this energy is received by each and every planet, star, etc. in the solar system, so too does every cell in our body embrace the energy of our soul, our very own solar system. In addition, the microcosmic and macrocosmic souls are ever exchanging energies and this is the strongest synergistic relationship in existence; it is also why spirituality is so important to our Fólk and Sovereigns strive to knowingly nurture this relationship.

Mortal men value life overmuch; Gods not at all, as they know that death is but a necessary conclusion, a cessation of Breath, a purification which, like life itself, is certainly sacred, though the two are inseparably linked and should be seen as such. Death as a whole (in the extant wisdom teachings) is interesting in relation to the Gods: we learn that all of the most renowned will fall in battle at the Ragnarokr, as do their opponents, presumably to make way for the next generation, the next age of things to come, as the wheel turns and evolution takes its course.

Every person who dies does so because the Breath of Life, the spirit, is expelled from their body; they are no longer able to accumulate *oðic* energy. It doesn't matter if one passes of old age, is killed in battle, dies of immolation, drowning, disease, etc. the final act remains the same: the expulsion of Breath, our *önd*, the very life-giving animating principle without which none can exist in this realm. After death the body returns to the wooden form from which it was found by the Gods prior to their gifts, signifying that the soul has left the body.

The topic of immortality has fascinated Fólk from the moment men first realized we were corporeal beings who age, wither, and perish over time; it is a concept that has even consumed some people's lives completely, yet remains elusive and illusory simply because it does not, and could not, exist as many envision it. Immortality is a misnomer, unconsciously employed to describe a concept difficult for most to comprehend. Mortality is the destruction of the physical body and cannot be anything else; once the body has this quality it cannot suddenly have an indestructible nature, nor is it possible for the body to exist perpetually, regardless of how advanced scientific procedures at prolonging life become. What most confuse with immortality is the Eternal Existence of the soul, the *laeti* of *önd* and *óð*, what the Voluspa refers to as aldabjarn or born of Eternity.

Existence is the energy expended by or exerted upon an organism, thus, if either is Eternal then so too will be the existence of that organism. The law of entropy states that the more energy put in to something specific, the more chaos is created, however, this only highlights the notion that destruction is essential to recreation. Effective Evolution is defined by intent, the amount of energy expelled in the pursuit of perfection, the annihilation of the inferior in favor of the superior. This is Sovereignty and the constant exchange of energy will lead us along the Path to Eternal Existence.

There are three states the soul can enter into after death and they correlate with both the rate of vibration each achieves and the three realms of existence: Extinction, Entropy, and Eternal Existence. Extinction is extinguishing the active and animating principle and banishing it to Niflhel. Entropy is the state of stasis the soul maintains in Hel awaiting rebirth. Eternal Existence is the endless afterlife among the Gods in Asgardh. Likewise, each of the three is reached through a gate dedicated to their individual purpose.

When one ventures through *nágrindr*, the gate of death, they step foot upon *náströnd* (the strand of death) where they are isolated as an outcaste; this strand of land in Niflhel is the place an individual's soul is banished to once they have offended nature. Exile is Extinction for Fólk who place an importance upon a noble reputation and renown. The Voluspa tells us that *náströnd* is far from the sun, which is as severe a punishment as one can receive when we consider the importance of the sun's life-giving properties; it goes on to speak of venom dripping down from above, reminiscent of Loki's punishment after he had murdered Baldr. The Voluspa also asserts that Niflhel is reserved for oath-breakers, murderers, and sexual deviants; these worthless ones would wade through wild rivers and in Tacitus' Germania we find that those who were stained by abominable vices were drowned in bogs and mires as "infamy ought to be buried out of sight." This muck and mud would certainly be away from the sun, in the darkest part of Hel, Niflhel, a fitting and proper punishment for malicious miscreants.

The gate of Hel, *Helgrindr*, opens onto the *Helvegr* or Helways, which lead to this abode, that of rebirth and renewal where Fólk await a return to Midgardh. The meaning of the Old Norse Hel (from which monotheists usurped their version) is "to cover" or "hide," which implies covering the body with either dirt or some sort of shroud to keep it from the sun as though it were unworthy of exposure to Fólk or Gods, of being laid bare to any and all who would examine the life of the individual. The notion that Hel is a state of stasis or Entropy expecting rebirth is best illustrated by Baldr's death: we know he was murdered by Loki through Baldr's blind brother Hodhr, however, he was sent to Hel on a funeral pyre to indicate there was no shame attached to his death. Interestingly, while Loki was punished for the murder by being bound and tortured with dripping poison, Hodhr was slain by Vali, laid upon the pyre and sent to Hel to join his brother. Both will be reborn after the Ragnarokr. This demonstrates how little importance the Gods placed upon death itself, as well as the fact that Hel was seen as the abode of rebirth, not punishment.

Burial itself implies rebirth and the need to live again, as that which is given to the earth shall be reborn from it. The natural world substantiates this metaphysical concept through the physical: a rose sprouts from a seed, matures, blossoms into a beautiful flower that many will gaze upon with wonder and awe, only to wilt with age, decay, perish, and rot into mulch, becoming fertilizer, decomposing into the earth to nourish the next seed, germinating new growth. This process repeats itself perpetually as the natural order of cyclical time and evolution. So it is with Fólk: when man dies what remains is that which shall become the next generation, either here in Midgardh, or in Asgardh. A botanist may attempt to consciously cultivate the perfect rose through repeated germination, refining this rose until a specific specimen is cultured and the same can be said for Fólk, who seek Sovereignty through Effective Evolution, intentionally reaching for the intense and infinite.

In the end, Entropy is the state of inertia a soul stays in until such time as it is revived. The straw death mentioned in the mythology likewise confirms this concept; during the Heathen Era straw was seen as something of small worth or significance, too insubstantial to provide support in a desperate situation, such as the Ragnarokr, and so someone who was considered unworthy of entering Eternity when they died were believed to have been the recipient of a straw death. This type of death was the result of having lived an empty life, without purpose or pursuit of anything worthwhile, the noble deeds and extraordinary acts that garner good reputation and renown. Those who die a straw death end up in Hel, which originally did not have a negative connotation per se, but was simply seen as the abode one's soul inhabits until they are reborn to take another shot at worthing themselves according to their Skuld; this is what the straw death implies, the return of the soul to Midgardh, another attempt at worthing one's self, unless of course the individual lives an ignoble life as an oathbreaker, murderer, or sexual deviant.

In Grimnismal we learn that "all worlds are open to the *Aesir* when ketils are heaved from the Hearth" and in this context *Aesir* should be viewed as synonymous with *aethel, óðal, aryan, aire*, etc., the noble souls that will attain Eternal Existence in the afterlife. These Fólk, descendants of the Gods, were traditionally laid upon the flames, a funeral pyre being the ultimate sign of respect for the fallen; ketil is a kenning for the body, which will be heaved from the Hearth fire to join the Gods in Asgardh in the abode most appropriate to how they lived their lives. *Valgrindr*, the gate of the slain, is that which leads to this realm. Immolation allows the soul to ascend through the smoke into the atmosphere (atmo-: *atman/ athem*) or what was once referred to as the aether (*aethel/óðal/aryan*) of Asgardh where it joins Mimir's Well. Conversely, to bury the body is to trap the *Laeti* in the earth, here in Midgardh, preventing it from crossing the bridge between this realm and the next, or joining the Gods. The God Ullr, protector of the Hearth fire, is the first to welcome all ascended souls and guide them through the proper gate to the appropriate abode, denoting their place in the afterlife. This place being determined by deeds during life: noble deeds to Valhalla, no notable deeds through *Helgrindr* to Hel, and ignoble deeds through *nágrindr* to Niflhel.

Eternal Existence has a threefold quality: physical, conscious, and metaphysical. The physical is one's heritage, the legacy perpetuated by their progeny, who prolong the genetic lineage into Eternity. The conscious comes from the reputation and regard remaining in the memory once an individual has passed: if one is remembered by many or for having achieved something exceptional then that memory will carry them into the infinite. The metaphysical is the most ambiguous of all, as it is both mystical and mysterious, requiring an element of faith for Fólk to fulfill and is the force that propels most religious practice today. Interestingly, these three qualities correspond perfectly with the three things all religions have in common: where we come from (physical), how we should live in this life (conscious), and where we go when we die, or the metaphysical. More important to our Fólk, however, they likewise correlate well with the blood/body (*Lá ok Litu Goða*), consciousness (*óð*), and spirit (*önd*), the gifts given to Askr and Embla.

Sovereignty alone holds the key to Eternal Existence for our Fólk, for though each of us is inherently divine and our soul is indestructible, it cannot partake of its own permanence without proper preparation: the physical and philosophical discipline along the Path of Odhinn.

On the purely physical, the importance of procreation can best be illustrated through the words of Tacitus:

> *"To limit the number of children or to destroy any of their subsequent offspring is accounted infamous."*

The significance of gaining glory by achieving noble deeds that would be remembered and subsequently etched into the genetic memory for all Fólk to follow is found in the Edda:

> *"Both cattle and kinsmen perish,*
> *you too shall some day die*
> *though the one thing that stays the same*
> *is the regard and respect you give your name.*
> *Both cattle and kinsmen perish,*
> *you too shall some day die*
> *though the one thing that stays the same*
> *is the renown and reputation you gain and attain."*

The modern word die actually comes from the Old Norse *deyja*, meaning "to expire," literally to breathe one's last breath and it is this release of the spirit after seizing Sovereignty of the soul that results in Eternal Existence. To become Sovereign, however, one must expose, embrace, and effect their individual Skuld, what should be, pursue it passionately to perfection, and exercise absolute authority over the self.

Ultimately, those who place their trust exclusively in physical preservation and existence will realize the futility of such faith, as their conviction will dissipate with the decay, disintegration, and destruction of the body; they will experience death as an end, while those who become Sovereign, achieving a state of supraconsciousness will welcome dissolution as the beginning of Eternal Existence.

Our earliest ancestors struggled against the forces of nature for survival and it was only after beginning to understand basic laws of environmental elements that they were able to achieve some sort of victory over them, i.e. rain required shelter, the cold demanded coverings for warmth, etc. At this point they likely only had a rudimentary notion that death had any significance whatsoever. As our Fólk gained more knowledge of the natural elements they likely struggled less with them and could focus more on the hunt for food and it is at this point that sacrifice of the self for the whole took on a sacred context. The hunter was prized for his prowess and the loss of even a single one would reverberate throughout the tribe, for both the hunger that would result, as well as the fact that he had given his life for the Fólk. It is natural that this would take on a spiritual significance and special honor would be paid the fallen. Once we began to settle on specific tracts of land to cultivate it and raise livestock the next phase of progression would be to turn our weapons on one another in a struggle for space, substance, and eventually expansion, which continues today; thanks to monotheism we can add religion to the list of things we wage war over. Nevertheless, the shift from hunter to warrior would be a natural one, as would be the way in which we would honor those who fell in battle: to this day Fólk around the world pay homage to those who perish in armed conflicts and it should ever be so.

Conflict is inevitable and it has been so since the dawn of man; the durable blade is one forged in the fires of ordeal. From the moment we take our first breath until we expel the last we struggle to exist and so it will always be. In the same way, we will continue to honor our dead and have faith in an afterlife, if for no other reason than we want the best for those Fólk we have an emotional connection to. Many modern adherents mistakenly believe that Valhalla is the end all be all to our way of life, that we lead a noble life here in Midgardh, die a warrior's death, to feast in the hall of the slain until Ragnarokr; a small segment sincerely believe this to be the ideal despite the fact that it excludes the majority of our Fólk, particularly women, whose contributions exceed men's in many ways. In truth, it takes all types to make a tribe thrive and the afterlife is no different: there are many halls one can and should seek out, just as worthy in their own way as Valhalla.

That said, those who do profess to be dedicated to Odhinn and to entering Valhalla to prepare for Ragnarokr, take this commitment too lightly today. Valhalla is the home of the elite, those willing to literally give their lives for the Fólk, to sacrifice for the whole in order to achieve victory over the forces of darkness and destruction. Most have lost faith, genuine faith that comes from both belief in our way of life and loyalty to duty (our obligations as descendants of divinity), thus Valhalla has been bereft of Fólk since the reign of monotheism began. We live in a soft society today, one where warrior is a symbolic term used to designate any sort of perceived or perverse struggle. Monotheism has weakened the fabric of our faith to the point that many Fólk feel as though the war were lost before the battle has even begun; as such, it is even more imperative today (than any other time in history) that the Sovereign step forward and fight for our future. Thus is the task for Fólk of faith, for the way of the warrior is the path of wisdom.

The notion of Valhalla has likely existed in some form or fashion from the earliest time, evolving to meet the needs of the Fólk as those needs evolved. In fact, it was Odhinn the Reformer in the Ynglinga Saga who recognized a need for worthy warriors to combat chaos at the Ragnarokr and dedicated those who fell to weapons to the Sovereign Self; presumably, these are the Einherjar said to inhabit Valhalla, though it should be remembered that not all Einherjar go to or remain in Valhalla, thus the two should not be seen as synonymous. What Valhalla represents is that the battle never ends, nor does life in the sense of the soul, but we continue to evolve even after relinquishing the physical body. The Ragnarokr certainly denotes a physical battle here in Midgardh, however, metaphysically the war will be waged between the forces of chaos and order, dark and light, and to the victor will go the spoils of spiritual superiority; these are the lesser and Greater Holy Wars spoken of by Julius Evola. Esoterically, Eternal Existence is a Higher state of consciousness than is possible in this realm and while the eternal battle between light and dark is that of conscious versus subconscious

SOVEREIGNTY: THE EMPIRICAL PATH OF ODHINN

awareness (the desire and drive to know all there is to know), this is the conflict of man becoming here in Midgardh, not that of those who have attained supraconsciosuness. Symbolically, we can see this best by Baldr the bright being in Hel through the Ragnarokr, the light being covered until Surtr, "the black one," razes the ground to make room for new growth and Baldr will be reborn to shine brilliantly once more.

Perhaps one of the most misunderstood concepts in our wisdom teachings is that of Einherjar. First, this is the plural of *einheri*, most often translated as "one who fights alone," though can also be defined as "inheritors"; the former comes from separating *ein-* as alone and *-heri* as fighter, while the latter is taken as a whole and it is in this sense that it is synonymous with Sovereignty. While it is certainly true that all of the inhabitants of Valhalla are Einherjar, not all Einherjar go to Valhalla; many who are chosen by Freya take the Field of Fólk to become *fylgjur*, while others assume appropriate roles in Asgardh. As elite warriors, the Einherjar of Valhalla prepare to take the plain of battle, *Vígriðr*, though as inheritors they are those who fulfill the gift for a gift by realizing their inherent divinity; the Gods gave us the gift of *ørlag*, the ability to attain Sovereignty, and it is our obligation to return this gift by becoming Sovereign. Either way, Einherjar walk the way of the warrior, that of the Path of Odhinn.

An interesting hypothesis for Fólk to explore is that Thor may very well have been the first mortal to attain Eternal Existence by following the Path of Odhinn. Thor is the only one ever specifically referred to as *Einheri* and in this sense should be seen as a hero akin to Hercules. The significant stanza, however, is found in Harbardh's Lay, one too many Fólk are quick to dismiss:

> *"To deny it is insignificant; to succeed is difficult*
> *long is it to the stock and long to the stone*
> *the way of the weak winds to the land of men*
> *Thor will find Fjorgyn, her son seeks*
> *the Path to Odhinn's realm she shows her children"*

This entire stanza refers to the Path of Odhinn. Those who elect not to step foot upon this Path are without meaning, while those who seek Sovereignty will need to demonstrate dedication and discipline to succeed. A stock is a block of wood and the allusion is likely to the state in which Askr and Embla were originally found by the Gods. Fjorgyn is mother earth and as such her children are those born of the earth, in contrast to the aldabjarn, those born of Eternity; more important perhaps is that she is likely the feminine representation of the Sovereign Self (as Hlodhyn), thus is Odhinn's counterpart. For Fólk then the Path can be said to wind its way from the realm of the giants (Utgardh), to that of men (Midgardh), and finally into Asgardh as the home of the Gods, those born of Eternity, and abode of Eternal Existence.

Another interesting interpretation of Einherjar comes from the Grimnismal, where we are told that 432,000 Einherjar will exit Valhalla to wage war against the wolf and if we see in these single days it becomes significant to the duration of the Wolf Age: according to the ancient sexigesimal system of reckoning, in which a base of 60 was used, this 432,000 would be exactly 1,200 years; of this last, 100 years would bookend the actual Wolf Age as the twilight periods after dusk and before dawn. Using this as a foundation, and knowing the Ages descend into degeneracy, we can conclude that the Battleax Age was 4,800 years, the Sword Age was 3,600 years, the Wind Age was 2,400 years, and the Wolf Age will be 1,200 for a total of 12,000 years. How this would correlate with more modern "scientific" calculations is still a work in progress, however, these time periods are all momentous.

Either way, we know that the four Ages of man are decreasing periods of illumination, with a final Age of darkness wherein degeneracy, immorality, and a lack of spirituality will reign before the wheel turns; between each of these Ages is a Ragnarokr, a twilight period, marked by a paradigm shift of some sort. The last of these twilight periods, being fraught as it is with senseless violence, ignorance, and sacrilege, will culminate in a turning point for our Fólks' evolution, brought about by devastating destruction, completely destroying this degenerate people to make room for a more highly evolved Fólk. These last are Nietzsche's *Übermensch*, Fólk who followed the Path of Odhinn to Sovereignty. The Einherjar.

Many Fólk misunderstand Ragnarokr, even among modern adherents to Odhinism. Just as every religion has its own cosmology and theology, so too does each contain as eschatology, an end of the world scenario, even if only the end of the world as we know it, rather than total annihilation as such. The Ragnarokr is one such, often confused as an event or incident alone, though it is a period of time, representing the turning of the wheel of cyclical time, the evolution of both men and Gods. Our eschatology makes no unrealistic claims of total victory or overcoming chaos completely to create a heaven on earth or perpetual paradise of some sort; instead, our Fólk have long known that the Wolf Age would see our world sink as low as it possibly could before a renewal was required, and the Ragnarokr represents such a revival.

Ragnarokr is often translated as "doom of the Gods," however, this is not as comprehensive as it could be; it could just as likely be translated as "withdrawal of advisors," referring to a period of time during which Fólk will have difficulty generating advice from the Gods, or genetic memory. This is why Ragnarokr is often referred to as a twilight period: twilight is the point between the illumination of light and the dejection and desolation of darkness. Jacob Grimm has defined *Regin* as "the powers that consult together and direct the world" and though this term is often used as a kenning for the Gods, "the advisors" is just as appropriate. It may very well be that the specific Ragnarokr described in the Voluspa refers to the end of divine guidance altogether and the elevation of the Sovereign, indicating that our Fólk have reached a point where they no longer need the *Regin* to hold our collective hands, what Nietzsche would refer to as moving beyond good and evil, and this is ultimately the purpose of evolution, both spiritual or otherwise.

Either way, most of us have heard the refrain "it's darkest before the dawn" and this is what the Ragnarokr represents: a period of imperfect clarity following the Heathen dark age, what we call the Wolf Age, which is itself marked by monotheistic madness and desperate degeneracy. Many Fólk view the Voluspa stanzas regarding the Ragnarokr as foretelling real world events, everything from a nuclear winter for the *fimbulvetr* to the sun going supernova. One of the more interesting theories is that of the 12P/Pons-Brooks comet that passed close to earth c1523bce, believed to have brought warfare into the world; this comet will again pass the earth in 2024 and it could very well be that this will bring about widespread destruction.

Nevertheless, *Líf* and *Lífthrasir*, Life and Longing-for-Life respectively, indicate the fact that our Fólk will survive whatever the Ragnarokr turns out to be here in Midgardh; like Askr and Embla, these two come from trees to repopulate our world, which implies that at some point the Fólk-Soul will awaken to its impending extinction before it becomes too late. The fact that the Ragnarokr represents the cyclical nature of time, evolution, and regeneration on the macrocosmic scale is seen in Muspellheim and Niflheim: when these two homes of fire and ice came together in Ginnungagap the result was Audhumbla, Ymir, and all of existence; conversely, at the destructive end it is the *fimbulvetr*, three ice cold winters without a summer, that will begin the Ragnarokr and the fires of Surtr that will conclude it, ushering in a new era, the Fridhr Age.

    In the final analysis, death is never to be feared, let alone mourned, but celebrated, emphatically embraced even, as the ultimate achievement and culmination of a noble life. Odhinn is well aware that he will fall to the Fenris Wolf during the final battle, yet does not attempt to avoid it or change his *dómr*; instead, he does not hesitate to lead both Gods and Einherjar into the fray, embracing his death as the greatest honor, and it is this faith and conviction that the Sovereign must reclaim. Courage is found in those whose spirit is the strongest: convinced the *laeti* is infinite and indestructible, the individual reflects this fearlessness instinctively, knowing without a doubt that Eternal Existence is the destination the Path of Odhinn leads to.

SOVEREIGNTY

"You solitaries of today, you shall one day be a people; from you who have chosen out yourselves, shall a chosen people spring, and from this chosen people the Übermensch."

— Friedrich Nietzsche

Sovereignty is the substantial synthesis of all potential and possibility, the distinctive dominion over innate powers, and Absolute Autonomy through integral independence and individuality. Sovereign has the dual meaning of supreme ruler or power and independent, dependent upon no external source outside of one's self; supreme in this sense being absolute, related to supra- or "above," thus divine. Sovereign in every sense is spiritual superiority, the supreme Self embodying elite, foremost, principal, Heathen, individual, King/Queen, et. al.

A Sovereign needs neither doctrine, dogma, nor divine intervention; only eyes that see, an ability to feel, and a mind that thinks. Sovereignty is an empirical Path, one that relies on contemplation and experience rather than revelation as such; it is existential in the truest sense, as personal responsibility and existing as an individual are of paramount importance. Discernment is the one-dimensional insight of the Intellect and knowledge comes from this, while wisdom is the experiential understanding of this dimension. Actual awareness is the three-dimensional concurrent comprehension of Intellect, Impulse, and Instinct, thus realization is existential. Knowledge cannot sustain the spirit alone; instead, it requires the energy of emotion and demands the right action of experience to give life to knowledge. This then is the Empirical Path of Odhinn.

Sovereignty is synonymous with *theomorphosis* to the extent that it is the transformation of man into god. Any process that has as its principal and pivotal objective, differentiation that affects actualization of one's inherent nature efficaciously, is transcendental, thus Traditional, while egalitarian emphasis is a profane regression, as it accentuates the secular similarities of substance over spiritual superiority to the detriment of divinity. First and foremost, Sovereignty is self-exploration, thus becomes a journey of discovery and development, transformation and transcendence that Tradition evinces as the Empirical Path of Odhinn.

Sovereignty then can be affirmed as the Alchemy of Individuation. Alchemy is often translated as the art of transformation and it is through Effective Evolution that we are capable of morphing from man into god. Like the Greater and Lesser Holy Wars of Evola, the Alchemy of Individuation takes the form of both interior and exterior transmutation, that of spirit and matter respectively, the Law of Embodiment brought into balance.

Alchemy should first be understood in its simplest form, that of the transmutation of an inferior substance into a superior one; Individuation is the realization of one's inherent nature and through this, the attainment of godhead. The Alchemy of Individuation then is the elevation of self to Sovereign Self, *óð* to Odhinn, that of the fully realized, independent, and individual state of supraconsciousness; Alchemy is a rainbow bridging Asgardh and Midgardh, spirit and matter, the art of the hermetic philosophy that cloaks in occultic knowledge and esoteric texts enigmatic emblems meant to relate the secret sciences of life and death, nature, and Eternity.

As any blacksmith can attest, impurities are destroyed through extreme heat, and the ascetic alchemist is capable of generating inner heat as inspiration that incinerates imperfections until what remains is relatively free from fault or defect. Additionally, the alchemical transmutation of lead into gold is analogous to the transformation of the physical into solar energy, with the aim of achieving Eternal Existence. Jung believed alchemy to be a Western proto-psychology dedicated to the achievement of Individuation, while Evola saw it as a secret science of human and natural transformation. It has been said that the ideas of Carl Jung and Julius Evola are incompatible, that they are and will always remain at odds with one another, however, Odhinism, and in particular Sovereignty, is the ground upon which the two would have discussed philosophy and the psyche, bringing into balance their notions of spirituality and alchemy. Sovereignty sees in alchemy a syncretism of the two, a mixture of magico-religious practices and psycho-spiritual beliefs reminiscent of the pact that saw shared worship among *Aesir* and *Vanir*.

The manner in which an individual thinks, moves, feels, and rests reveals their connection to their inherent self and a strong bond between an individual and their *óð* will be mirrored in the manner in which they think, move, feel, and rest. The body is both a tool for transformation and a reflection of the inner self; it is individualized *Ørlag*, the medium necessary to the manifestation and attainment of Odhinn as Sovereign Self. *Lá ok Litu Goða* is not only flesh but the means by which each of us relates to and interacts with the soul, how we respond to Impulse and intellectual urges; the creation and nourishment of this connection is the initiation and art of spirituality respectively.

Alchemy can be characterized as the science of life that studies and controls consciousness; the alchemist is aware of a concrete connection between energy, ego, and matter, thus alchemy is the art of manipulating both spirit and self in matter, in an effort to effect evolution or balance internal chaos. The seed of life was planted for the soul to evolve, grow, and ultimately reach a state of perfection that mirrors the universal order; just as ultimate reality is self-created so too must we be Creators of our own reality through Effective Evolution.

In alchemy each step or phase represents not merely an inner awakening or initiation, but a practical physical procedure performed in the terrestrial realm as well: for every philosophical truth there is a ritual to reinforce that fact to the extent it can be verified. Thus the practices of the physical become confirmation of spiritual development. Blót is held at significant solar and lunar points, as these contain the most powerful and beneficent energies; the planets likewise play an important role in ritual as they too emanate *oðic* energy. Everything in alchemy is composed according to the tripartite structure, known as the three kingdoms: mercury (energy), sulphur (individualized essence), and salt, the physical body. These correspond to *önd*, *óð*, and *Lá ok Litu Goða* respectively; the art of the alchemist is to combine these three in perfect proportion just as it is for the Sovereign.

To this end then Individuation is the process of becoming a person, an integrated personality that we consider one individual; it is self-realization, a search for totality, the discovery of the divine in one's self. A Sovereign must become independent, separate themselves in a manner consistent with their individual Skuld. Excellence is effected through noble deeds, actions, and accomplishments: one's Worth. Self-realization can only come about through becoming the supreme ruler of the self, the discipline that allows for complete control of one's mental, physical, emotional, and spiritual faculties.

Individuation entails becoming aware of and comprehending the Persona, the Ego, the Shadow, the *Anima/Animus*, and finally the self. The Persona is a complicated system connecting the individual conscious with society, while the Ego is the center of this consciousness, the I of identity. The Shadow represents unknown or little known characteristics of the Ego, those thoughts and feelings Fólk deny in themselves, but see clearly in other people; the Shadow is the inferior base animal nature in all Fólk, the part that undertakes impulsive and ill-considered deeds. The *Anima* is the personification of all female psychological tendencies in the psyche of men, including feelings, moods, intuition, receptivity for the irrational, the ability for personal love, a feel for nature, and a man's attitude toward the unconscious. Jung asserted that facing one's Shadow was the "apprentice-piece," while confronting the *Anima* or *Animus* was the masterpiece; in early European spirituality it was held that to see one's *fylgja* or *fetch* meant the individual was *fey* or doomed to die.

Individuation is a natural inherent process that manifests from within; the experience of the self which culminates in individuation is the realization that we are divine, unique, and yet connected to the collective unconscious in a way that is beyond mortal comprehension. The initial objective of Individuation is the integration of all aspects of the personality and progresses into the process of becoming completely conscious of the self, the procedure by which one explores every facet of their *Ørlag* and unites the archetype of the unconscious with their inherent nature to produce a perfected state, one that transcends the mediocre and mundane to the superior and Sovereign. The personality can be deformed by lack of experience or education; our modern world does not give enough opportunity to experience the archetype of the Shadow. Once we do, however, we can trigger the transcendental function wherein one unifies the opposing tendencies of the personality, the goal being realization of all aspects of this personality as they were initially instilled in one's center and the development of the potential unity.

This Alchemy of Individuation is epitomized by Odhinn, the very framework from which Sovereignty becomes a spiritual, philosophical, and transcendental way of life. In all of the spiritual and sacred texts or teachings around the world, throughout the history of man, none give a stronger example of Sovereignty than the Norse Allfather Odhinn. In Odhinn the monotheist would find a supreme being to be worshipped and obeyed without question, while the polytheist sees one god that reigns over others; the Sovereign, however, recognizes Odhinn as an equal, the first among equals to be sure, in that he intentionally sought out, realized, and revealed the Path for Fólk to follow should they be willing and worthy. Everything Odhinn as Sovereign Self represents is summed up in...

> *"Wounded I hung*
> *Sacrificed myself to my Self*
> *On that tree that none*
> *May ever know*
> *What root beneath it runs"*

Like Odhinn himself, Sovereignty is achieved when the lower self is cast aside in favor of the Higher or Sovereign Self. Man is self, while godhead is Self; one either embraces their base nature or that of the divine. What the Sovereign sacrifices is not what defines them or makes them an individual, but all that stands in the way of Higher purpose, possibility, and potential. Sovereignty is not monotheistic, atheistic, nor polytheistic, but metatheistic, moving man beyond deification of outside forces into the elevation of one's self to divinity. There is no doubt that the time for deism has come and gone, though we cannot move beyond this by denying divinity as atheists would have us do either. Rather, the natural progression from belief in many gods to "one true god" can only see its culmination in the Sovereignty of the self, the elevation of each individual to godhead. Absolute autonomy is achieved through Sovereignty, the evolution from simple to complex organism, from the mediocre masses to chosen and ultimately the *Übermensch* as Nietzsche understood it. In this way Sovereignty can best be understood as theomorphic existentialism.

The symbolism of Odhinn's ravens is significant to the Sovereign, for, while *óð* is the potential for Odhinn as Sovereign Self, *hugr* and *munr* are likewise the potential for Huginn and Muninn respectively. The Sovereign Intellect is one that considers only objective truth (rather than subjective perception or divine discernment) and is the Wisdom to Power of Odhinn; the Sovereign Impulse acts upon necessary sensation and stimuli, rather than the profane desires of the material world and is the Will to Power of Odhinn. Odhinn then is the ultimate equimotive and it is this balance that the Sovereign seeks for the self.

It may be wondered why, in a spiritual system such as Sovereignty, there is a concentration on consciousness and the simple answer is that we are not aware of our own excellence: it is only through our realization (conscious awareness) of our innate divinity, the superb nature we are born with, that we are able to even locate the Path. The paradox of perfection is perpetuated by the profane notion that we are all flawed in some way, that our very birth is a blemish; in reality, like the acorn has within it the ideal oak, so too are each of us exactly what we are supposed to be. The notion that a newborn child is corrupt, somehow guilty of a sin, is absurd, abject worth at its worst; the result of teaching our children from the earliest age that they are defective in some way is that they ultimately seek spirituality beyond their self rather than recognizing and realizing the perfection within. It is simply the separation from Source that occurs at birth that perpetuates the perception of imperfection; conversely, once we reconnect with the Source, we become aware once more of our perfection and can pursue it along the Path through Effective Evolution as we seek Sovereignty through what should be.

Each of us has unconscious, subconscious, and conscious domains within our *verald*, the universe in which we exist as individuals, corresponding to Instinct, Impulse, and Intellect respectively; to the degree that the former correspond to the latter, the conscious is our self, the subconscious our Shadow, and unconscious are patterns of propensities. The unconscious is unique, however, in that there exists a personal unconscious from which come inclinations and intuition, as well as a collective unconscious, the

Sovereignty: The Empirical Path of Odhinn

Source itself wherein the paradigm of patterns and perception exist; this collective is consanguineous, passed on genetically one generation to the next. The framework for Sovereignty can be found in the motto of many Heathen Fólk for countless centuries: *TRÚA Á MATT SITT OK MEGINN*, which translates as "to trust in one's own Will and Power," thus to be completely self-sufficient and Sovereign over one's self.

As a self seeking spiritual harmony, each of us can only become consciously aware of the Path and step foot upon it once; this initiation creates a paradigm shift in consciousness that becomes permanent immediately and can only be experienced a single time, as it is evolutionary and expansive. The self of Intellect and Impulse is a function that allows us to distinguish ourselves from others and a construct that orders our psychological qualities. The self in this sense is temporal, only giving us an identity in this life when kept at a base level of existence. Conversely, when an individual steps foot upon the Path seeking Sovereignty, it begins a journey that can never allow it to be profane again: it is required to embrace the essence of inherent Instinct and balance conscious and unconscious realms to achieve a supraconscious state. The Sovereign Self is the central archetype in the collective unconscious, as the sun is the center of our solar system, and both symbolize order, organization, and unity, bringing together our personality and planets respectively. Consciously attaining this Sovereign Self is the purpose of the Path, as it is the most complete expression of the highest possible unity, that which we refer to as individuality.

The collective unconscious is a vast reservoir of archetypes consisting of characteristics many Fólk have in common, unique to the Fólk-Soul, and which we inherit at birth; many arise from an inner necessity rather than a conscious pursuit. These archetypes are the result of various experiences of Fólk as represented by the numerous Gods and Goddesses; these archetypes will perpetually manifest themselves and alone they are neutral, without value judgment attached to them, though together they make up the entirety of the Fólk-Soul.

The personal unconscious consists of hidden aspects of our self that continuously attempt to realign our conscious awareness, to bring us into balance, primarily by influencing behavior and action in a way that compensates our conscious efforts to the contrary; conversely, the collective unconscious seeks to control the spiritual development of the archetype, the pattern of perfection, and though there seems to be a barrier between the personal and collective, there can be no doubt the bridge is our blood, the genetic memory of all potential and possibility. Reality is articulated through consciousness (Intellect) and its ultimate objective is to become aware of all things; the subconscious seeks complete control of one's Impulse (their Will to Power), while the personal unconscious ever strives to attune both of these to the Instinct, to develop the natural ability to utilize instincts without effort. With all of this in mind, the process of Individuation reaches completion when the Impulse and Intellect are reconciled with the collective unconscious to form a supraconscious state, that of the Sovereign Self. In the final analysis, Sovereignty is existential theomorphism, the empirical transformation of man into god.

The content of an archetype is unconscious, though it undergoes a transformation when it becomes conscious, when it comes into the light and is perceived; the manner in which it is transformed is entirely dependent upon the conscious state of the individual in which the archetype has arisen. An archetype is experienced as image and emotion, as well as Instinct; its content is primal, only taking form as it becomes conscious, being shaped almost exclusively by experiences had by the observer, both cultural and spiritual. Heritage then plays an integral role in the development of the self because it is instrumental in shaping the archetype; conversely, a lack of ancestral traditions, practices, etc. prevents proper understanding of the archetype. The environment in which an individual develops can deform, stimulate, or stabilize their growth or lack thereof; it can and does interfere with and influence the evolution of the self by removing the necessary and natural stimuli needed to nourish their inherent nature properly.

In the conscious recognition of the awakened archetype we take the preliminary step upon the Path that leads to Sovereignty and ultimately each of us is solely responsible for that first footfall, as well as pursuing Higher consciousness along it. This initial interval, however, requires an initiation, something sadly lacking in society today. In the Heathen Hof all those who propose to seek Sovereignty are instructed to initially climb the peak of the nearest mountain, alone, and commune with the Gods, for...

> *"[In] Nordic-Aryan tradition the idea of the mountain is often associated with Valhalla, the seat of heroes and of deified kings, as well as with Asgardh, the seat of the Gods situated at the center pole of the earth... this is a very high divine mountain on the peak of which beyond the*

SOVEREIGNTY: THE EMPIRICAL PATH OF ODHINN

clouds shines an eternal clarity from which Odhinn observes the world... it is up here on these peaks beyond which lies another country—and from similar experiences—that one can truly perceive the secret of that which is imperium *in the highest sense of the word...such a tradition is formed only when a heroic vocation awakens as an irresistible force from above and where it is animated by a will to keep going, overcoming every material or rational obstacle."*

– Julius Evola

It is only among the most elevated ascents that, alone with our self we can connect with something greater than that self, marking mountain climbing as a method to gain spiritual liberation, and it is this emancipation that enables us to step foot upon the Path. Individuality demands the destruction of all bonds, breaking barriers, and shedding shackles. All initiation should be trying, pushing the limits of physical, mental, and emotional endurance; only then can it be considered spiritual. Most Fólk have heard of the "second wind" that comes from persistence, persevering beyond what one believes their boundaries to be, and any initiation worthy of being called such or seen as a preliminary step upon the Path, consciously seeks such superhuman effort; the Sovereign must be disciplined and dedicated to the superior. There is a point for all Fólk at which the physical limitation is reached and spiritual reserves must be relied upon, though many never know what those boundaries are, let alone try to explore the frontiers or further from their comfort zone; the Sovereign seeks out the unknown with abandon, striving to live with no limits, beyond or above time.

Sovereignty synthesizes Intellect, Impulse, and Instinct through contemplation and action as Will to Power: for every philosophical truth that we must comprehend, there is a corresponding ritual to reinforce that particular truth. Each of us must transcend the temporal before we attain Sovereignty and this starts with Initiation, the foundation of which is a strong spirit in a methodical mind and beautiful body; these three aspects in proper proportions and balance bring about the condition necessary to achieve Sovereignty. Initiation is only that, however, a beginning, and this phase lasts only as long as the initiate requires to reach the next subsequent step along the Path. There are no shortcuts along the way, and though there may be the occasional deviation or debris, so long as one devotes all energy with discipline and dedication to focusing on what should be, they cannot fail to realize it.

Initiation in this sense is essentially a fresh start to our interior development, as it assists us in consciously comprehending our evolutionary experiences. Ritual, contemplation, *staða*, etc. are but exterior shadows, imitations, assurances of things to come, as true initiation can only begin from within; for it to be successful in shifting the paradigm, an initiation must be made up of an energy, a force unlike any the initiate has as yet known. The near-death experience exacts an amount of vitality (or *önd*) equal to what is necessary for the survival of the soul as such; the spirit knows that the body has limitations and will compensate for the confines of the physical, as it's indestructible and instinctual disposition demands it do. Life and the longing for life, or Eternal Existence, cannot possibly be fully understood until death or something similar has been experienced; it is only the most traumatic and extreme experiences that become permanently imprinted on individual memory, thus mark the genetic memory with an immortal impression.

The first step upon this Path is that of liberation, the realization of true freedom, by destroying all bonds, as attachment is anathema to the Sovereign.

> "...*liberation*...*to overcome the brotherly contamination, the need to love and feel loved, to feel together, to feel equal and joined with others. Purge yourself of this. Beginning at a certain point you will not feel united with somebody because of blood, affections, country, or human destiny. You will feel united with those who are on your same Path, which is not the human path, having no regard for human ways.*"
>
> – Julius Evola

This should never be reduced to an excuse to be selfish. A Sovereign has respect for the independence and individuality of others and a sense of dignity that prevents them from forcing their Ideal on others, even when these notions are needed, necessary, and true. Sympathy, pity, compassion, charity, etc. are an insult to the Sovereignty of another and a display of weakness and insecurity on the part of the self; these have long been considered meaningless bonds, unnecessary fetters that tie the self to another. No mercy should be shown the self, let alone any other, and in expressing these impulses, an individual shows lack of respect for the other to govern themselves properly, implying that they are incapable of Will to Power and at the same time robbing them of their pride, their worth, and confidence. Conversely, such outward demonstrations exhibit frailty and fallibility, evoking and expending energies better utilized against any and all that would attempt to limit the Sovereignty of the self in any way. Humanity as such is to be completely conquered with no compunction, subjugated so thoroughly that Sovereignty is comprehensive and incapable of abdication.

The self is source and solution, equilibrium as the archetype of harmony and what should be, our uniquely inherent Individuality and Individuation; it is the Path as well, along which we become aware of our self, see it for what it is, not what we would wish it to be, and pursue Sovereignty through supraconsciousness. The ego evinces duality, the polarity of existence, while the self sees balance and all conflict is a chance at conscious recognition of Divinity, friction being fundamental to the very framework of existence. Without conflict there is no change, only stagnation, and we must consciously and consistently consider both sides of any conflict to find truth; thinking in absolutes such as good and evil entangles the mind in myopic methods rather than opening oneself to omniscience. Assessing any situation without prejudice or prejudgment of good or evil offers significant opportunity for self-awareness.

Dissatisfaction with the modern world is a direct result of the inherent drive to strive for ever more, to grow, thrive, and evolve; most notably, for those unique individuals whose moral, spiritual, and physical evolution are not a mere byproduct of "chance," but who seek to actively pursue the highest value and virtue. The present plebeian perspective does not seem to measure up to the ideal of what is right, good, or proper simply because what is contrasts with what should be, rather than bringing these together to give life to what is becoming. This comes from living in time instead of against, beyond, or above it. When dissatisfaction with contemporary cultures, customs, and community becomes overwhelming, it is those with the strongest innate desire for evolution who step forward to present a new orientation, and so it is with the Sovereign. Society often calls these Fólk rebels, social misfits, or some such arbitrary appellation for daring to question the status quo, that plebeian perspective of the communal mindset, yet history offers ample evidence that it is the former that bring about necessary change, and they do so through Effective Evolution, the conscious and comprehensive realization of what should be. It is this that constitutes true liberation.

The second phase is Worthing oneself and the Path of Sovereignty is paved with accomplishments that leave an indelible mark on the Fólk-Soul; the Sovereign must Worth themselves to merit their inherent divinity. Worth is the self-sufficiency found in existing exclusively for one's self alone, insisting upon internal dominion. Relinquishing control of the self to external forces, permitting dependence rather than demanding independence, allowing some thing beyond one's self to influence its reign, all diminish the value of that Sovereignty, Worth waning in the process. Self-knowledge and self-sacrifice are the means by which self-mastery and self-realization are achieved; self-centeredness and selfishness are self-defeating and self-destructive. The self must evolve within the constructs and boundaries of the whole to achieve realization or Individuation, for beyond these borders lay the plebeian perspective of modern society, the status quo of the masses that accentuates mediocrity as the means by which man as socio-economic factor is to be measured.

Effective Evolution is not Darwinist scientism, but rather spiritual Sovereignty, wherein striving for the superior is a result of Will to Power. First and foremost, Effective Evolution is personal growth with a purpose: consciously Worthing oneself in an active attempt at attaining the Absolute. This concept is unique to the Fólk-Soul, the intentional pursuit of superior spiritual realization we have sought since the dawn of consciousness. The foundation for evolution must first be formed on the simple premise that a higher form exists and from this evolution is defined as the gradual development of an organism from a simple form to a complex one. So long as something superior seems just beyond reach, man will ever strive for that which is greater than their self.

During the nineteenth century Charles Darwin put forth the theory of natural selection to explain how an exclusive minority can adapt to their environment, with little effort, so rapidly and thoroughly as to far surpass these surroundings, and move beyond mere survival to a superior state of existence that leaves the former majority stagnant and often self-destructive in their inability to adjust or advance. This last certainly characterizes Fólk since the reign of monotheism began, most notably in areas that have become predominantly multicultural and/or racially diverse. More than anything else perhaps, Effective Evolution is ensuring that our children are stronger spiritually, mentally, emotionally, and physically than we ever were, thus better prepared for a future that becomes more unpredictable with each passing moment.

Key to Effective Evolution as spiritual nourishment is that we receive exactly what is needed for growth when it is necessary; it cannot be forced or hurried, nor can steps be skipped. The Path is initiatic, so understanding one concept is based upon fully comprehending another; only through incrementally increasing one's awareness by degrees can they comprehend deeper, hidden knowledge. To be concerned with more advanced wisdom than one is prepared or ready to receive is regard for the self-centered egoist, not the spiritual seeker interested in realization. With every equivalent expansion of energy an induction occurs that increases in intensity and if this power becomes permanently and easily accessible, not temporal, then the individual is evolving properly towards the *Übermensch*.

Significant and substantial spiritual nourishment can be said to derive from two primary sources. The first allows the ability for discernment of and adaptation to realities beyond the material or physical, as well as the acceptance of these realities as reflections of unknown or unfulfilled potential. The second allows the ability to express incorporeal realities using metaphor, analogy, and symbolism (the language of nature), as well as the use of symbol to direct and even predict future deeds aimed at bringing possibility and potential into existence. The former can best be comprehended as contemplative, while the latter remain in the realm of intuition, though both rely on regarding the spiritual and physical as equally real and alive. There are separate laws which govern each, though the balanced life is one which honors and upholds both simultaneously.

For the Sovereign these two sources are symbolized by Odhinn's ravens, Huginn and Muninn, as Intellect and Impulse, contemplation and action, Wisdom to Power and Will to Power respectively. They are known elsewhere as the Paths of Power:

> *"Paths of Power yield to the man who stares beyond his own reflected gaze. The inner reckoning, leap beyond the known reflected surface, beckons. The Paths open not by act alone, but by decision; who has decided he cannot live but in Power, that is so."*

The Path of Intellect is paved with the cobblestones of contemplation, commencing with a thought and leading to a logical conclusion, which allows for growth and spiritual nourishment. Thoughts themselves are real things on their way to becoming tangible in the physical realm; it is for this reason that, during meditation, we mentally wrap ourselves in a veil to physically isolate the mind from disruptive energy outside of our self. When we think Higher thoughts we bring about divine deeds, as contemplation is creativity to the point that all potential is available and by harnessing the creative energy necessary to transform thought into action, we manifest possibility. To contemplate is literally to create a temple, a sacred space in one's mind, that emanates into their immediate environment, in which to connect to cosmic mind for observation and meditation; more than this, however, contemplation is the coming together or joining of the universe with the individual, melding the two (the framework of the cosmos or pattern and man's mind), to consider and create. This can be understood according to the laws of Traditional thought and Logic:

1. The law of Contradiction = a proposition cannot be both true and false simultaneously, nor can anything that exists both have and not have a given quality.

2. The law of Excluded Middle = a proposition must be either true or false; there can be no mean point, thus an organism cannot be both alive and dead, an environment cannot be both chaotic and ordered, etc.

3. The law of Identity = a proposition implies itself; the best way to explain this is through the declaration of Rene Descartes *cogito ergo sum* or "I think therefore I am."

The Path of Impulse is laid upon the idea of intuition as immediate insight or comprehension of some ideal, concept, event, etc. by the mind through a seemingly inexplicable means and this often leads one to "feel" something is right or wrong, with little to no logical deduction or application of reason. This source of spiritual nourishment derives from action and emotion, and as such, is founded on the three laws of motion:

Sovereignty: The Empirical Path of Odhinn

1. A body remains at rest or in motion with a constant velocity, unless an external or internal force acts on the body.

2. The sum of the force(s) acting on a body is equal to the product of the mass of that body and the acceleration produced by the force(s) of motion in the direction of the resultant of the force(s).

3. For every force acting on a body, the body exerts a force having equal magnitude in the opposite direction along the same line of action as the original force.

These two Paths of Power correspond in many ways with Cognitives and Emotives, their functions being only one of degree, in that pursuing the former is a conscious act done with full awareness of one's intent, while the latter are natural states. Herein, however, the seeker finds the one essential element imperative to their ascension: in recognizing one's self as innately one or the other, to become truly Sovereign, one must actively strive to incorporate their opposing polarity into their inherent nature. A Cognitive consciously pursues the Path of Impulse, while the Emotive ever strives to faithfully follow the Path of Intellect. It is the intrinsic desire to realize divinity that drives the seeker to Sovereignty, while it is the lack of longing that Odhinn feared most for Fólk, an apprehension that was well-founded considering the current state of spiritual stagnation.

A path is the way which is typically travelled by another previously; the Path is that which was forged by Odhinn for the Fólk. A path ordinarily leads from one point to another; the Path is the journey of *óð* to Odhinn, that of the self becoming the Sovereign Self. Extinction is deviating too far to return to the Path, while Entropy is a boarding house along the way, often referred to as Hel, where one rests briefly before continuing their journey; Eternal Existence is the ultimate destination the Path leads to, said to be Asgardh. Midgardh then is the vehicle, our body, which walks along the Path, while Utgardh is the brambles and briars to either side of this Path, the untamed chaos and disorder one can get lost in should they deviate too far. Finally, *Hamingjar*, or synchronicity, are the seemingly coincidental events that tell the seeker they are headed the right direction, the signposts guiding us along the Path of Odhinn to Sovereignty. To this end the following can be considered cornerstones paving the Path:

Sovereignty

- The self exists as a separate universe, unique and unparalleled by any other; this universe should be the focal point of one's existence, for only through completely comprehending its order and operation can one attain Sovereignty, let alone understand the multiverse around them. All others are likewise the center of their respective universes and that Sovereignty must be maintained at all cost.

- Explore the natural elements, inherent nature, and power of your universe, considering each carefully so as to discern the purpose of your existence; this is a dynamic journey that allows you to pursue Effective Evolution as the means of achieving Sovereignty.

- To know your self is to know divinity and you must be willing to accept your self exactly as you are, as you are exactly who you need to be. Repressing or resisting an innate Instinct or inherent inclination is self-destructive; both will create chaos in your universe, as each is an emanation of the natural laws that govern all existence, and as with other laws, cannot be compromised without consequences.

- Once you have become fully aware of your universe and the purpose of your existence has become apparent, pursue this with your entire being: Will to Power through Effective Evolution is the surest way to attain Sovereignty.

- Develop a heightened awareness that brings into balance all faculties, characteristics, and qualities, then direct them towards Effective Evolution, devoting every effort to achieving a supraconscious state.

- Learn how best to harness and utilize those energies you hold dominion over in your universe and control those you have yet to fully comprehend; these energies are the laws of your universe, the power you have to create and destroy. By understanding and properly using these laws you can elevate the self.

- Extend control of your conscious awareness to include the ability to manipulate outside forces to your will through the precise perception, accurate understanding, and ordered government of your universe; in this way alone will you necessarily gain influence over the external multiverse.

- Remain vigilant to the possible invasion of your universe by enemy forces determined to destroy your self, as they are ever-present in the modern world; most cannot comprehend Sovereignty and seek to vanquish what they do not understand, while others strive to destroy any form of individual spirituality altogether, as its existence obliterates the very foundations upon which their dogmas are built. By keeping the filter of Truth through natural law firmly fixed over one's senses, you will only allow into your conscious awareness all that benefits the self and keep out that which is destructive.

- Never allow the will of another to hold dominion over your universe, as you abdicate the throne of Sovereignty in doing so; you are the Supreme Self of your universe and any interference or influence by an outsider is counterproductive to the governing of that cosmos. Conversely, keep out of another's universe unless invited; while you should always seek to enlighten others, do so with pure intent, as it enhances your abilities to both resist and manipulate outside forces. Be cautious, however, because entering another's universe leaves yours vulnerable and should only be attempted by those with ample experience and noble judgment to prevent losing one's own Sovereignty.

Rúna: The Mysteries

"...down beneath the tree...on the wood they scored...primal law for the sons of men."

— Voluspa

"Know how to carve know how to stain
know how to advise know how to ask
know how to invite know how to offer
know how to test know how to sacrifice."

— Havamal

Rúna can best be summed up with this last: rather than referring solely to the symbols we know as the runes, *rúna* means mystery, the primal law laid by the Norns and fundamental framework for all of existence. *Rúna* has many aspects such as *seiðr*, *spá*, *útiseti*, *galdrar*, Blót, among many other mysteries not meant for the masses; it is metaphysical and incapable of measurement by mechanistic means.

Sovereignty: The Empirical Path of Odhinn

A mystery is first defined as a religious truth known by revelation alone and it is this that should begin any exploration of *rúna*. We know that the Gods revealed the knowledge of runes (likely Heimdall rather than Odhinn) and that there are various sources that reveal other spiritual practices, beliefs, and explanations, however, none can be more accurate or easily comprehended than that of the genetic memory: any and all answers a Sovereign seeks can be found in their blood, the fount of wisdom our ancestors bequeathed to us.

Rúna is gestaltic and every aspect works in concert with others to form a whole. All of the elder European wisdom teachings maintain that the Titan, or giant, nature must be destroyed to develop divinity and for Odhinists this refers to all that is related to Utgardh, the outer garden beyond our self, where chaos and disorder dwell. Ymir's dismemberment demonstrates that those descended from him, all giants or not-gods, are of the world, temporal, and time is tied thoroughly to the terrestrial. Conversely, the Gods are Eternal, timeless, thus truly spiritual and metatemporal. To ascend to Asgardh then, all that is temporal must be shed so spirituality can shine like the sun, and it was the four gifts given each of us that allows the freedom to pursue potential and possibility.

Odhinism does not have a revealed canon as such; the closest we come is the Eddas, a collection of poems meant to be didactic rather than dogmatic. Language is the single most important factor in how Fólk impart information, sustain their spirituality, and maintain culture; poetry has always been the primary way our Fólk accomplished this. All language is saturated by the spiritual worldview of its speakers as it emanates from the Fólk-Soul and a foreigner could never hope to fully comprehend the customs or culture of the native; thus is the reason the knowledge and wisdom of our Fólk is virtually incomprehensible to outsiders, just as that which derives from others (such as monotheism), is unable to be truly integrated into our Fólk-Soul.

Odhinism embraces Effective Evolution; we know the Gods and Goddesses of our Fólk are real, living, breathing entities, as well as symbols of that superior spiritual element we seek and these same deities are guiding us towards. As their descendants, each of us has the inherent ability to become gods in our own right and *rúna* is the means through which we worth our self through Effective Evolution and attain Sovereignty.

Our Fólk have always attempted to categorize everything so that we could fully comprehend it, however, spirituality can never be considered completely uniform: every experience is different and each individual experiences them in disparate ways, thus there are as many empirical truths as there are people in the world multiplied by their respective experiences. As a whole we are spiritual entities, though most Fólk today believe themselves to be biological beings striving for some sort of spiritual experience; in reality, we are spiritual beings striving for Sovereignty through a physical existence. When we speak of empirical we refer to experience as sensation and perception. Personality traits are relatively consistent patterns of thought and behavior.

Contemporary spirituality is a mere phantom of what it could or should be. Even within Odhinism too many concern themselves with attempts at reconstruction, while others simply go through the motions of the practices compiled from Sagas and tales told of the Gods, without satisfying the spiritual aspects imperative for true growth and nourishment. It is pointless to try recapturing fragments forfeited to time, based on theory and supposition, for it cannot be done with any exactitude: some integral piece will always elude the reconstructionist and reconstruction fails ultimately due to removal from its roots, losing its spiritual value once it has been uprooted.

Furthermore, while it can be held certain that culture and spirituality are reliant upon language, no form of monotheism is found in an Aryan dialect: Jesus spoke Aramaic, thus neither himself nor any of his disciples likely even knew an Aryan language. Conversely, all forms of Heathen thought and teachings derive from the Fólk-Soul and are expressed through the language of that Fólk, not any other.

The word god for example is a uniquely Aryan one, not at all related to another family of languages, let alone those the monotheistic faiths fall from. It is likely this term was initially applied to the role of shaman, the one who was held in high regard for their psychological and spiritual nourishment of the Fólk, and was a source of wonder for their ability to embrace the ecstatic consciousness of the divine. Later this label was transferred to tribal deity and even broadly to whole groups of Fólk, such as the Goths, Visigoths, Ostrogoths, etc. as an honorary epithet meant to denote those who had attained a level others had not. Gods are considered omniscient, though this all-knowing state is not being aware of all things there are to know at once, but in knowing all truths, thus all possibilities; the Gods cannot have a false belief, as all potential is within their grasp, and as Creators they reveal that potential according to their individual Will to Power and Impulse.

The concept of god as we know it today comes from the proto-Aryan *ansu-* meaning spirit (cognate with ON *áss* or god) and *-deiw* meaning to shine (cognate with ON *týr*), which gave life to the Sanskrit *asura*, Avestan *ahura*, and Old Norse *Aesir* and *deva/daeva/tívar* or *vánir* respectively, referring to sky and earth deities, though eventually combined to a simple understanding of **gheu*, "to call" or "invoke," from which we get god.

The importance of a true understanding of what god is comes from the words worship and contemplation. The first literally means worthy of reverence, while the second is to create a temple in the mind. Worth is what is good or important enough to justify, has value, and excellence of character or quality as commanding esteem; this is an extremely significant concept for those seeking Sovereignty, especially considering that the archaic meaning of the word worth is "to happen" or become, particularly to become noble. Nobility is not and cannot be automatically acquired by virtue of being born, but rather is the quality of achieving a superior state; being noble is not merely expressing the ideals or regurgitating the lines one has memorized to appear noble or worthy of respect, but living a life that demands respect and reverence from others. Nobility is what you do when nobody is watching.

The word worship is an interesting one. Many Fólk today see in it some sort of subservience to another, though, like most of the misunderstood concepts in contemporary society, this is due to the slave/master relationship all monotheism is founded upon. Instead, worship comes from the Old English *weorthscipe*, literally translating to "the quality of worth," thus being Worthy, of value, or meritorious. The OE *weorth* is directly related to *wyrd* and cognate with ON *verdh*.

The notion that god created man in his own image has fascinated Fólk for some time now. On a macrocosmic scale this refers to the universe as a whole and the laws which govern it; on the microcosmic level we see that man is subject to the laws of this world, in the same way: the earth in relation to the universe and man in relation to the earth. While our Fólk have a long-standing practice of creating our gods in our own image, likely from the fact that we believe the Gods to be our ancestors, it can be seen in the gift of a godlike appearance that it is indeed the Gods that created us in their image.

The Gods are above time, as they exist in Eternity, where time as we know it does not exist, thus knowing beginning and end simultaneously through all potential and possibility. We, as Creators and descendants of the Gods, have at our disposal the same potential and possibility, as it resides in Mimir's Well, our genetic memory, and takes only Will to Power to reveal and realize. No word in any of our languages prior to monotheism applied solely to religion as we understand it today; instead, every word which relates even remotely to religious or spiritual practices also incorporates ideas of custom, culture, Tradition, and law.

Rather than representing some sort of monotheistic concept, Odhinn has the fundamental meaning of inspiration in its truest sense: the inner breath, the spirit within, which we must comprehend and connect with to realize what should be. If anything in fact, our earliest Fólk would be considered henotheistic.

Perhaps the practice most misunderstood by many Fólk is that of *Seiðr*. *Seið* is simply the Source; not a place or a person, but the well from which all potential, possibility, and power originate. The Source has no beginning nor end as it is *Aldr* (Eternal) and exists apart from all, while also permeating the world and existence. *Önd* comes from this Source and is the constant interplay between *óð* and Odhinn; it is the way in which we tap into *Seið* most successfully and harness it with intent and purpose that we can alter reality.

Seiðr then is sorcery, marking the *seidhkonur* and *seiðmaðr* as sorceress and sorcerer respectively. *Seiðr* has been interpreted and defined in a number of ways in recent years, running the gamut from an evil black art to beneficial magic, and this has caused considerable confusion, when in truth, the Ynglinga Saga gives us a clear explanation of *Seiðr*:

> *"Odhinn knew and practiced that craft which brought most power and which was called Seiðr and he therefore knew much of man's fate and of the future, likewise how to bring people death, ill-luck, or illness, or he took power and wit from them and gave it to others."*

From this then, *Seiðr* is related to *spá* (prophecy), divination, and *niðlingar*, or curses, all of which rely on intuition to be effective and intuitive practices demand a relinquishing of control, marking the reason "lack of manliness followed so much that men seemed not without shame in dealing with it" and "the *gyðjur* were therefore taught the craft." One who specialized specifically in prophecy was known as a *völva*, while those who practiced the casting of curses were *Heið*, and *Seiðr* did indeed become an exclusive realm of our women Fólk, for good reason.

It is widely believed that intuitive people can tell the future or predict events with accuracy and though this may seem extraordinary to the average person, there is a logical explanation for this: intuitive Fólk are attuned to the Source, their Instinct, the voice of our ancestors, archetypes, and recognize the patterns that are cyclical, their repetitive nature allowing an unconscious recognition of situations that seem similar to those that have occurred some time in the past and determine the likely outcome of present circumstances; even predicting further ahead based upon these self-same patterns of existence.

It was Winston Churchill who said, "The further into the past you look, the farther ahead you can see" and the veracity of these words are no more apparent than to intuitive Fólk. In the recognition of a cyclical pattern, prophecy becomes possible and the fact that our ancestors relied so heavily on prognostication and divination proves not that they were superstitious as some claim, but quite the opposite: they were far more in tune with nature and the *Seið*, than we are today and understood their inherent instincts to be the Source from which all true knowledge and wisdom derive.

When one understands the philogenesis of the ancestral memory and its role in determining future events (based primarily on previous ones) with accuracy, it comes as no surprise that Fólk were and are capable of such prophecy. In reality, all Fólk are capable of prophecy with enough discipline, dedication, and the proper preparation; we have the necessary tools and most simply lack the desire or belief necessary to succeed at a high level. The truth of the matter is that prophecy was once much easier for Fólk primarily because we were at one with nature and still connected to Source in a significant way.

Ideally prophecy is and should be the principle domain of our women Fólk, as it is through their inherent desire to nourish and demonstrate emotion, coupled with logical deduction, that they are capable of clairvoyance. It was the rise of misogynistic monotheism that saw the destruction of worship women received for their divine nature and abilities. Even today, however, many Fólk absentmindedly mention "women's intuition" in a humorous or insignificant manner, often without even realizing the reality of what this truly is or how powerful: women are more naturally adroit at foretelling future events, as they are capable of immediate insight without conscious contemplation. This likely comes from the fact that women are also more adept at relinquishing control and being pliant by nature, while men typically are rigid and domineering, these being opposing polarities between feminine and masculine mysteries. In this way it should surprise nobody that prophecy and divination are a product of intuitional recognition of the cyclical patterns of life itself, which often requires a complete release of conscious control to achieve.

In nearly every instance of prophecy in our wisdom teachings a woman is the source of the knowledge, from the Voluspa to Baldr's Dreams and even Hyndla. So too in Lokasenna is there a reference to *Seiðr* being a woman's practice. Eternity is so real that no being can ever KNOW the future; if the future were set or fixed there would be no freedom, experience, or free will. The Norns cannot possibly know the free will choices of men, but only the outcome of those decisions, however, after ascertaining how Fólk are likely to choose in any given situation or circumstance it can appear as prophecy or prognostication to the uninformed. Every individual imagines a future, either consciously or not, and these fancies create the energy necessary to manifest that future. The ability to become aware of what should be may seem extraordinary to many Fólk, however, we all have the potential to "see" the future, just as we have the Will to Power to create it: that which we know can be made manifest.

Prophetic prognostication can only come about through generalities, however, never specifics; this is why so many prophecies remain open to interpretation by individuals claiming insight. As with language and spirituality itself (the purest form of which rely on symbology, analogy, subjectivity, et. al.) prophecy must be metaphoric for the imagination to grasp it and create the reality of the future.

Source is *Aldr*, Eternal, beyond time or its constructs, thus has all possibility and potential instilled innately; any individual who has the ability to tap into the *Seið* then would likewise have all potential and possibilities at their disposal. Because time is cyclical, none can know specifics about the future, but only the culmination of events that must come about at some point due to their cyclical nature coupled with the knowledge of all possibilities and potential that allows an accurate prediction of future events. This foreknowledge is founded upon awareness and understanding rather than some sort of supernatural source.

The exact meaning of *Seið* has been lost to us, but likely derives from the same root as seethe, to heat or become heated to a high degree. The symbology for inspiration and intuition in our wisdom teachings is often found in a ketil or cauldron, which would signify bringing something to a boil. On a more exoteric level this refers to the emotion necessary to tap into the Source, while on the esoteric it speaks to the heat generated by the ascetic as alchemy. Trance is the primary practice behind *Seiðr*, the sleeplike state of altered consciousness that imitates death in its complete and total relinquishing of conscious control to consider what should be.

Spá craft is specific to seeking what should be as prophecy rather than divination for guidance or to answer a particular question. The most famous and significant example of *Spá* craft is the Voluspa, the seeress' prophecy. A *völva* is a woman dedicated to a prophetic form of *Seiðr* and, significantly, the Voluspa is clear in demonstrating that it is knowledge of what is that leads to the wisdom of what should be. *Seiðr*, however, is only one of two Paths of Power:

> *"Paths of Power yield to the man who stares beyond his own reflected gaze...much a man can hold, but this I know: none may hold the Seiðr; who holds not, nor expects, lives in Power."*

The first part of this refers to contemplation, which is dependent upon consciousness, thus Intellect, while the latter specifically citing *Seiðr* is alluding to trance, the subconscious result of emotion or Impulse. Both are required to practice *Seiðr*. The second Path of Power is *gandi*, or magic, and comes from inspiration and Instinct, which require control and discipline. This is also referred to in the Ynglinga Saga:

> *"Odhinn also knew where any treasure pit was hidden and knew such songs that the earth and hills and rocks and howes opened themselves for him and he bound with spells those who might be dwelling therein, so that he could go in and take all that he wished. By these crafts he became very renowned; his foes feared him but his friends took pride in him. But*

most of the crafts he taught the goðar; they came nearest to him in all wisdom and wizardry."

This passage speaks to the use of natural forces, necromancy, and a sort of spiritual dowsing, all of which are found in the spells of the Havamal and each demands discipline to make work, the means by which one harnesses the *meginn* of the Source to a specific end and that which we refer to today as magic.

Magic is often misunderstood by many Fólk as some sort of supernatural or miraculous practice, confused and compared to the illusions of sleight of hand artists, prestidigitation, and the New Age absurdities such as wicca. Instead, magic is, at its core, Effective Evolution, wherein one is able to inspire or draw forth the natural energy ever present all around us towards some end or purpose, to manipulate forces with intent, or summon from nature the necessary power to create or alter reality. In this way, the microcosmos embodies the macrocosmos, becoming, in effect, the Creator: creativity is magic, the Will to Power which produces extraordinary results.

It is imagination that has been lost to contemporary culture, creativity stifled in the process. This is not the more mundane imagination of simply thinking of passive possibilities, but the active principle of creating a conscious reality through contemplation of the subjective until it becomes objective manifestation. The legends and deeds of the Gods only seem fantastic to the modern mind that cannot imagine such a reality. The Sovereign, however, can visualize any possibility and through Will to Power realize it as reality.

Magic in its truest form can be defined as a holistic approach to nature, physics, and spirituality in gestaltic form and these can easily be seen in the three realms of Odhinism: Utgardh, outer realm or nature, Midgardh, middle realm of physics, and Asgardh, the indwelling or spiritual. The first represents everything outside of our self in the material world of our environment, the second is our physical self as the dwelling or cauldron to which we are subject to the laws of physics, and the last is our spiritual self, the inner world of the soul, our unique universe, where the Gods exist, thus our potential for godhead. This final is where magic and Sovereignty meet, as it is desire made manifest.

Magic can best be understood as repetitive ritual action undertaken to bring about a desired result, most notably in what is referred to as sympathetic magic, wherein the imitation of, or enacting, a specific outcome will result in it coming to fruition. This can be seen in the Law of Embodiment, in that of Extraversion, which states that we create our own conscious reality and the true magician can alter another's as well.

Many modern scholars like to lump Old Norse terms, concepts, words, etc. together for ease of interpretation and because none of them are practicing Odhinists, the distinctions are either beyond their comprehension or not important enough to warrant thorough examination. Such is the case with *gandi* and *Seiðr*, magic and sorcery respectively. There is a distinct difference between the two, in that the former relies on nature and the natural world to alter reality, while the latter depends upon the Source of all existence, the ineffable and empyrean wellspring of power few can even understand, let alone utilize or attempt to quantify or qualify. The magician, like the alchemist, views the cosmos as a creation and reflection of the imagination of godhead: concentrated imagination generates and exerts a tension or force on the very fabric of the cosmos, attracting an energy that enables the magician's images to manifest into reality. This is the reason magic has been defined as "the controlling of supernatural powers".

Many Odhinists consider themselves sorcerers rather than magicians, in that they realize the *Oðic* force is the Source from which they draw their power, the *ásmeginn*, while magicians garner their power primarily from the *meginjörð*, the energy of the earth. All Odhinists recognize the fact that the runes represent the very framework and foundation of all existence and we know that all potential and the potential for all are contained in these seemingly simple symbols. The magical uses of the runes are best summed up as deriving directly from conscious effort and intent, actively utilizing *meginn* to produce a desired result toward a specific end by focusing it through a concentrated exertion of energy directed at a particular purpose interpreted through the lens of genetic memory.

As Pliny the Elder so succinctly described in his "Natural History," magic is the "uniting in itself the three arts which have wielded the most powerful sway over the spirit of man" and these are medicine, religion, and astrology. Interestingly perhaps, is the fact that Pliny was clear in asserting that magic was not indigenous to either Italy or Greece, and though he supposes it was first invented in Persia (by Zoroaster) he also maintained that the ritual practices were so much more at home in the Celtic Isles and conducted with such a passion that it seemed as though it were they who taught it to the Persians rather than the latter having initiated the Celts; it is significant that Caesar also claims that Pythagoras had gained his knowledge of numbers from the Gauls/Celts as well. The fundamental basis of magic was and is the belief in the spiritual vitality of nature, the imminent, while its practices were transeunt as seen in shamanistic works and rituals. This spiritual vitality is *önd*, that principle given Askr and Embla, and which Odhinn is the ultimate manifestation of. This *Oðic* force is inherent in nature (so named and described most profoundly by Baron von Reichenbach) and permanently pervades the cosmos, as it does the soul, thus linking the microcosmic to the macrocosmic in *óð* and Odhinn respectively.

Óð is the principle that makes man what he is, that "human spark" that corresponds to the self, as it not only encompasses the ecstatic consciousness of the ego, but the Intellect and Impulse inherent in the divinely descended. *Seiðr* and *gandi* then are *meginvegur*, Paths of Power, and the most powerful tool to utilize these Paths (in relation to the self) is the Meginsmal, as this text offers a profound perspective of the Paths of Power and should be regarded as sacred scripture.

Önd is often translated as soul by scholars, though it should be seen as the Breath of Life or spirit rather than the soul. The ON word *öndverða* literally means beginning, though could be translated as "breath brings about." *Önd* is related to the Latin *animus*, Greek *anemos*, and Sanskrit *aniti*, which is interesting when we consider that the ansuz rune refers to the breath or voice of the Gods, what we know to be inspiration or inner spirit. *Önd* is the *meginn* of the aether, the *oðic* energy drawn from the sun, the sky, and our surroundings; it is the solar, nuclear fusion of all elements in the air around us. The Greek *pneuma* and Latin *spiritus* are the metaphysical equivalents of *önd* as Breath of Life, that which possesses mysterious vivifying powers often likened to the wind itself. In this, we find a correlation between the breathing in of *Oðic* energy and its perpetually existing state all around us in wind and air. Taken a step further, the Greek atmo- or "air," Sanskrit *atma* or "breath," and Germanic *athem* or "self," all refer to the principle of life, the individual self known after enlightenment and can be seen also in the Greek aether or "upper air" which is related to the Germanic *aethel* and ON *óðal*, meaning noble or of a higher degree. The Greek *atmosphere* literally refers to an enclosure of air and it is from this that New Age philosophy gets the concept of the akashic record, though Odhinists have been well-aware of the collective unconscious, the Fólk-Soul, since prehistoric times.

The significant aspect of *önd* is the *meginn* created through the synergism of *óð* and Odhinn; this is an extremely elastic and tenuous material, conveying all energy to and from Fólk partaking in the exchange between microcosm and macrocosm. This *önd* can be likened to day and night: inhale at the point of light and hold with dusk; exhale at the point of darkness to hold until the dawn. Similarly with the solstices and equinoxes, thus is the means by which the macrocosmos and microcosmos mirror one another.

"Their race had not *önd*" is profound to those on the Path seeking Sovereignty, as this *önd* is Instinct and there are three fundamental types of instinct: order, chaos, and balance. These correlate well with Cognitives, Emotives, and Equimotives respectively. Of the three, balance is best and it was this that was given Askr and Embla: the desire and determination to bring into balance and harmony all order and chaos. Conversely, the instinct to chaos need not necessarily be a direct pursuit of chaotic activity, but can be the inability to create or build for the future, the lack of any desire or drive to maintain anything more than a material, mundane existence.

Today, more than any other time since receiving the gift of *önd*, many Fólk rely heavily on individual ego to define their lives, manifesting as materialism at the expense of our collective unconscious and its evolution; this imbalance has created chaos in our Fólk-Soul, from disregarding our inherent instinct, to harmony and wholeness, and this disorder is evinced in the overall decline of morality and degeneracy of the Western world. The breath is the bridge between body and soul, the physical and metaphysical, and is the immediate now, the present moment wherein we become. It is breath that can bring back into balance Instinct and inspiration for those Fólk seeking Sovereignty.

Proper breathing brings about relaxation and realization. Assume a comfortable position when focusing on breath, one which can be completely relaxing. Start with eyes closed and breathe in deeply for three seconds, hold it for three seconds, and exhale for three seconds. As you do this feel every inch of your body, be aware of all, consciously relaxing with each exhalation, dispersing any tension or stress. With every breath begin collecting any negative energy you can sense and release it with exhalation: in through nose, out through mouth.

Note the quality of your breathing, where the breath is centered and feel your heartbeat, allow your thoughts to drift wherever they elect to go without becoming involved in any conscious consideration whatsoever; do not judge nor stifle them in any way, as this is your true self swimming through the stream of semi-awareness connected to the unconscious. When you feel ready, allow the intent of your contemplation to enter your mind, focusing your entire being towards worshipping in this temple, demonstrating reverence for that which you are consciously considering.

The most effective techniques are those that bring breath properly into balance with contemplation to create conscious reality. While *önd* is the Breath of Life, *óð* is consciousness, the self; where breathing is the active aspect of *önd*, contemplation is the conscious and consistent cultivation of the connection between *óð* and Odhinn (the self of the individual and Sovereign Self of Divinity) with dedication and intent. Aligning awareness with ascension is an affirmation of the divine present in each person and it is in this way that we will our self to the way things are rather than how they seem.

Contemplation is an attempt to attune one's self to Source. All life is vibration and attuning to the Source is seeking balance and harmony between the oscillation of divinity and development; spiritual nourishment and growth is empowered by what the mind focuses energy towards, that which we continue to think of. Contemplation, then, is the expression of our individual Impulse, our desire, to develop awareness and attunement; if *galdrar* is speaking to divinity then contemplation is listening to what is divine within each of us.

Contemplation requires the complete balance of *önd* and *óð*, allowing Instinct to guide Intellect and Impulse according to our inherent nature. By doing so, the ascetic builds their storehouse of *meginn*, drawing from *Seið* the energy necessary to nourish their spirit and gain spiritual nourishment through awareness and understanding. Each day Odhinn sends Huginn and Muninn out into the world, his universe, and what this entails is his balancing of Intellect and Impulse with Instinct to gain ever more knowledge.

Contemplation is by far the most powerful weapon in the Sovereign's arsenal, as it allows the self and spirit to interact in the divine. Only the individual can contemplate for themselves; others may be able to guide them to the base of the mountain, but ultimately each of us alone are responsible for and capable of attuning the soul with Divinity. The purpose of contemplation is to expand our conscious awareness by directing our focus and attention into the unconscious and achieving enlightenment by bringing the contents to the surface. Contemplation in this sense consists of inspiration realized as insight: immediate insight as intuition.

Instincts, of course, are a set of natural inborn tendencies and predispositions in favor of or against something and are the very archetypes of the ancestral memory, the philogenetic pantheon. These instincts can be seen as the lessons learned by our forebears, passed down or "taught" us through morphic resonance: these are the experiences of thousands of years of trial and error extant in our blood and carried from one generation to the next.

Intuition, on the other hand, is the recognizable manifestation of man embracing their inherent nature, exploring it, and fully comprehending it; to be truly intuitive is to act automatically upon one's Instinct in any given situation, doing what feels right with the confidence that this can be completely trusted.

Contemplation is a key component to the quest as it is through the intent of seeking what should be that we know our self and can subsequently achieve Sovereignty. Anything the mind dwells upon becomes part and parcel of the self, spiritually and physically; the goal of contemplation is to become a conscious companion of creativity and this can only be accomplished through intentional ideals. Lost in Eastern and New Age notions of meditation is Impulse: feeling is far more effective than thought, though the two together can consistently create any reality and it is for this reason that contemplation is considered so significant to those seeking Sovereignty. Whenever one is able to <u>feel</u> the thought they contemplate throughout their entire being, they are moving beyond the mundane and mediocre to metaphysical and meaningful mindfulness.

Mindfulness is the intent to be present here and now, entirely engaged in what is, rather than what seems to be, while contemplation is the focus of familiarization with the qualities of mindfulness. The physical sensations and stimuli experienced as a result of energy coursing through the body during contemplation is real and measurable, as this *meginn* releases endorphins and engages the endocrine centers, from adrenals to gonads, pineal and pituitary glands, as well as thymus and thyroid. We know today that regular contemplation can change the way the brain functions, as well as its structure; it is like a muscle that becomes stronger through practice and proper training. This last is the reason ritual is so important to spiritual nourishment and Sovereignty: it enhances our emotional and evolutionary abilities. The Old Norse *yggr* is cognate in this regard with the Sanskrit *yogin*, both referring to one who masters the mind through focus on complete control of body and breath.

Contemplation can best be defined as memorizing a pattern, while paradigm finds truth in the tension of juxtaposition between two correlative constituents. The primary distinction between meditation and contemplation is found in intent: while the former requires one to relinquish everything and think of nothing, the latter demands the focus of intent towards a particular purpose. Some of us need an external focal point and any sacred symbol will suffice (from the sunwheel or swastika to the runes, black sun, helm of awe, valknot, Hammer, or any other), though again the selected symbol should be one connected to one's intent and helps them focus the mind towards it. When utilizing a symbol in this way, we merge with it completely, regulating our breath, heartbeat, and mind in symbiosis with the symbol synergistically.

If the head is the temple then it is the home of the soul, the Intellect, Impulse, and Instinct. Today we know this to be true, in that Intellect is left brain logic, while Impulse is right brain creativity; Instinct is drawn in from nose and mouth as the Breath of Life. It is our duty to ensure that the soul in this temple is worthy of reverence (i.e. worship) and do so appropriately through contemplation. Scientists have found that focusing, or contemplating, on something spiritual lights up the frontal lobe of the brain, which supports the notion that to contemplate is to create a temple or sacred space within which we can worship.

Contemplation also activates the part of the brain associated with positive emotions, causes the aspects attached to memory and learning to grow, improves attention and the immune system, produces antibodies, and helps with pain management, among other physiological benefits. Contemplation could and should replace pharmaceuticals for controlling depression, stress, anxiety, and other mental disorders.

After relaxing focus on the fact that each thought is energy you are attempting to accrue, acquiring this *meginn* to put towards a particular purpose. As each of us consciously creates our own reality, we can bring about any change we want through wisdom and Will to Power. *Ásmeginn*, as the divine power garnered through spiritual nourishment and power (in this sense) signifies one's Sovereignty, their independent freedom, control, thoughts, and feelings; it is harmony with the Higher Self that constitutes creation and confidence.

There is no such thing as good or bad contemplation; it is all part and parcel of the body/soul dynamic. It is most beneficial when done at the same time and place each day. Most important, however, is to not be discouraged; contemplation takes practice to master. Attempt to hold the feeling in harmony with thought, without having to repeat any mantra, and open your palms to potential power and energy.

Spirituality must rely on symbolism simply because all that is in the spiritual realm is obscure and abstract: soul, spirit, Intellect, Impulse, Instinct, self, etc. None can be measured by mechanistic means, let alone with any exactitude, thus remain recondite. Man, however, has the unique ability, among all animals on this planet, to comprehend and communicate by way of symbols, to translate an approximate intuition of a design into a precise knowledge. Without symbols, man could not consciously consider, let alone understand, a considerable amount of both spiritual and secular wisdom, from philosophy to mathematics. It is believed that mathematics is inherent, that it is not a learned ability, but instead hardwired into our brains like the need to breathe or eat, and that without mathematics civilization itself would not be possible; while this is likely true to some extent, without symbols expressing mathematics (or any fixed idea for that matter) would be virtually impossible.

Numbers are perhaps the most profound symbols known to man, as they are capable at the same time of expressing potential or possibility and perfection; there is nothing that cannot be expressed numerically. Numerology helps us understand cyclical time, as well as the patterns pervasive in people's personalities. Three, for example, is considered the oldest sacred number and remains the root of all existence. Carl Jung maintained that three is the number of the soul, the solar principle, masculine, and celestial, while four is the number of the body, the lunar principle, feminine, and terrestrial.

Either way, it is nine that is and has always been the sacred number of the Sovereign, as it is holistic, complete unto itself, and is the number of divine man as Sovereign Self. Nine is the perfect number, in that it is the only number that when intensified, always returns to itself; no matter what number nine is multiplied by, the sum of the answer is always nine. Contrary to contemporary belief, there is no ten, there is only Eternity, the circle from which cyclical time comes and returns to. Nine is in fact the last number and as such symbolizes perfection.

Mircae Eliade maintained that nine formed a part of a more archaic symbolism than the number seven; the latter he considered of more recent Mesopotamian, hence Oriental, origin. The fact that our Fólk found nine to be the most sacred number from the earliest time is indisputable and our wisdom teachings can in fact be substantiated through this spiritual symbol, as all of the eldest emanations of the Fólk-Soul are saturated in the symbology of the number nine.

Perhaps the single most significant symbol demonstrating this is the Valknot, the knot of the slain; it is certainly the most profound for Fólk seeking Sovereignty. Not only is the Valknot the singular symbol of Odhinn, but also represents everything essential to the Path of the Sovereign Self; as the mark of the Einherjar, the Inheritors, it depicts several important ideals. The three triangles represent the realms of Asgardh (above), Midgardh (below), and Utgardh (outside of both); the points of these triangles are nine in number, that of divine man, as well as the worlds of Yggdrasil. It has long been known that only those dedicated to Odhinn wear the Valknot and that remains as true today as it has always been, as only those on the Path dare display such a powerful symbol.

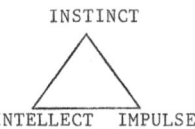
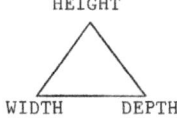

The first triangle (at the top) is that of Asgardh, where Eternity as cyclical time exists, that of Urdhr, Verdhandi, and Skuld. The second triangle (at the bottom) is that of Midgardh, the spiritual and that of completion, the soul containing Instinct, Intellect, and Impulse. The third triangle (outside the other two) is that of Utgardh, the three-dimensional framework of the terrestrial, that of the temporal which sits just outside of the other two. Together, they comprise the Valknot of the Sovereign Self.

Additionally, these three triangles represent the three phases of divine development: Thund, Yggr, and Odhinn or growth, worthing, and ascension respectively.

Sovereignty: The Empirical Path of Odhinn

The swastika, on the other hand, symbolizes the sun or solar principle first and foremost, then the importance of the sun itself. Deosil *fylfót* represents the active masculine *oðic* force emanating from the sun, while the widdershins swastika is the passive feminine principle of sister Sunna herself; the former likewise symbolizes forward motion or evolution as well. As noted by Jung, where three represents the soul and celestial, four designates the physical and terrestrial, and this is found in the *fylfót*, with its four "legs" pointing in the four directions, seasons, etc. The Sanskrit *svastika* literally means "be in good health" and derives this definition from the impact the sun has on all life, from plants to people, and without which life as we know it could not exist; the Old Norse *fylfót* means "four-footed" and is a more direct symbol of solstices and equinoxes as the sun's influence on the temporal and terrestrial.

Closely related to the swastika is the Sunwheel or "Eye of Odhinn" as many Odhinists refer to it; it is a significant symbol to Sovereigns as well; it is likely the oldest mandala in the world and represents the Eternal and indestructible soul, the self as Sovereign. The vertical line is the positive, active, and dynamic principle of *önd*, representing unity, oneness, authority, absolute, and the connection between higher and lower; it is the aspect of this symbol signifying the sun and spirit. The horizontal line is the negative, passive, and static principle of *óð*, representing the earth, body, malleability, the physical, and balance; it is the aspect of the essence of Eternity, the indestructible and ineffable.

Together then, the Sunwheel is the symbol of the soul, the Eternal duality of all existence and complimentary character of the universe. *Önd* and *óð* exist only in relation to one another; they represent the rhythm of existence and are inseparable in their pulse of reciprocation, as they alternate perpetually. *Önd* and *óð* can never conflict, only complement one another and as such they symbolize the Absolute: equilibrium, the point of perfection of balance and harmony of the Sovereign Self.

The single most significant symbol to Odhinists is Thor's Hammer, or simply the Hammer; it is used as both an amulet for protection, as well as a sign for blessing, and is the preeminent power symbol, signifying both creation and destruction. In the hands of a blacksmith a hammer is capable of creating tools, weapons, and other implements, while in those of a warrior it is a weapon that can destroy shields, structures, and people alike.

In the Heathen Hof, the sign of the Hammer accompanies the intoning of the four gifts given Askr and Embla: *óð* for consciousness (which we conceptualize in our heads), *önd* for the Breath of Life in the chest, *lá* to the left shoulder for the blood pumping through our hearts, and *litu goða* to the right for completion of the Hammer signifying the body.

By signing the Hammer, we create a filter of sorts to cover our consciousness, one that allows in only truth and reality; in this sense then, the Hammer is what protects Asgardh and Midgardh from Utgardh, the chaos and disorder of the outside world. The sign of the Hammer predates that of the cross used by many monotheists by a significant amount of time and is just one of many beliefs and practices usurped from Heathens.

Sovereignty: The Empirical Path of Odhinn

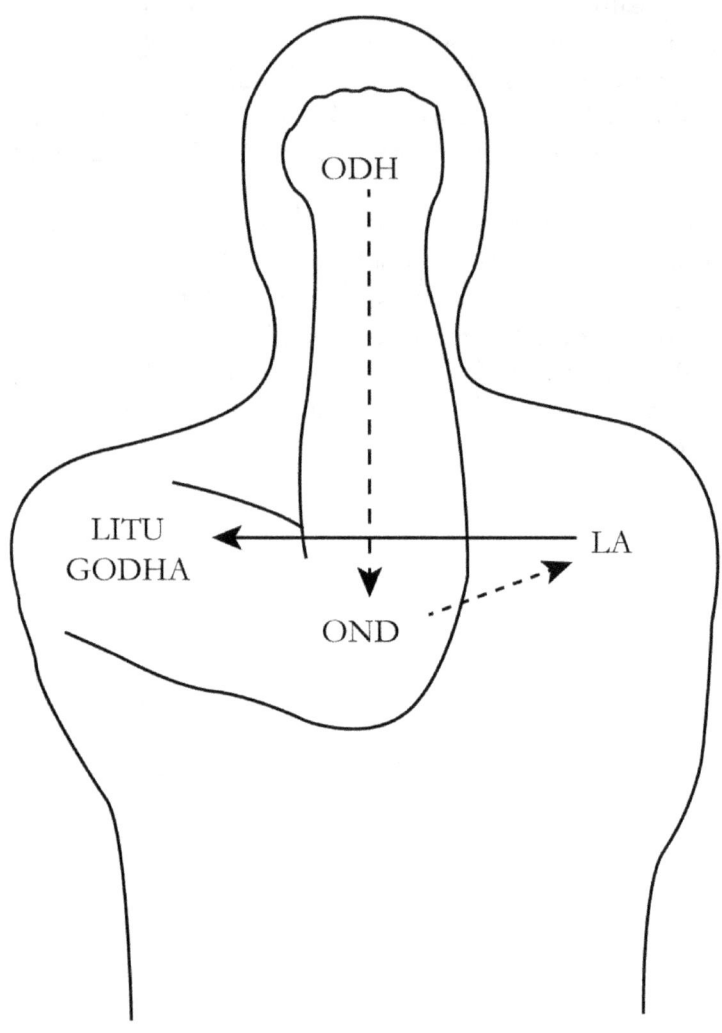

"The king is doing what all men who trust in their own strength and power do: he is blessing the horn in the name of Thor by making the sign of the hammer over it before drinking."

-Heimskringla

It could be argued that the tree is another, for it was held sacred by the Celts long before any other. In the Edda we are told Askr and Embla were trees before being given the four gifts of the Gods, while Tacitus made it clear we worshipped in groves and forests, as it would not be "consistent with the grandeur of celestial beings to confine the Gods within walls." Many Celtic rituals revolved around the tree, while Ogham is based completely on trees. Most significantly, however, is the Tree of Life, the *axis mundi* or world-pillar which represents all of existence; the world-tree is the Eternal Existence of Higher evolution, the enduring cosmic axis between this world and others, earth and sky, the pillar perpetuating our very existence.

The tree is a very powerful symbol and the symbiosis between man and tree is indisputable. Additionally, perhaps the best way to examine evolution and the symbolism of the spiral is through the motif of a tree expressing all existence: the age of a tree, its duration of growth and evolution, can be measured by its rings, as a series of timelines that emanate outwards from the center just as man does from *ørlag*: like ripples in the well as layers of *Urð* are laid, the rings of the tree mark every moment. What a 3,000-year-old sequoia has witnessed throughout its life must be profound to ponder.

It is no coincidence that the tree is the first thing mentioned in the Voluspa, as well as the nine dimensions within it, the entirety of existence. The Tree of Knowledge (ON *Laerað*) co-opted by monotheists as that of "good and evil" sits in Midgardh, on the border between "beyond" and "against" time, while that of Life (likely ON *Mimameith*) rests in Asgardh, "above" time. These two trees became one (ON Yggdrasil) through Odhinn's Ordeal and those who would become Sovereign must do likewise: "hang" upon the Tree of Knowledge to gain the wisdom necessary to move beyond time to the Tree of Eternal Existence. Friedrich Nietzsche recognized the importance of this Path and through his philosophical trilogy of morality encouraged "all good Europeans" to move "beyond good and evil" to the superior state of consciousness he referred to as the *Übermensch*, from the slave morality of the masses to the master morality of the Sovereign.

SOVEREIGNTY: THE EMPIRICAL PATH OF ODHINN

The best depiction of the World-Tree is:

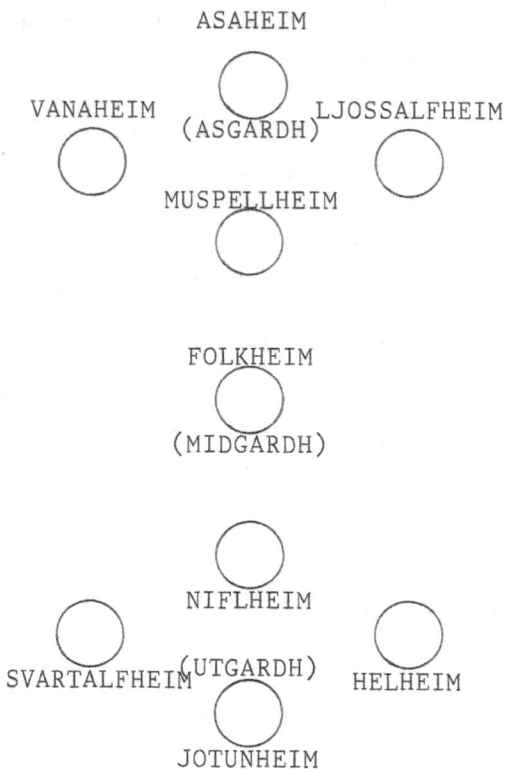

ASAHEIM: Higher influences/Divinity/archetypes/Fólk-Soul
VANAHEIM: growth/evolution/balance/continuity and community
LJOSSALFHEIM: mental influences/Intellect/guidance/logic
MUSPELLHEIM: vitality/activity/energy/movement/Impulse
FOLKHEIM: life/manifestation/freedom/individuality/consciousness
NIFLHEIM: resistance/passivity/dormancy/inertia
SVARTALFHEIM: emotional influences/creativity/materialism
HELHEIM: instinctual influences/suppression/stasis
JOTUNHEIM: confusion/change/crisis/chaos/lower influences

TWENTY-FOUR PATHS

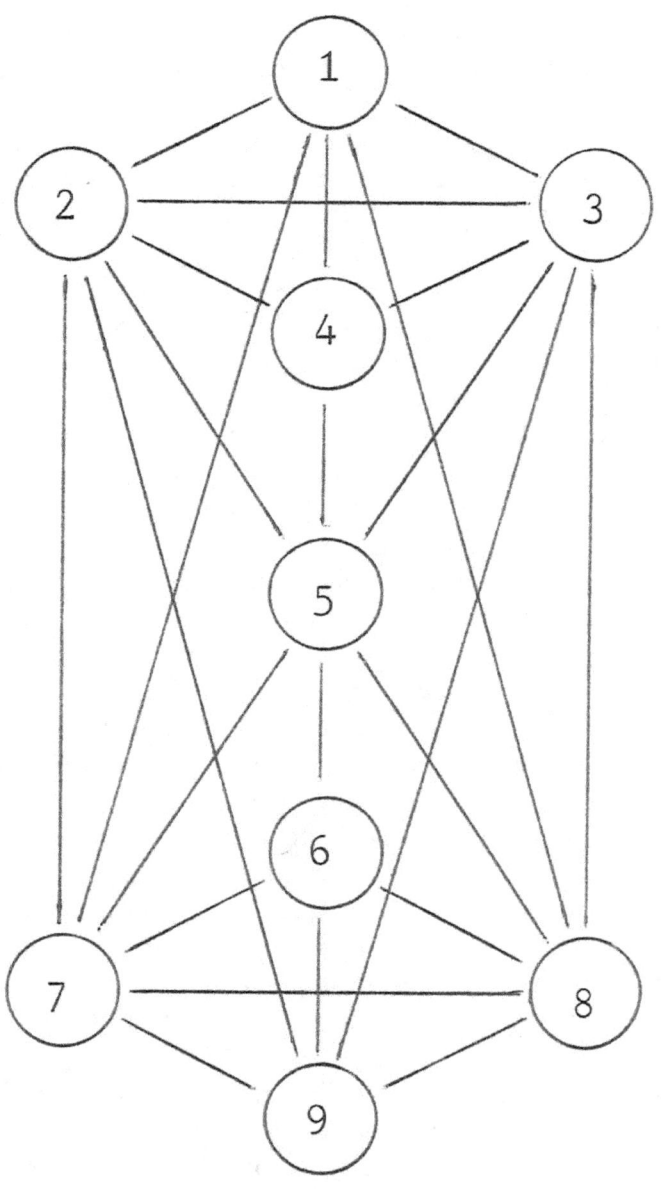

NINE WORLDS OF THE WORLD-TREE

Sovereignty: The Empirical Path of Odhinn

There are exactly 24 paths between the nine worlds of the tree and these correspond to the runes; conversely, there are 24 vertebrae in the spine, the trunk of man's tree. From the root to the head (ON *höfuð*) can be found nine *grindr* (or gates) that must be opened to achieve Sovereignty. The process is symbolized by *niðoggr*, the dragon or snake that from below flies forth to betoken the arrival of the "great godhead" who holds all power and rules the land; this is the Sovereign.

As we unlock each gate, we move further along the Path in seeking Sovereignty and in the physical realm this is accomplished through *bóndi*, or binding one's self to Divinity. This practice consists of *staða*, the physical positions or postures the body is placed in to develop discipline, to suppress unnecessary movements and gain full control of our nerves and muscles, particularly those areas of the body not typically controlled by the Instinct; *galdr*, or the chanting of sounds of power through control of *önd* (the Breath of Life), to bring the mundane breathing of oxygen into balance with the life force of the aether; and *óð*, the contemplation which brings the physical and metaphysical together in a manner that alters ordinary waking conscious into the deeper awareness of the unconscious where the Divine dwells. In this way, the Sovereign "bind" themselves to ultimate reality and attains an Eternal Existence.

Many mistakenly equate *staða* to *yoga*, though if there were a Sanskrit equivalent it would *asana*. *Staða* begins from a recognition of the human situation, the physical and terrestrial: man is bound by the laws of process and suffers as a consequence of this bondage. *Staða* proceeds by a focus on knowledge of the self; self-knowledge may be said to be both the essential method and ultimate goal of *staða*. Self-knowledge, however, is a relative matter and depends not only on the depth and clarity of insight, but also on what is seen as the self to be known. A change from the identification of the self as the body to that of inhabiting the body is the most crucial development for *staða*, as *staða* identifies the individual less with the body than the embodied, bringing forth the indwelling in the process.

Staða is about control and discipline, the power of the Sovereign to direct their energy to a specific purpose and intent; this is accomplished through complete control of the body, breath, Intellect, and Impulse. There are essentially two types of power the Sovereign can draw from: *ásmeginn* and *meginjörð*, the power of the Gods and that of the earth respectively. These streams are harnessed through *bóndi*, with *staða* being a significant aspect of this, the personal transformation of psychological and physical integration. The exchange of energies between man and the divine engages Effective Evolution efficaciously.

Each posture is meant to be held for at least 30 seconds and flow into the next in a fluid progression towards perfection. At the completion of every *staði* the practitioner will gather all of the energy from the position itself, let it flow through their body, and release it into Utgardh with force of will, allowing this energy to emanate outwards as a sign of sheer power. This very act is invigorating, cleansing, animating, and most of all electrifies one's *hamr* to the point that others become aware of their power.

Staða is more effective when combined with *galdr*, the vocalization of vibrations we call sound. All life is oscillation and attuning to that movement allows the manipulation of the *meginn* as magic to alter reality. Actions, emotions, and contemplation create vibration that are physical and formative, experienced as an energetic effect; this *meginn* combines with patterns to produce paradigm shifts cultivating constructive and creative configurations. When we make sound, speak, sing, etc. our voice oscillates at a level that allows all around us to attune to it and for us to attune to all around us; in this way we impart intent, image, even internal impressions to any empathetic receiver.

Which leads to the ideal of the garden, where all of existence is cultivated not through agriculture, and certainly not by means of multi-culture, but simply through culture: the customs, accomplishments, and worldview of a particular people. Like the plant whose existence depends upon burying its roots deep into the earth seeking food and water, and sprouts up into the open searching for sunshine and air, man is dependent upon the same and certain soils nurture and nourish particular plants and peoples; any that are uprooted and placed in foreign soil are sure to perish long before they have an opportunity to blossom. Today, Western culture is cultivated by sickened soil, and the seed is sterilized; the only way to make the garden suitable again is to raze it, purify the soil through a controlled burn to revitalize it, and allow new seed to take root. Thus is the Path of Sovereignty.

> *"Without Sovereigns, true Sovereigns, temporal and spiritual, I see nothing possible but an anarchy; the hatefullest of things."*
>
> – Thomas Carlyle

A Note to Female Fólk

The use of man or men throughout this book does not designate the male or masculine to the exclusion of the female or feminine. I adopt the understanding of men and man proposed by Freya Aswynn as part of the definition of Mannaz in her monumental work Northern Mysteries and Magick.

More importantly, however, as I have written this from the empirical perspective, that of my own personal experience, I cannot, with any exactitude examine, nor offer the feminine view of Sovereignty. That said, there is absolutely no doubt that everything I have written pertains equally to women as it does to men.

The trifold Path I explore through Thund-Yggr-Odhinn is likely found in the Gullveig-Heidhr-Hlodynn dynamic, this last translating roughly to The Yielder for want of a better term, possibly denoting the feminine, fruitful aspects of relinquishing control to attain ascendancy. What I do know is that Freya's search for self, *óð*, is her journey to achieve Sovereignty as embodied in Hlodynn, the feminine form of Odhinn. Interestingly, Hlin, one of Frigga's names we're told, would be the shortened form of Hlodhynn. Freya and *Óðr* are said to be married, which is mirrored in the

A Note to Female Fólk

Greek *heiros gamos*, the holy or alchemical wedding. The "thrice-burnt" event in Har's Hall is likely an initiation and the counterpart to the trifold ordeal of Odhinn. Perhaps it was this initiation that led to the first Fólk war in the world, or maybe it was the fact that Freya revealed the Vanic mysteries of *Seiðr* to Odhinn, though whatever the reason, it can be no coincidence that this was a FOLK war, and Freya is given FOLKvangr, the field of Fólk, likely as the counterpart to Frey being given Alfheim as his "tooth gift".

As a side note, some 12 percent of women are tetrachromats, which means they have four cones in their eyes able to differentiate color, while most Fólk have only three, some even two. This may explain why some women are far more intuitive than men or even other women, and why it is almost exclusively women that can see *hamr* or auras. The only other tetrachromatic creatures are birds, which is significant considering our Fólk view birds as having great "sight" or wisdom; Freya has a falcon's cloak, while Frigga is said to have that of an owl. Odhinn, of course, has Huginn and Munnin, whom he sends out into the world each day to "see" for him.

Nevertheless, I cannot speak to this with any certainty, but can only hope to inspire a great lady to step forward and offer a feminine perspective. In the meantime, may my words find a warm welcome in the hearts of my women Fólk. 14/14

MEGINSMAL

1. I am the union of fire and ice, where their streams meet. I am energy and have no state. Nothing I grasp, and what have do not hold. I am only I who knows and all that I am is that knowing. I am, for I know myself to be apart from what I am not

2. Selves change, world is Eternal. Self reappears, goes about in new forms: self is Eternal. World about changes; worlds come and go. I release it and selves change beyond the selves they are. Ginnungagap is Eternal, void between fire and ice; it cares not for me, nor not-for-me. The void I have formed; the void forms me. The Gods both were before and follow too. Conscious became the void, became first thought, and gave first word and it was Odhinn.

3. Energy goes on, takes new forms; it merges with, emerges from, the play of selves, best tribal minds, the oldest souls. With each living and each dying they self-merited through successive higher lives, progression to Godhead. Huginn creates itself best formed mind of tribe and this goes on, becomes immortal. Ginnungagap is hereby

thought in minds of Gods and men formed thereof and from itself, ancient milk of that first Aurochs. Lived much and many becomes that force compassion, troth to the ways of men. Looked with care upon itself became Ginnungagap and it spoke: Frigga.

4. Faced stone and storm, the dying and birthing of worlds before ours was thought to be. Faced with no concern for hurt nor loss, went on as consciousness; went on in all of storms of worlds. Pure courage was born to the void; pure ardent valor came to the world before worlds and spoke the holy spark in darkness: Thor.

5. Frigga nurtures young shoots of life; Freya is pure beauty and Baldr is pure light. All their own right self-won, self-determined. Each spoke to us in the travail of birth; in each cloth tied to bough, in each ale cast from horn I give to them and they to me in turn.

6. Green Man Frey came not one great harvestman, nor came he one swain o'plenty; long ago, who forestayed Earth's embrace, wrote himself large in the home of the Gods. No, ever he grows anew in each fair freeholder, every ardent swain, and bringer of harvest, his is all that lived thus and ever shall. Should none harvest, still he is; should none love, yet he is.

7. Thought itself too hard a darkness, burst to flame, bright lit, fair and beauteous it spoke Baldr. In the High Sun, when the wheel on ground is cut becomes anew, for timeless the Gods and true.

8. The Gods give back to me the cycle, time from time; they redeem to me what is forfeited in change from one threadbare cloak to the next. All forgotten here, the Gods beyond change anchor our timeless core.

9. Who opens may see, from life to life; who opens must sit out his thoughts. Who opens, her shall the Gods speak of time and cause, of life to life renewed. Who sits in the halls of men? The changeless ones. Who sits renews. Who watches renews. Who cleansed of his own voice heard theirs, renews. And Askr and Embla Odhinn and Frigga formed, and from the void gave Huginn and Muninn, gave *laeti* too. And the void moved in smaller ripples and it spoke *wünsch*.

Open is the way to see the void, open to who reflects it as Ran's daughters Knakve's dance.

10. An illness came and took the frail. Lady of small green things helped some, the *vitki* others. The lady who spun and wove, she never faltered, though it struck about her house; at her stoop she lay unrobed in Summer sweat. In the cold day brisk drove the herd with only a shawl about. In Ostara's cold water she was seen by the men o'weirs.

11. They came to ask the weft-woman "Why never afflicts you?" and she told the five purities: I sweat Baldr's gaze but may not return it; this be the first. I lay in Sunna's smile and ask she probe my innards with light, the dark moon chase; this the second. I sit the cold fast water until it is faster than my thought and rumbles out cares for three. Drink I only from skins I fill at the high stony brooks and eat not the day; this every month for four. I sit and do not ponder, do not do. Once it be wind in rushes, they sweep me clean. Again a brook rushed past and next it was leaves before a storm. Last dusk it was a thousand calling frogs. Into the shadow I gaze, where none will look, or to tan grasses, wind-rustled, they sweep me clear. Or in the babble of brook the play of Sunna's greeting washes eyes as stone-speech cleanse the ear and thus be five.

12. Opening is active, for the mind I must put aside is active; I take the active urge to be passive, to allow in the knowing of the Powers. Comes only in the active self, then puts itself aside. The opening I either do by act of will or quite undo by unthinking, for the mind I know stands aside the Path of Power. By such paradoxes do I advance, for life is known by precept but I lived by riddle and so must be thought.

13. Three states has the life of man: youth, prime, and old. Three streams his time, for water comes down divided. One branch beneath the high Sun dry fish, cut peat, and herd to market drive. One branch the tales around fire, the time of Thing, the boy given knife and rope, the girl given loom and ladle; to both to sit, to pray, to grind soot and stir. The third lie still in stream its course of dreams, of quiet, of fire or moon gazing.

14. Paths of Power yield to the man who stares beyond his own reflected gaze. The inner reckoning, leaping beyond the known reflected surface, beckons. The Paths open not by act, but by decision; who has decided he cannot live but in Power, that is so.

15. Feasts and draughts arise for who holds abundance. Who holds someone sorrows at her loss; who holds what should, shall ever regret what is. Much a man can hold, but this I know: none may hold the *Seiðr*. Who holds not, nor expects, he lives in Power. Who holds not, nor clutches or seizes, is much given, but little estate will build. Who holds little can be little riven by grief. Who holds not but accepts and looks forward with good anticipation gathers pleasantry and is beyond sorrow.

16. Never is there time before the field be tilled; never is there time before the nets need tying, that I can sit and learn. Never is there time to bend the limb to keep the age-dragged gait away. Act beyond, beyond fatigue; act beyond, beyond what is not to be worked with, beyond comfort, and beyond known headlands. Who sails beyond creates new charts; if the new land comes not here, still a man is richer to have sailed for it. In his next voyage shall she send him to a better journey. Never is there time to strive, yet time must find; never the man is so busy that he may not stop and look about. Even busy, two in the warves: one sees the sky, one not. Always one may be aware.

17. I can refrain from too much trencher and too many cups. I can curb the tongue from boast or threat. I can be still and learn or sit in *hörgr*. Even with poor food, even with a humble cottage, much can understand. Even a town sweeper can be of Power and all hear his thought or see his glow.

18. Faith is participation; faith constructs and creates experience. Like from the mold cheese is taken thoughts our experience create, but are also influential. Who can hold the image of the higher world will reach it. He whose logic deconstructs experience lives only in his head. Sweet the sleep of the one who tires in striving to know. Sweet is the touch of woman's roundness to man and sweet the hard

shoulder of man to woman, but the touch is the moment; no place full happiness is in this wald.

19. Know the spirit mound is there, is here, and I access it; do not construct or imagine. Stand anew at each threshold, not knowing but at ease with what is known. Walk briskly in, knowing nothing still, and know the impress of Eternity on mind. Calm the heart, calm the deep, the mind which opens to all forms of Power. Bliss is in moments, the calm of morning before the house awakens, waving grain, awaiting the Sun's taking off dew before the scythe; moments are bliss or it is not at all.

20. He came to the *hörgr* after far trekking to the fiery realm trading amber; whereof to consecrate this place he knows? For I have seen of ewe and fat shoat, the people of robes kill and the notched stone soak. Here they make holy as should we; the *gyðja* gave that to kill and not to eat would Vidharr or Ullr offend. "Consecrate," she said, "this circle, the warrior with his sword motion, the craftsman with her banner, and the brewer with his mead. All with their gifts of mind, this Thor loves best, as keeps the hill. Consecrate thus with your essence given the Gods."

21. Faith is participation; it is choosing not to choose and turning to decide that all is undecided and awaits, Eternal journey. It is influential to know that I can journey and all realms of experience are open to my tread; share with another and they travel also. Believe that what I behold is "just imagination" or "just expectation" and I am moored tight to my own shore. Can or cannot, real or imagined: either way I'm "right." The can or real are richer and connect me to a deeper journey. Bliss is in moments but the moments are far longer than they seem; each is endless if one but let it be so.

22. Once smithied the sword is ever near my grasp. Will becomes reflexive once built. Thor's forge smithies greater evolution; it constructs a higher world by efforts Hammer. Then Odhinn, laughing releases it all and I ascend the glass mountain to the Gods.

23. We are reborn; Self is Eternal, ever new in new surroundings. It is reborn; world is Eternal, itself remade by our returning selves. Truths are created; Law is Eternal. Self is Eternal; worlds are Eternal. All are in flux to higher matters bound; all need my mind's flight to higher cycles bound.

24. Scarcity, hardship, direst necessity; these were the woodsman's companions. Once his axe struck hoard beneath an ancient oak, as had set there in ancient time. Into a hall, to hold a hall, he took companions. Hungry he acted, though the table high with breads and shields of meat. Why, know they, of him, pushed away from table? "Act ever scarce," he said, "pair wanting to the musts and always I'll have enough." Embracing want would never want again.

25. Freedom is a puff of wind. He is not free, the stag who with hoof scrapes beneath the snow for greens; he is not free though I saw him for a moment at the cliff, as if he overlooks the valley as lord. It is a moment; it is releasing and not doing. From Impeccable it arises. Who does well worries less than who does poorly his craft. Who does to perfection may then release them, all outcomes great and small; only the impeccable can release. Only from the perfect arrow's flight can the archer, before it lands, turn his head.

26. Seeking the Golden Age within, all who do must seek it in their intention; then it may come to be. Why a dark age is thus is that most less willing and less able to see. Cleanse sight and hold clear the vision; pure earth, land loved by each, no serfs, all waters clean of hides and wanting little, each is content. Of kings and councils few, and these nearby.

27. Cultivate stillness in reflection; in the business and busyness of life it is not idle, must be sought. Cultivate stillness in all passions, as the watcher, never judging or reacting. Clear like moon, like lake and still, Heimdall watches over all. Observe detached yet act, for greater truths are in commoner places found. At the wharves and in the commons are greater matters chosen. Wholeness, I know, is facing squarely my situation. Plan that direction to the Higher goals, what for Earth and for your Fólk be good. Further the way where you can. Wholeness is forged from deciding and acting.

28. Wholeness is creative and by intention lives, birthed in the freedom to act, to choose. The Gods leave me free that I may be co-creator. Freedom is momentary; it arises in the impeccable act and in releasing that act from care. Send out my choice, create, detach it from myself. Self goes on; world is Eternal.

29. Worlds change; Self is Eternal, reborn into different matrices that we call "worlds." Vision is Eternal, beyond Time, smallest cell of Ginnungagap, seeking the Golden Age and my own Godhead, holding the sight. Releasing into being what worlds we have; the seer by knowing knows. The diviner by stave and stone. The man of Power holds his vision tightly at the highest reach of self. Released into being his flight is the flight of all whom he touches.

30. Though cozy abed with beloved, each sleeps ever alone; each is born alone and dies thus, though a foeman with reciprocal strike die too. In all only the Gods accompany us throughout, ever task-giver, ever bearer of constitutions, and ever the tendencies of breed. Always the Norns and the Gods engage each life. The wise keep with them, in turn, while the fool may fear or trivialize and is ever alone.

31. When choice presents be kind; less thought takes the kind man than one of guile, a freer mind and lighter step has he. Easier for self it is to release the higher act. Be noble, good, kind, where the helping furthers the Higher Life.

32. Be passionate but fair, forceful and swift to scour out sickness. No kindness to the world-destroying worm, no kindness show to the Sun-darkening wolf. Act as the talons of the Gods in Nature, vermin destroy lest they gnaw the slender thread of food.

33. What the world manifests is what Ginnungagap thought; its Hugr is awakening. The worlds yawn at the cusp of every Age. Hugr calls to Higher Thought, greater knowing. In the scheme of things be kind when you can; when you cannot, be hard, and in either case, be Noble.

34. The *Seiðr* is no destination; it is a trackless journey. It is the eyes of the mind, travelled in the attention; it is decision, deciding what to

envision, for what envisions, in some ways comes to be. It is the trackless expanse for the steppe-wanderer, happy for the quest. Whether another arrives or not we cannot know, but journey in joy and without expectation.

35. Self and worlds change; Gods are Eternal. Tribe is the medium of transformation. Go to the crossroads and uplift them. In retreats only the self is rested. Through several selves, through the tribe, uplift to detach, struggle to attain the Higher, release all gains and gain detachment.

36. Selves are reborn; worlds are Eternal. Selves thought beyond the cycle of cause are to Godhead born. In passionate involvement cleanse, protect, elevate the tribe. By example of we, the flax-Fólk, will other tribes progress. Self changes; Gods are Eternal. Heighten the self to seek the realm of the Gods.

37. Act passionately with clear vision where you see your way and step lightly where the Path ascends in scree. Live fully here, yet live apart. Sustain, achieve, and yet release. Hold tight the moment and shape it intensely, yet give to quiet reflection and release, for matters only the shape of acts, the shape of intentions and the thoughts of souls. Be these High, they know it to mirror thoughts of the Gods. Polish slate to clear act and choose for clear and higher selves to come and may his thought enter every moment. Act for my future selves, be better, higher born, for worlds change; self is Eternal.

38. World that is known builds from thought; as seer it is unlearned, forgotten. As sword-wielder I cut it free. Cleansed of talk, I confront the world. My talk deconstructed I float without anchor in the Eternal. Much is beyond thought. The *Seiðr* has no end, for the Gods are without end and advance also. Cultivate awareness; reach for Godhead. There is no truth but there are truths. What is real we create as do those unseen.

39. Without, ideas are drawn by the Norns and inner sight to experience. The warrior invents in every instant, unencumbered by thought. Without knowing, everything shines new, every moment. Without

knowing, all is lived, not thought into being. Without knowing, all is fresh, and the paths to stream yet is filled with surprise, with wonder. Patience to the hunter his pursuit quiet treading. The fisher-Fólk of silent waves and Sun on water see. The warrior, he by careful movement given, invents each moment, invents his life anew.

40. Impeccable and earnest warriors come to battle for meaning. Some men of arms but most were in any work but war. Found only battle, urgency, fear, pain, squalor; found small friend-circles to bind same-chosen hardships and there found meaning. Still the father threshed, the mother baked; still the younger carved the wooden bowl and spoon. Filthy and hurt, his pike he hung by fire, hollow his cheeks. What meant, what known, the same, the threshing, the pot for water to stream, what meant was how he came again and that was all. The same place began anew, rich in remembered valor, with the scythe he wend.

41. Eight steps to be *goðar*, yes, but few the journey make. For all there is eight steps advancing in your state. First, have long sight over many lifetimes, be still and listen, ask her and listen what is not from past fulfilled. Second, live with passionate attainment, for outside reflects within and matters well-resolved do bring to peace. Third, do fully the mind apply, yet with full detachment, for never man knows all the winds and currents. Fourth, cultivate noble character, helpful, kind when can be. Fifth, with compassionate bearing, help all ascend upward by example, goad, or teaching. Sixth, make full intention through higher plans and seek their completion. Seventh, cultivate stillness apart and in the core of the business of living. Eighth, create openness to Powers, openness to forces unseen, full know what moves beneath the flux of worlds.

42. At the crossroads camped many diverse men at the Summer High Sun. *Goði* cooked for the lot of them, cleared the vessels and sat; at fields edge apart from camp, he hew the willow branch of creek near road. Strange shapes upon it cut and the ploughman said had a glow. "Only a cuckoo's days Sun," said a merchant. "With his thoughts made it thus," offered a maid and she was right also. Next morns light, he stood at hills edge like tree with ancient branches, blown by storm or bent by frost, then still and stared. Glanced over, far to see

and said the smoke-meat: "He watches over the shrubs, how silly!" Heard this the houseman's daughter. "No dad, the small ones sport where he does look; can you not see them?" and both were right. At the next road to Uppsala a miller saw him and remembered as he and son the full sacks wend to market. Another encampment he sat at waters edge, high Sun to his back and clear the sky. "Feel it tremble," spoke the miller and fell silent. "But distant cloud-fire," said the son and both were right. At fire that eve, all knew the *goði*, but none knew his years. The eldest of the market road knew him when a youth, he hoary then, nor whence he came; none could guess, he would not tell as he to temple wended.

43. Great compassion is a transformation. Freya's tears and Tyr's gripped fist changed ages in greater and smaller lives. Compassion is power. Great is Heimdall's Sword, red-flashing; in superb compassion Thor his great hammer wields. Not from anger, nor from hate does the hawk fly over the field to search for vermin. Great compassion like Higher Love is for the evolved only; Higher Life is hardness, the hardness of sea-winters and fields, the forests and squares. In its busyness its reaching for the world, the Higher Man overreaches. Who stomachs not the struggle withdraws, deludes from his own I-ness, which thinks itself beyond the world and draws apart. The Higher Man in struggle is at peace, treats with compassion where is meet and with the talon when is needed.

44. Completeness is the shrouds well tied, the chamber well swept and ordered, and the child full-taught. Wholeness is the spine relaxed, the life well-thought, with winter's stores dried and hung. Fulfillment is the son grown to father, the daughter to mother, and the ship coursing home. Final is the purpled haze of Shedding-time, beech leaf fallen, and the warrior's self-known last moment. Completion is the nock released from its grip, the message sealed and sent, the fork behind on the Path taken. Hold not to the doing, nor the making; create and release, work, plan, prepare, for there is wholeness, but after that allow and never expect.

45. Grounding is the well-fleshed horse a'pastured, the grave barrow with blue glow, and the stones stood beneath at four points. Weary but full

comes the fisherman home from his trawl and bowman from the day's hunt. Complete and whole comes the warrior without wound from axefield, or the wife, taut-bellied to labors.

46. Fulfilled the pilot who senses the rocks near placid coast or the wayfarer who the highwayman intuits to change his course. Fulfilled the gleaner who knows dry day to harvest. Fulfilled and complete who knows a fellow's needs and fills them; when each for each does, friend it is called. Complete is the one with much given to high and noble act, yet needs but little; her shall the Gods fulfill.

47. Beneath waves, within wind, all is motion; fastness is what I think to see it still and understand. The Gods change; like moon upon waves, we reflect them. Within flux Ginnungagap called out for order and it spoke Knakve. When its awareness shined upon the sky-sent Sons of Heimdall, when oaks and ashes speech and mind were given, called they out for order and spoke it: Tyr. Beneath had always been an order, though none divined it, at the heart of storm and birthing of worlds, always the first: Ginnungagap.

48. Before the fish are laid to dry is the thought; before the thatch is laid over is the thought. Silent she weaves between cottages, selling loaves, the Deep-Minded. Between the busyness of life is contemplation. No unnecessary actions, no frivolous occupations, no idle chatter, pleasant but aloof from gossip, erect and alert she goes; who knows her age? The superior woman. Between cottages between chores, her inner world, the silent salt marsh at roads edge, silent passes. Between the business is thought; before the fire, while others stare like beast, is her contemplation. After linen and wool are on grasses dried in sun before the brook in contemplation. In the Hof early and at the stones with time picked from between the businesses of life is her meditation. She is not a healer; she is not a seer, but those who seek advice find that she tells well the knots of a man's decision.

49. None should too much hoard; great ownings of some beget great misery by most and none should have too little. All from the market road, the tavern hour should have, and plenty. From windows should women lean and talk together, and men at shores before the nets be

gathered. By the huntmans fire is talk that long endures in ear. A new road the royal council declared, new markets would bring and great goods from the coast, would all grow in weal. Rather came more beggar and landless merchant, crawled over the work-camp; came more brigands to work the road and the toll-takers too. All ended we had less than more. Weal is but for few together banded, the same as chat by nets or hunting plan. Few to share is weal, for much is not needed, nor the knobby knees of soulless men.

50. Another's land desire not, said she from the peaceful land. All councils unpaid, sit to serve, time given after duties, need no taxes save to build when all have need. They built the quay and some brought bread. Others their carts with sand, some of stone, and some brought rope, did the Fries. These and their labors given built quay, roads, and temples. No tax needed they, nor slaves, nor wars. Great owning creates great dearth and high-paid councils brings the death of armed peasants sons.

51. In the peaceful land all owned roundel, though all owned different, and none owned another, but only worked with. The Folda-woman, she wove wool and raised her lamp to Freya. The augerman with leaves and roots the foaming crock tends. In the peaceful land, each her advantage is yet another's too.

52. Happy he dug barrow as the face flushed pale and blood left more. He was not sad, went to the hill that his mound be seen. "These clothes," he said, "to the wooden maid I give"; waited in the happy hours, though leaves took care, for deaths ships tide. Feared not the wayfarer of skins and oar the sky stroke or the roiling, coiled beast. Happy he goes to storm and wise, the waves her daughter's dance; puts out all thought, great ocean mind, was called, eyes gray and deep who said before the hill he had climbed "This voyage but begets another."

53. In the Eastern wood, he tracked, was ill and wasted. Sky overshadowed his plan of march and thorns had torn the flesh. On the dry bed he climbed, ice-free, a narrow passage, then disputed by bear. Bloodied he smelt, weak he seemed; no way to flee, he threw his life away. His staff he seized and made pure act beyond fear, beyond hunger,

the huntsman knew fear; he went on and beyond fear lay panic. He moved through panic, came detachment; released pain, fatigue and detachment, came he to resolution. Drove the wind-broke oak rod deep to innards, not waiting, without the moments thought; in pure act of resolution he threw his life away and thereby won it.

54. From groans of maid and swain do the shudders of the low chair come. There is deference to maidly brightness, yet wraps the shuttered gossip about the shuffle-footed crone. Strength of bow and staff is first conscripted, first the stout son, foemans iron will feel. Fine curves of prow with cargoes, worms, and scratched at rocks are ruined, so the maid her forms brings child, the form to fade. Elder the warrior oozing-scarred and gap-toothed the soothing ale, gone the splendid youth the battle quickly ruined. Only the wit sharpens long past the eyes are dull. Only the hammered hide rings strong long past the stout arm lifts the smithys sledge. Mind and soul alone will time alloy.

55. Potter at her fire stared but briefly. White-hot the ox it blew. Away she looked and the black fire saw. Mariner reckoned his way by star and moon, looked long upon her and the dark ring saw. Took in the darkness, silent after watch, and sweated out the Power. Crewman cried "moonstruck" or "fool" as warm coasts plied and slapped their arms. He was unbit whom the dark power oozed out, a yew its resin. Alone in the stone-hut the herder saw not his fair face these many weeks, far beneath the Maidens Shields. He turned from fire and warmed the back. He opened to the Great Eye and the Black Sun rose.

56. On the voyage bread soured in the spots of rage; on the voyage peas and barley emptied. The one ate of the dew, as others famished, and sat eyes upward, then closed; rubbed his belly those long days as others perished. Breathed deeply the fogs with ale and water gone, as others from fog huddled. In the cove he walked the surf while others lay and groaned, did Aegir's man.

57. Frey's man at Harvest went out with girl-child gathering barley. Bronze-armed and strong he had scythed; they gathered and tied the

sheaves. In the shade of a stack he paused to tell her of Gods, of kings, of ships, memories from him flowed while she lay her head on his hard shoulder in the late noon heat. Freyja's dame stoked the hearth, bread-baking, while the stout son split wood. A highwayman came as beggar, came to rob. With outstretched bowl, he reached over the gate to seize the antlered grip; she without stop split his skull with ladle even as he seized it.

58. Happy the maid of valor and the swain of peace; their young shall prosper and their mated powers increase. Happy the fox who climbs the berry bush when hare is scarce. Well is the wheelwright who hunts the winter marsh; well is the potter who loaves bakes beside his wares. Pleasing to the Gods is the father who shines on his young like the Sun, with play and speech oft given; pleasing to the Goddesses the mother who takes her lass to haft and steel, to cooperage and thatch. For the wise one says, "Fólk are everywhere by halves," and the half lost must the other soon learn.

59. Twelve years at rope, sail and helm, the weathered face made good the mariner's craft and knew the secret rudder of far routes. Came another to toil at sea who saw himself at once a leader of crews, but had not the hard gales and lonely stars for companions. So came to Thing one who had talked his dream, knew much before he learned the Gods. The hoary *gyðja*, her knowing came of long hearing and longer recitation, all the ways of Gods and men, for knowledge asks a barter, but the self-important would ever lead the Thing though little knowing. Seven years before the wind a captain makes. Seven years the lad to master of the ship and eight who would be master of Godly whale-path, the harbor of mind.

60. Eight steps makes the *goði*. First, hear the old ones, know what has gone before. Second, seek solitude in quiet green places, or in fells and crags to prove the runes. Third, journey foodless, sleepless, past the world of men and behold Powers and spirits teach you. Fourth, return to loom, plough, or flock, doing busy in the ways of men, and seek quiet moment for the voice of the Gods. Fifth, act as seer, warrior, caster of the lots of the Norns, as healer, or as scribe. Sixth, reach and bring another to the Thing, *goðar* to train. Seventh, to the

world of men apply the Thing-spoken wisdom. Eighth, learn and live the herders stone hut and the crossroads of men, at once in both and speak the Thing.

61. One walks bent with age soon enough; bent and broke with care the warrior is his Fólk. The lonely border watch, the snows before short poppies and lupines break the steppe. Bowed with concern the leader, priest, and seer. The knight straightens in the act, like a well-strung bow, he launches cares. Bent ill is the man who shoots not forth his acts. Like a marmot the face of the man who, after many years, but uses his paws to gather and his teeth to gnaw; full cheeked and beady-eyed the man who lives as squirrel. The knight is neither bent nor rat-faced; is fully formed, be he priest, merchant, or seer, for any can be knightly.

62. Bent with heavy limbs the oak; bent with nuts full the oak. Shading, tall standing, robe of Sif, the oak. Knowing has its costs: full hang the fruits, low hangs the bough. Who does the work of the Gods in Midgardh, let ever her head not bow and her back not sag; lift straight as Sifs shoot and give shelter. Light of step is the rat and light on wind is the noxious weed; one is food for fox or cat and the other trampled by the goat in the shade of the noble oak.

63. Some at Thing were amber-men and apart they drew. Flocks were fatted and bartered. Sons brought to flail and spear; apart they did not age. Like the crag-tree, there from the grandfathers grandfathers tales they stayed. Yet all behind, the island fell to sea; dark ones walked and drove their skin ships and never they cared for it all. They had no gold, but each gloried in his own glow in the mountain fastness. Their plant withered but the flower in cool high place endured, seeing only its own beauty, changeless before time.

64. One age prior had from the crag descended Rigr, sired Sons of the North. "This mortal vessel I am not," he declared, "and I will return whenever the times have need. Not the self-reflected flower, I go the seed and glow and fruit, life after life. To my shining-ship bear me, when this time is done."

65. Some transformed through time, some in the lust of combat, then released; some transform by kindred minds blended to Powers. "I transform through you, though I die many times to be with you," said Rigr, "some for Power, some for perfection, some for their amber sheen, but I transform that you transform, as darts against the gathering gloom. Once I was bended at care, then let it go in my best bows release. In my quietest stealth and bravest position took the field of valor; while others held the Shield, I held also the Sword."

66. At market came the man of Power, only a glimpse, to stare, then he fades from sight. Simple lives the *vitki* and none may know where. His sons upon the Hawks path flown, he tends far borders, rushes, and fens; he quickly speaks out his staves, for who have not will envy. Who envy will wound with tongue or harm with the spear. He finds those who will counsel, does the man of Power; none find him, nor is he known to others but as a herder of swine. As the woolen men were about with men-at-arms he reached into his cart announcing, "Mats of rushes! Well-woven mats of rushes!"

67. Others huddled at the storm; she went about in simple thread, hands raised to Erde or Tyr, stood still, tall, proud, palms opened. Others took to shade but in the heat of day she tread slowly. Others made busy in the night, but he gazed to the dark heart at the arch of trees. Others huddled warm, when barefoot in the snow she trekked. Freedom in cold, freedom in hard, freedom is in hardships found.

68. The youth thought him mad; he gazed into shadows in the noon slumber of High Summer. In the snow he sat or stood until it melted about. At the marsh he sat, rubbed the juice of roots about to keep the biters away, yet stayed and sat. Now and then one sees him. A boy asked of him, why gaze or sit? The hermit answered, "Much do we do between birth and death and most of it no matter; in all that Grimnir does, he becomes aware. When he hung upon the tree, he became aware; when he bade Mimir speak, he was aware. Much passes between birth and death; what means any of it if I am not aware?"

69. Yet how is to gaze to be aware? "In each place and force a spirit dwells before, after, and always; they show the world before and after. They show our world at the time of hidings, when people of stones and the people of oaks, when the Fólk of staves and ravens are banished and they show that we shall return again, in the night after the next Sigurd." Now and again, Fólk see him at marsh or skerry stone and none think him mad.

70. Even among good Fólk come disputes. Before the Thing may be brought it must be first in the common-house before Elders. Before wind bends the tree and rains the fields fair faces smoothness line, much is endured and much more learned. Go thence to the Elders. If between kin the common ancestor has gone before, ask always that same from the Living Acre be present; failing this, seek next who dwells behind. If betweens kins, let each an Elder attend and together seek Tyr's council. Should not resolve, the Elders locked, priest, priestess, or seer ask to guide their way and make new choice beyond each position. Failing this, then matters wend before the Thing, where Tyr and Odhinn, Saga and the Norns sit as matters come to Elders of many a kin as sit in council wise.

71. She went to well early to draw for potation of wormwood, for his head was still in his cups, the light of day did wound. She early chopped wood; for he could not. He tended not the ox and it feasted bloat weed; no ox to cart, no cart to haul, no eggs to market, though the children took from nest.

72. In the talks of markets, another ask, how could she suffer thus? The frau quoth, "You must endure; you must be a warrior in life." The *gyðja* near, trading her beads, replied it was false to be a warrior in life unless first you be a warrior by choice. "The warriors choice first make," saith she, "the good steel to arms, the high ground to hold, the early march on slumbered foe; to fight well who chose poor position is fool more than fighter. Well picks the spearman his ground and the bowman his hillock. Then fight well who must. The stubborn wight an ill-chosen stand may make, for warriors be ignorant or old, but rarely both."

73. Dark was the storm in the East; dark were the riders, short with horsetail hair. Where they took land are people as burnt. From the horsemen keep your daughters and from the horsemans sons; from the skin house princess keep your sons, for they go not to streams and drink sour milk.

74. Where now they trade and farm, are heads like hares, short, swart like elves, beware! Look only to the light of us, the fair-browed, whose brows do not meet. Look only to the tall of us, strong going and high-minded. Look only to the fair-minded and clever, good at trading stave and equal of temper. Look for the quiet and earnest or the well-spoken and sincere. Here seek they maid and swain. Though some be comely too, the dark with dark belong as geese by feathers nest else all is confused.

75. Once we all were of flax and heather; that was in grandmother's days. Then came from the East in fathers time, making the half-dark; now dark with flax and either with half-dark until neither wood duck nor goose remain.

76. Two brothers there were as courted two sisters, both toothsome swains. The Binder held all that he had, be it fit or not, but Free-Fisted held only were it weal. Binder courted the lass whose bright smile and full form promised strong youths, but her water was foul, far too oft sailed and loved not but slated face. When tired or fled she, with magic, he by her hair bound her, or stick made to keep her. From Goddess his wish and bound her fast.

77. Free-Fisted found her sister much the same and set her free; he slept alone while Binder made a goodly home for stout children. Often they fought and never was it kempt and never was it peaceful. Soon they slept apart did Binder and Foul. Free-Fisted went long years alone; when he met Fine-Spirit he did not seize her. Though they drew water at the same stream, each smiled, but carried skins apart. They met again and grew to court, to happy home and stout child. They prosper at the Mothers hearth, the house in peace.

78. The hooded-robed came and we hid in forests to Thing. Dark soldiers they brought from the South, so we spoke in barns and hid the two horses amid rushes. From him they stole land, for he would pay no tax; from him they fined goats, for he would not tithe. Land gone, he settled the *vík* between the holders grants.

79. They would not suffer him to hunt, so weirs and traps he set. Since spring thaws over the low hearth flowed, he with sons built poles, thatched high. The rich taxed his foot upon their trail, so he make float to town. Then skins and fish he brought to market could not sell, be they not blessed by the hooded ones, thus he bartered for grain and cloth. Offered they to "save" him, would say at barter; he would not and to the Gods was ever true. What they took never he stopped, but made anew; what they dammed he flowed around like waters of first budding.

80. *Seiðr* goes far now from the land of men, for the new priests are barons and the new kings heavily tax and many in chains. Those who pray not with them and know not one of four their sheep and bushels must with Ullr the wild hunt join and pick Friggas down.

81. Darkness comes, the carts of cut stone hauled by tax-slaves for the hooded ones to build. *Seiðr* you shall speak man to man and woman to woman, shall whisper true to grandson brave. Turn to the heath and know it, for beyond this time, Sigurd shall rebirth to us, yet many his dragons and fierce then, say the *gyðja*. Slay he or be slain, the sons of his warriors shall set to the shaven wood again our way. Until then speak it to moon, to heath, to hidden men in places remote. Speak to star and perfect every word where naught hear but whose mind blend with mind. In this time shall speak it often and truly that in far time it be little changed before it come to birch again.

Glossary of Old Norse

ÆSIR (plural of ÁSS) = sky gods, in contrast to the earth deities of the *VANIR*
ALDABJARN = born of eternity
ALDR (also ÖLD) = eternal, time/age
ÁLFAR = elves or fairies
ÁLFABLÓT = sacrifice to the elves
ÁLFHEIM = home of the elves
ALLSHERJARGOÐI = priest of the host
ALTHING = Great Assembly
ALU = ecstatic magic
ÁR = year, time
ASAHEIM = home of the Aesir
ÁSBRÚ = bridge of the Gods
ASGARÐ = garden of the Gods
ÁSGRINDR = gate to the garden of the Gods
ASKR = ashes; first man
ÁSMEGINN = divine power
ÁSS = God
ÁSYNJA = Goddess
ÁTT = family or race
AUSTRI = east
BERSERKR = bear-skulled; elite warriors
BIFRÖST = rainbow bridge
BLOÐARN = bloodeagle
BLÓT = blood sacrifice or offering
BOÐN = bowl of offering
BÓNDI = binding
BOLLI = bowl used for offerings
BRAGARFULL = chieftains cup or boasting horn
DÍSIR = female ancestors
DÓMR = doom or fate
DRAUPNIR = the Dripper; Odhinn's ring
DRÓMI = fetter; second attempt to bind Fenris
EDDA = grandmother; the name of a collection of poems or lays, likely deriving from the same root word for "to know"
EINHERJAR = inheritors; one-harriers or those who fight alone

EMBLA = embers; first woman
ETIN = giant
FENRIS = marsh-dweller, likely identical to Grendel; the Wolf who will swallow Odhinn at the Ragnarokr
FETCH = male tutelary spirit
FIMBULVETR = great winter
FÓLK = those descended from the Gods
FÓLKLÆTI = Fólk-Soul
FÓLKVÍG = civil war
FREKI = ravenous; one of Odhinn's "wolves"
FRIÐR = peace among Fólk
FYLFÓT = four-footed, as a swastika
FYLGJA = female tutelary spirit
FYLGJUR = tutelary spirits; ancestral guides
GALDR = magical chant/incantation
GALDRAR = enchantments
GAMBANTEIN = diviner's twig; a magical staff
GANDI = magic
GANDLIR = magician
GANDR = magical item
GANDUL = magical animal
GERI = greedy; one of Odhinn's "wolves"
GINNING = chaos or illusion
GINNUNGAGAP = chasm of illusion: the Great void; primeval chaos
GJALAR = Bridge to Hel
GJALLARHORN = Horn of Resounding; Mimir's drinking horn; trumpet of Heimdall
GJOLL = rock Fenris bound to; river boundary for Niflhel
GLADSHEIM = Home of Happiness
GLEIPNIR = open one; the fetter that ultimately binds Fenris
GOÐI = priest and chieftain
GUNGNIR = Odhinn's spear
GYÐJA = priestess
HAMINGJA = synchronicity or guided fortune
HAMR = ethereal shape or aura
HAVAMAL = sayings of the High Ones
HEARTH = a group of Fólk sharing a firepit
HEIÐINN = Heathen

Glossary

HEIÐNI = Heathenism
HEIÐR = honor
HJUKI = the symbol of the waxing moon
HLAUT = sacrificial blood
HLAUTBOLLI = sacrificial bowl
HLAUTTEINN = sacrificial twig
HLIDSKJALF = shelf of battle; Odhinn's seat
HODDMIMIR = forest of Fólk memory
HOF = temple
HOFGOÐI = temple priest
HÖRGR = stone altar or holy place
HRÍMTHURSAR = sooty-giants
HUGINN = Sovereign Intellect
IDA = plain of the Gods
IDAVALD = forest on the plain of the Gods
IDISI = Dísir
IFING = river surrounding Idavald
JARL = nobleman
JOTUNHEIM = home of the giants
JOTUNN = giant or outsider
KON = king
LÁ = blood
LÆDING = chain used on Fenris
LÆRAÐ = tree in Valhalla
LÆTI = soul; óð and önd together
LAWSPEAKER = one who makes legal decisions
LÍF = life; survivor of Ragnarokr
LÍFTHRASIR = longing-for-life; survivor of Ragnarokr
LITU GOÐA = Godlike appearance
LJOSSALFHEIM = home of the light elves
MEGINJÖRÐ = power of the earth
MEGINN = power
MEGINSTAÐA = power positions
MIDGARÐ = middle garden; home of Fólk
MINNI = remembrance drink/toast
MUNINN = Sovereign Impulse
MUSPELL = end of existence by fire
MUSPELLHEIM = home of Muspell

NÁGRIND = gate of the dead
NÁSTRÖND = strand of the dead
NIÐAVELLIR = dark fields
NIÐI = dark one; new moon
NIÐOGGR = one full of darkness
NIFLHEIM = the dark home
NIFLHEL = the dark Hel
NORDRI = north
NORN = weavers of Worth
NÝ = new one; the waxing moon
ÓÐ = self or consciousness; spirit; Intellect/Impulse
ÓÐAL = ancestral home/property
OÐINN = Sovereign Self
ÓÐLING = descendent of Óð
OÐROERIR = exciter of inspiration
ÖND = breath of life or vitality; Instinct
ØRLAG = primal law; the four gifts given Askr and Embla
RAGNARØKR = twilight of the Gods
RÚNA = mystery or occultic knowledge
RÚNAR = sacred symbols; secret hidden lore
RÚNSTAÐA = runic positions
SEIÐ = source
SEIÐKONA = sorceress
SEIÐMAÐR = sorcerer
SEIÐR = sorcery
SIGR = victory
SKÁLD = poet
SKULD = the norn of what should be
SON = bowl of expiation
SPÁ = prophecy
SPÁKONA = prophetess
SPÁMAÐR = prophet
SPJÖLL = spell
STAÐA = positions, as in yoga
STALLR = indoor altar
SUÐRI = south
SUMBEL = a series of three toasts
SVARTÁLFHEIM = home of the dark elves

TAUFR = talismanic object
THING = assembly
THRALL = slave
THUND = roaring one; Odhinn's initial phase on the Path
THURS = evil-minded giant
TÍVAR = gods
TRÉFÓT = three-footed, as in triskele
TRÚ = troth or faith
URÐR = the Norn of what is
ÚTGARÐ = outer garden; all that is beyond oneself
ÚTISETI = sitting out
VALGRIND = gate of the slain
VALHALLA = hall of the slain
VALKNOT = knot of the slain; symbol of Odhinn's chosen
VALKYRIE = chooser of the slain; Odhinn's maidens
VANAHEIM = home of the *Vanir*
VANIR = terrestrial deities, in contrast to the sky gods of the ÆSIR
VARGR = wolf or outlaw
VÉ = sacred space; brother of VILI and VITHRIR
VERALD = world
VERALDIR = worlds/dimensions
VERÐANDI = the Norn of what is becoming
VERÐR = worth
VESTRI = west
VITHRIR = windy; brother of VE and VILI
VÍGRIÐ = plain of battle
VILI = will; brother of VE and VITHRIR
ÝGGDRASIL = world-tree
ÝGGR = terrible one; Odhinn's second phase on the Path

Other Words & Terms

ARCHEGNOSIS = literally "principal knowledge"; as used in this book, refers to the original spiritual wisdom that Odhniism is founded upon.

ATAVISTIC = the appearance of some characteristic in an individual that is shared by a distant ancestor, the characteristic itself, or a person with such a characteristic.

CONSANGUINEOUS = of the same blood or having the same ancestor(s).

ERGRIFFENHEIT = the state of being seized or possessed; in his monumental work "Wotan," Carl Jung refers to Odhinn as ERGREIFER ("one who seizes") of men, likely alluding to the way in which the Allfather has influenced Berserkers and other great men throughout time.

EUHEMERISM = the notion that the Gods of mythology were simply deified human beings or that mythology itself is based upon traditional accounts of actual people or events.

EXISTENTIALISM = the belief that existence takes priority over essence and that man is completely free, thus fully responsible for his actions.

FÓLK-SOUL = the sacred and spiritual principle that connects a group of people related by blood or biology.

GESTALTIC = the integrated patterns that make up all experience and have specific properties which can neither be derived from the elements of the whole, nor considered simply as the sum of these elements.

HEIMLICHE ACHT = the "hidden tribunal," a term used by Guido von List to refer to the notion that all truly spiritual or sacred wisdom teachings contained a three-fold interpretation; in the Heathen Hof these are known as the mundane meaning, the exoteric and the esoteric.

HENOTHEISM = the belief in one's own deities without denying the existence of others.

METATHEISTIC = beyond the belief in a God or gods.

MORPHOGENETIC FIELD = a space within which a form comes into being; in developmental biology, a field around a morphic unit that organizes its characteristic structure and pattern of activity.

MORPHOGENETIC RESONANCE = the influence of prior structures of activity on subsequent similar structures of activity organized by morphic fields.

PHYLOGENETIC = the line of descent or evolutionary development of any animal; the origin and evolution of a division, group, race, etc.

THEOMORPHIC EXISTENTIALISM = the belief that man can become Godlike by prioritizing existence over the essence and accepting that he is totally free, thus fully responsible for his own actions and omissions.

THEOMORPHOSIS = the developmental process of an organism from simple to complex, specifically from man into Übermensch.

ÜBERMENSCH = often translated as "superman," though is more appropriately defined as "overman" and refers to that state of evolutionary development wherein one becomes superior or Godlike.

UR-FÓLK = The first Fólk; original or primitive people, often seen as the Hyperboreans, having come from the far North.

WELTANSCHAUUNG = a comprehensive conception of the universe and life; a personal perspective of the world, often influenced by the world around us.

www.ingramcontent.com/pod-product-compliance
Lightning Source LLC
Chambersburg PA
CBHW071959070526
44583CB00015B/1262